The Koreas between China and Japan

The Koreas between China and Japan

Edited by

Victor Teo and Lee Guen

CAMBRIDGE SCHOLARS
PUBLISHING

The Koreas between China and Japan,
Edited by Victor Teo and Lee Guen

This book first published 2014

Cambridge Scholars Publishing

12 Back Chapman Street, Newcastle upon Tyne, NE6 2XX, UK

British Library Cataloguing in Publication Data
A catalogue record for this book is available from the British Library

ISBN (10): 1-4438-6024-7, ISBN (13): 978-1-4438-6024-6

CONTENTS

ACKNOWLEDGEMENTS

The editors gratefully acknowledge the assistance of the colleagues who have made this book possible. A great debt is owed to the School of Modern Languages and Cultures, University of Hong Kong, for making the logistical and financial resources for this project available. We are grateful to Dr Kendall Johnson and Dr Dixon Wong, present and former heads of the School, respectively, who have been so supportive of the project. The editors are also tremendously grateful to Miss Lolo Yu, Mr Richard Edele, Mr Samuel Wong, Mr Watson Lam, and Dr Rebecca Wong for all their assistance in the organization of the workshop at the university and the subsequent production of this book, as well as to Dr Benedict Young and Ms Penny Iremonger for assistance with preparation of the manuscript. We would also like to express our sincere thanks to the learned scholars who have taken the time to come to Hong Kong to attend our workshop, for undertaking the many revisions required as well as their forbearance in waiting for this book to materialize. Although the materials cover only developments in the era of Kim Il-sung and Kim Jong-il, there are nonetheless, numerous invaluable insights contained therein concerning the patterns and complexities of East Asian International Relations. Finally, we would also like to convey our sincere thanks to the editors and staff at Cambridge Scholars Publishing for their confidence in us and for making this book possible.

CHAPTER ONE

CONTEXTUALIZING THE KOREAS BETWEEN CHINA AND JAPAN

VICTOR TEO

On December 19, 2012, the official announcement of North Korean supreme leader Kim Jong-il's demise was finally issued, two days after his purported death on December 17, 2012. A week after this announcement, on Christmas day, Prime Minister Yoshihiko Noda began a two-day working visit to Beijing to discuss, amongst other things, the impending fortieth anniversary of the Sino–Japanese normalization of relations. These claims notwithstanding, there was no question that at the top of the Sino–Japanese diplomatic agenda was the situation on the Korean Peninsula. This was especially pertinent given the domestic developments within the Democratic People's Republic of Korea (DPRK) over the past decade, as well as the challenges of her very rocky relations with the major powers in the region. After the death of the DPRK leader Kim Jong-il, the Korean Peninsula situation was once again catapulted to the top of Northeast Asia's security issues—and especially between China and Japan, North Korea's closest neighbors. Long recognized as one of the three hotspots in East Asia (the other two being the Taiwan Straits and the Spratly Islands dispute in the South China Sea), the contrast between the two political entities cannot be greater.

South Korea, one of the four roaring "tiger economies" with a population of 48.8 million, has an annual Gross Domestic Product of USD $1.5 trillion (USD $31,000 on a per capita basis). South Koreans enjoy one of the highest standards of living in East Asia, and the Republic of Korea today is world-renowned for her technological expertise, demographic vibrancy, and forward-looking social policies. Located within Northeast Asia, South Korea is one of the main areas of world economic growth. The last decade has seen a sharp spike in the popularity of Korean cultural products across Asia, and the Hangul wave is the driving force behind South Korea's soft power. In contrast, the images we encounter of North Korea in our everyday narratives are strikingly negative. From the relatively scarce news reports emanating from the DPRK, it is clear that North Korea's economy is in an abysmal state. The DPRK government has difficulty feeding its population of 24 million. North Korea's GDP per capita was higher than South Korea's at the end of the Korean War; but by 2011 the average North Korean was earning only one-thirtieth of the average wage of a South Korean. Human rights abuses are rampant within the DPRK and many freedoms that South Koreans enjoy are unheard of in North Korea. Communist propaganda and personality cult programs dominate the airwaves, as opposed to the K-pop and Korean drama shown daily on television in South Korea. In short, everyday life in North Korea is best summarized by the Hobbesian formulation—it is "solitary, poor, nasty, brutish and short." The difference in political and economic systems and social institutions that originated from the armistice, in place since the 1950s, has created two Korean nations constantly at odds with each other, to the extent that it is now increasingly said that, perhaps, North and South Korea should remain as two separate political entities in perpetuity.

This volume examines the question of the Korean Peninsula in the context of changing relations between Japan and China during the era of Kim Il-sung and Kim Jong-il. The trajectory of Sino–Japanese relations over the past decade has left many concerned scholars and policymakers wondering if there could be any issues of strategic importance that Japan and China can agree upon. These two East Asian giants have disagreed on almost every single issue that has cropped up between them in the past decade: China's nuclear tests in 1995; the Taiwanese independence movement and the Taiwan Straits Crisis in 1995/96; the annual disputes over the Senkaku/Diaoyutai Islands; the demarcation of their sea border; sovereignty and drilling rights in the East China Sea from 1999 onwards; and, in addition, a host of historical issues, ranging from textbooks to apologies. Given the volatile political nature of Sino–Japanese relations over the past decade, it is difficult to perceive how Sino–Japanese relations can move concretely beyond diplomatic niceties to substantive cooperation on items of major strategic importance. But there is one issue that China and Japan do not have significant differences over—the security situation on the Korean Peninsula. The North Korean issue is one of the main areas where both China and Japan can work together to enhance strategic cooperation. This is indeed not only desirable but necessary, as it builds political trust between these two strategic rivals, and also provides a critical platform for China and Japan to engage with each other, on an issue of mutual interest in their foreign relations.

Technically, North and South Korea are still at war. Their 1953 ceasefire has produced an abnormal situation, in which the uneasy tension belies the facade of peace and tranquility on the Peninsula as well as the continuing rise in prosperity in Northeast Asia more generally. North Korea has shown that it is increasingly willing to disrupt this fragile peace, with its nuclear belligerence throughout the 1990s, its firing of the Taedopong-1 missile over Japan, and its incursions into South Korea. Almost two decades have passed since the Berlin wall collapsed, but the predictions that the Communist regime in the DPRK would implode have not materialized, and Kim Dae-jung's sunshine diplomacy seems to have had little effect beyond his and President Roh's tenure. On the other side of the thirty-eighth parallel, South Korea has spent a disproportionate amount of resources preparing for reunification across a wide range of possible scenarios—from the collapse of the regime in North Korea to reunification with a "one country two systems" scenario; or from a peaceful political settlement to all-out war. At the same time, it has also ambivalently sent aid worth billions of won to North Korea annually. In practical terms, any security scenario or political solution between the North and the South is not simply an issue of the two Koreas. Any negotiation, conflict, or settlement will involve the great powers in the region—namely the United States, China, Japan, and Russia. Of these four powers, China and Japan stand to be the most affected by any settlement, as the Korean Peninsula effectively straddles the strategic location between China and Japan. As such they are intimately concerned, as neither wishes to be dragged into a war started by Korean belligerence, South Korean aspirations, or US adventurism. The situation of Korea, thus, has the same critical salience for both China and Japan and, hence, this is one of the most pressing issues which could upset both their developmental agendas and political aspirations.

In Chapter Two, "Leadership Rivalry and Crisis-Driven Cooperation: Dynamics among Mutually Distrustful China, Japan and Korea," Dong Xiang Rong, from the Institute of Asia–Pacific Studies in the Chinese Academy of Social Sciences, provides an overarching historical analysis of the situation on the Korean Peninsula. This chapter argues that due to historical, ideological, and other causes, the relations between China, Japan, and the Republic of Korea have never been ordinary "triangular" relations. After the collapse of the Imperial Tributary System centered on ancient China, Japan sought to play a leading role in the region through the colonization of Korea and the invasion of China. During the Cold War, Japan and Korea kept close alliances with the United States, and so what China faced were not two individual countries, but an alliance or quasi-alliance. After the end of the Cold War, the essence of such a structure has not changed: in the case of military conflicts erupting, Japan and Korea will follow the United States and fight against China. However, there is some evidence to suggest that over the last decades the framework has changed to become an ordinary triangular relationship. The three countries are working together to resolve the Korean nuclear issue, build a multilateral security regime, and prevent the emergence of military conflicts. Dong further argues that in the last two decades, ASEAN has played a crucial role in regional cooperation, while the big three—China, Japan, and Korea—have been relatively marginalized under the "10+3" framework. Negative historical legacies have caused civilian hostilities and national rivalry between China and Japan, and this has had spillover effects into their competition for regional leadership. ASEAN's driver seat in the regional cooperation framework is the by-product of the leadership rivalry between China and Japan. It would appear that the possible way forward for cooperation in Northeast Asia is "crisis-driven" cooperation. This means that China, Japan, and Korea are more likely to be pushed towards institutionalized economic cooperation and security cooperation, whilst ignoring civilian mistrust and negative sentiments and other domestic political factors, when they are faced with nuclear threats and financial crises.

Leonid Petrov's chapter deals with an important source of conflict between the countries in Northeast Asia—historical controversies. Petrov notes that even as Japanese colonial and nationalist historians in China and Korea have clashed over the origins of their nations, there have been a variety of different historiographical conflicts that divide the regions. Petrov groups these historiographical conflicts into three categories: those that involve the possession of cultural assets of past civilizations and dynasties, those that pertain to the ways in which certain military forces colonized and maltreated the peoples of neighboring countries, and finally those that concern contemporary debates about the issues outlined in the former two categories. These conflicts, however, do not exist in vacuum and are often incited, exaggerated, and intensified by competition between these states today. This is currently the case even between North and South Korea. In particular, the Koreas are engaged in such disputes with both China and Japan. Petrov suggests that in order to achieve reconciliation and advance regionalism, issues of the past should be properly addressed and closed. This chapter suggests that history writing in East Asia, based on the democratic principle of deliberation, should be encouraged in order to engender an ethics of difference and tolerance. This approach would erode the monopoly of states in the writing of history textbooks, and help transnational interpretations cross borders more easily.

Kim Sung-chull, of the Institute of Peace and Unification Studies at Seoul National University, continues the analysis of the Koreas between China and Japan by looking at the issue through the normalization of Sino–Japanese relations, and the implications of the Koreas from the period 1972 to 1975. Kim argues that the Sino–Japanese normalization in 1972 provided Japan with a chance to expand the scope of its policy toward the Korean Peninsula (hereafter its "Korean policy"). The impact of the Sino–Japanese normalization on the Korean Peninsula was greater than that of the US–China rapprochement. Right after US President Richard Nixon's July 1971 announcement of his planned Beijing visit, Japanese "China fever" developed into high expectations about Sino–Japanese normalization. Given this situation, another fever emerged in Japan: the rising enthusiasm among North Korea–friendly politicians and businessmen regarding the expansion of economic and cultural exchanges with the North. For Japan, the Sino–Japanese normalization in 1972 meant expansion of the scope of diplomacy. For the two Koreas, the core element of the normalization was Japan's abandonment of Taiwan, a strategic front to which the United States has never given up its security commitment. Evidently, the normalization—and Japan's abandonment of Taiwan—contributed to facilitating Japan's "two Koreas" policy, by which Japan played a balancing role between the two Koreas. Japan's policy forced South Korea to accept the reality of the *de facto* existence of two Koreas, on the one hand, and emboldened North Korea to actively launch peace initiatives towards the South, Japan, and the United States, on the other. Japan's policy toward the Korean Peninsula was independent of the South Korean government's demand, wish, or protest, despite the fact that the South Korea–Japan quasi-alliance anchored by the United States remained intact.

Nonetheless, the dynamics of what is happening on the Korean Peninsula cannot be attributed only to Chinese or Japanese policies. South Korea is arguably one of the most important actors in directing events on the Korean Peninsula and, by extension, within Northeast Asian regional politics. In Chapter Five, Lee Sang-hyun, former Director-General for Policy Planning at South Korea's Ministry of Foreign Affairs and Trade and Director of the Security Studies program at Sejong Institute, examines the development of South Korea's role under the Lee Myung-bak government. Lee argues that South Korea seeks a constructive role in Northeast Asian regional politics under the Lee Myung-bak administration. The Lee government's foreign and security policies are collectively referred to as "pragmatic diplomacy." Among the items on this agenda, President Lee Myung-bak has placed the highest priority on revitalizing the ROK–US alliance and peacefully solving the North Korean nuclear crisis. Although the ROK's foreign policy is predominantly focused on restoring the domestic economy, developing the ROK–US strategic alliance, and making substantial progress on the North Korean nuclear issue, South Korea is turning its eyes to other regions of the world. Naturally, Asia comes first, not simply because Asia is where South Korea belongs geographically, but also because the region is becoming strategically important to South Korea's national interests. Although Asia is not yet a theater at peace, the region is, indeed, experiencing a burgeoning network of governments, corporations, and institutions, both formal and informal, across the region. At the same time, Asia is facing the risk that it will fail to develop the structures of cooperation necessary, both to seize the opportunities and master the threats that come with globalization and interdependence. Furthermore, the emergence of new, more powerful economic and military actors may generate rivalry and even conflict, manifesting itself in the classic security dilemma that has characterized much of Asian history. To avoid such dangers, it is imperative for Asian nations to develop a rich web of cooperative networks throughout the region. South Korea, indeed, wants to contribute to the creation of a thick web of networks between China, Japan, and Korea. South Korea can contribute in two ways: firstly, by helping find a breakthrough to the North Korean nuclear crisis using cooperative networks among Asian nations—particularly among China, Japan, and Korea; and secondly, by playing a mitigating role in the case of a potential rivalry between China and Japan.

In Chapter Six, "Sino–Japanese Relations and the Diversification of South Korea's National Interests," Park Ihn-hwi of Ewha Womans University examines the interface between South Korea's national interests and China and Japan in general, and Sino–Japanese relations in particular. The chapter begins by surveying the Korean Peninsula against the backdrop of Northeast Asia's political developments. Park raises the question whether the rise of China has been centered on the "regional security complex" of Northeast Asia in the post–Cold War era. Beyond that, this chapter also raises the question as to whether or not China would try to aggressively expand her external power in East Asia, and if so, whether the target area could be territorial integration in Taiwan, deeper diplomatic influence in South Korea, or invisible but realistic economic integration with many of the Southeast Asian countries. The chapter argues that in order to grapple with this problem, South Korea needs to define her national interests very carefully, and then separate them into two dimensions: regional and global. As a relatively small state surrounded by major regional powers, particularly China and Japan, South Korea needs to pursue parts of her national interests within a regional framework, and parts of Korea's national interests beyond the regional framework. Diversifying Korea's national interests, the country may apply theoretical rationale and policy options according to the nature of the issues, such as the Korea–US alliance, East Asian regional institutions, Korea–Japan political alignment, Korea–China economic interdependence, etc.

Jiang Lifeng, Professor Emeritus and previous Director of the Institute of Japanese Studies (incorporating Korean Studies), provides a very insightful analysis into the developing situation on the Korean Peninsula. Jiang's chapter argues that the Korean Peninsula issue has had tremendous implications for the development of Northeast Asia and Japan, and that China's cooperation would be vital for the eventual peaceful reunification of the Koreas. This issue of reunification is, however, still a matter for North and South Korea to work out in accordance with their own interests and timetable, and the Six-Party Talks remain one of the viable mechanisms to bring North Korea back into the community of nations in East Asia. Jiang's chapter lays the groundwork for the subsequent discussions on the viability of the Six-Party Talks as a mechanism for managing intra-Korean relations.

Zhu Zhiqun, John D. and Catherine T. MacArthur Chair in East Asian Politics at Bucknell University, provides an interesting take on the Six-Party Talks. Instead of looking at whether the talks will improve the situation on the Korean peninsula, he examines whether the talks could actually improve Japan–China relations. Zhu starts off by proposing that peace on the Korean Peninsula is one of the very few things that Japan and China are in agreement over. Third parties play a significant role in international conflict resolution. Major third parties include sundry nation-states, individuals, groups, and organizations. What is lacking in the current literature is discussion of other potential but less common forms of third-party facilitators. This chapter explores whether an issue, a forum, or a platform, in which both conflicting parties have vested interests and through which they frequently interact, can serve as a facilitator or mediator in conflict resolution. The research uses the Six-Party Talks as a case study for potentially mediating in the troubled China–Japan relations.

Ties between China and Japan have always been difficult because of their different interpretations of history, territorial disputes, and geopolitical rivalry. The two countries do not seem to be able to overcome these problems by themselves. Major state-level third parties in East Asia that can help include the United States, the two Koreas, and Taiwan. Strictly speaking, none of these parties has played the role of a mediator nor actively pushed for the improvement of China–Japan relations. Often these third parties actually perpetuate China–Japan disputes either by taking sides or by pursuing their own problems with one or both main actors. One wonders whether other forms of third party intervention, such as that represented by the Six-Party Talks, may help. This chapter suggests that historical baggage, opposing approaches, and different expectations, have rendered the Six-Party Talks a lost opportunity for Japan and China to move forward. It can be argued that this new form of third-party facilitation, like other mediators, can only work if Japan and China themselves have the political will and domestic support for improving bilateral relations.

Lee Guen, Professor of International Relations at the Graduate School of International Studies at Seoul National University, presents an alternative take on the case of the Six-Party Talks in his chapter "The Clash of Soft Powers between China and Japan: Synergy and Dilemmas at the Six-Party Talks." Lee investigates the dynamics of two different types of soft powers revealed during the Six-Party Talks, particularly involving China and Japan. In retrospect, the Six-Party Talks are the results of multilateral efforts by the United States, China, Japan, Russia, and the two Koreas to resolve the problem of North Korea's nuclear program, and the involved countries have applied various tactics aiming at both common goals and individual domestic and foreign policy goals. As the Six-Party process is based upon a premise that the nuclear question on the Korean Peninsula must be answered with peaceful measures, the whole process has been more of an arena for soft tactics rather than hard ones. That does not mean that coercive "hard power" was completely missing during the process, but rather that the strategies and tactics applied to the Six-Party processes relied more upon "ideational" resources than material resources such as military options or economic sanctions. The Six-Party processes have been mostly about venue-making, agenda-setting, facilitating and mediating, idea-seeking, and word-finding, followed by (supposedly) material incentives or disincentives.

Japan's soft-power strategy at the Six-Party Talks produced what Lee conceptualizes as a "soft-power dilemma"—the term referring to a situation within which soft power, despite being appealing and attractive to the domestic audience, engenders a threatening or negative external environment. Imperialistic nationalism is a typical example. Even if such nationalism mobilizes the domestic audience by its appealing nationalistic elements and slogans, that same nationalism can threaten other countries by sending aggressive signals to them. Japan's recent conservative turn may have appealed to the Japanese public by raising the issue of Japan's history textbooks, politicians' visits to the Yasukuni Shrine, taking a tough stance towards China, close cooperation with the United States, and the expansion of the Self Defense Force's international roles; but such a conservative turn also created much tension in relations with its neighboring countries, particularly Korea and China. On the other hand, China's soft-power strategy has manufactured what Lee terms "soft-power synergy." China's improved status on the international stage, and the acceptance of China as a responsible stakeholder by international society, particularly by the United States, has not only improved its security but also amplified the domestic pride of the Chinese people. The China threat thesis was gradually replaced by China's "peaceful development," and China became an essential player at the Six-Party Talks. Now it would be unimaginable to resolve the North Korea nuclear crisis without the presence of China. In a nutshell, this chapter argues that during the Six-Party Talks on North Korea, China adroitly used its diplomacy to produce "soft-power synergy" while Japan became stuck with a "soft-power dilemma." Borrowing from Robert Putnam's "two-level game" metaphor, this chapter tries to reveal the two-level dynamics of soft power by developing a refined conceptual framework of soft power and also by explicating a case study of Chinese and Japanese diplomacy at the Six-Party Talks.

Alexander Zhebin, Director of Korean Studies at the Institute of Far Eastern Studies at the Russian Academy of Sciences, provides an interesting analysis of the Koreas' role between China and Japan from a Russian perspective. In his chapter "Overcoming Obstacles for China–Japan Cooperation over the Korean Problem" the prospects for furthering regional cooperation and establishing a new peace regime in Northeast Asia are dependent, to a large degree, on China and Japan's ability, together with the United States and Russia, to reach a common vision for a future united Korea's place in the regional security system, a place mutually acceptable to the four "big countries." Of particular importance is the position of China and Japan. The heritage of numerous Sino–Japanese conflicts on the Korean Peninsula, starting from Toyotomi Hideyoshi's invasion in the sixteenth century, repelled with China's assistance, remain among the main obstacles for the development of Sino–Japanese cooperation over Korea. Beijing and Tokyo have different approaches to the solution of the nuclear problems on the Peninsula. These disagreements begin with responsibility for the current situation, the scope of the DPRK's nuclear programs, what part of them should be eliminated (only those meant for military use, or all of them, including those intended for peaceful use), the scale and depth of forthcoming inspections, conditions and character of security guarantees, and the economic assistance which the DPRK could be given. Beijing and Tokyo have differing visions of the future place of a united Korea in the regional and global systems of international relations. Tokyo sees this place within the framework of a tripartite alliance with Washington and Seoul. Such an approach can hardly satisfy Beijing, as she is likely to perceive such an alliance as a mechanism of containment or even deterrence against China. Tokyo is well aware of China's influence on the Peninsula and recognizes China as an important player in the region. However, the Japanese side, as a rule, prefers to forget about China's own legitimate security interests on the Peninsula and attempts to utilize China's influence almost exclusively for exerting additional pressure on Pyongyang. In spite of the above-mentioned differences, it is possible to identify a number of similar, or even identical, goals for China and Japan in Korea.

Hirosayu Akutsu of Japan's National Institute for Defense Studies contributes a chapter on "Japan–China Cooperation in Future Scenarios for the Korean Peninsula: Soft-Landing, Collapse and Muddling-through Cases." This chapter illustrates some major future scenarios leading towards a reunified Korean Peninsula and discusses Japan–China strategic relations in each of those scenarios. As an initial intellectual exercise, this paper focuses on two divergent cases, that is, soft-landing and hard-landing cases. The first case involves a situation in which the current North Korean nuclear missile controversy and other related issues are settled through the Six-Party Talks resulting in a unification of the two Koreas. The other case examines a scenario in which the collapse of the North Korean regime leads to an unstable or chaotic situation on the Korean Peninsula and in Northeast Asia. Possible responses of the United States, South Korea, China, Russia, and Japan, in both scenarios, are also discussed. This chapter then focuses on the likely course(s) that Japan–China strategic relations may follow in each of those scenarios, and points out several key issues stemming from the events and processes in the scenarios. In drawing up policy implications for a future Japan–China strategic relationship, based on mutual benefits regarding stabilization and peace-building on and beyond the Korean Peninsula, this chapter concludes that Japan and China could find many areas of cooperation and suggests that more advanced scenario studies should be developed between Japanese and Chinese experts.

This volume concludes with Victor Teo's chapter on the role of the Democratic People's Republic of Korea between China and Japan. The chapter outlines the evolution in Japan's and China's post–Cold War thinking and argues, contrary to what is commonly assumed, that North Korea's behavior is important for China's and Japan's grand strategy and foreign policy posture. At the same time, this presents an important opportunity for China and Japan to cooperate on an issue affecting their national security. Unfortunately, because of the domestic constraints and inertia of previous policy stances, these two powers have yet to capitalize on the opportunity provided to prevent the improvement in the strategic environment and work hand-in-hand to help ameliorate the issue on the Korean Peninsula. This approach illuminates how the DPRK is perceived by Tokyo and Beijing in a comparative perspective. This allows us to gain an insight into how North Korean issues are evaluated, interpreted, and manipulated in both capitals, while isolating and distinguishing their views from the United States' considerations is critical. Unless, and until, one understands how the Chinese and Japanese view the DPRK-related issues, one cannot be reasonably clear how Chinese and Japanese interests are juxtaposed against those of the United States, the dominant actor in East Asian politics.

This has important implications: Japan is often discounted as an international actor in DPRK-related issues because of the Yoshida doctrine, a cardinal pillar in Japan's foreign policy since the end of the Pacific War, that mandates Japan follow the United States in foreign and strategic affairs. China is often discounted as the patron and ally of the DPRK, suggesting that China can hardly act independently and judiciously when North Korean issues are concerned. These general assumptions are maintained surreptitiously in many narratives that dominate op-eds, media reports, and editorials. Some of these analyses are fairly accurate, while others are hardly fair portrayals of reality. Most of them make assumptions about the roles of the powers which must be scrutinized carefully.

This chapter highlights the important role of domestic politics in Japan in enhancing our understanding of North Korean issues, and argues that Japan's normalization agenda could be construed as the principal driver in her approach towards the DPRK issue. In other words, even though DPRK threat to Japan is a real, it is important to note that right-of-center Japanese politicians use it to drum up public opinion and electoral support, and predominantly to justify the normalization agenda. The normalization agenda, in part, drives Japan's DPRK posture. Likewise, in the DPRK, the united front posed by the US–Japan security alliance is an important theme in the DPRK's propaganda and official narratives. Japan, in particular, is significant as the "eternal" enemy, and remains essential to the official legitimating myths and in the DPRK leadership's exhortations for people to continually "sacrifice" in order to stave off threats from Japan and her allies. The differences in Japan's responses to the DPRK from the United States' position reveal, at best, cracks in Japan's long-professed stance in following the United States and, at worst, the beginning of an era where Japan is maturing strategically and might adopt eventual interdependence.

This chapter also argues that international opinion overestimates China's influence in North Korea. In understanding how the DPRK is debated and perceived through Chinese strategists' thinking, it reveals a schism in China's ability to operationalize its doctrine of Peaceful Rise and its image of a responsible power and the geo-strategic realities she faces. China has consistently refrained from "constraining" the DPRK, downplaying many real bilateral issues that dogged the Sino–DPRK relationship for many reasons. A regime collapse in the DPRK affects the People's Republic of China more than any other East Asian power—it has the most unthinkable consequences for China's northeastern region—economically, strategically, and demographically. Beyond that, the DPRK issue weighs heavily on China's often repeated principle of "non-interference" in the business of others. Even though the DPRK represents an important opportunity for China and Japan to cooperate and improve Sino–Japanese relations, domestic circumstances and strategic realities have made it difficult for both Beijing and Tokyo to seize this opportunity.

CHAPTER TWO

LEADERSHIP RIVALRY AND CRISIS-DRIVEN COOPERATION: DYNAMICS AMONG MUTUALLY DISTRUSTFUL CHINA, JAPAN, AND KOREA

DONG XIANG RONG

Introduction

China, Japan, and the Republic of Korea (hereafter Korea or South Korea) are three leading and vibrant countries in East Asia. According to the World Bank GDP rankings, in 2010 these three countries stood in second, third, and fourteenth places, respectively.[1] They account for more than three-quarters of the region's economic activity. However, in the regional cooperation map of East Asia, it appears that ASEAN plays a more critical role. China, Japan, and Korea are marginalized under the "10+3" framework. This abnormality needs to be investigated as it goes against the grain of theories on international relations. Why would a relatively strong China, Japan, and South Korea accept such a regional arrangement led by ASEAN? Why is greater cooperation among the three major powers in East Asia so difficult to achieve? The keywords here are leadership, rivalry, and mistrust.

As Gilbert Rozman has noted, while the EU paid increasing attention as to how power should be balanced in its horizontal composition, the struggle over East Asian regionalism has been much more about hierarchy

---

[1] "World Development Indicators: GDP (current US$)," The World Bank (2010): http://data.worldbank.org/indicator/NY.GDP.MKTP.CD?order=wbapi_data_value_2010+wbapi_data_value+wbapi_data_value-last&sort=desc.

and its vertical structure.[2] In order to become the accepted leader of the regional framework, China, Japan, and the ASEAN countries (Korea may also be included) have competed with each other under the shadow of the United States' hegemony over the last three decades. Now ASEAN is in the driver's seat and plays a central role, while China and Japan, both major powers, are still contesting the leadership position in the region.

In addition, institutional cooperation requires members of this community to surrender part of their sovereignty in order to accommodate supra-institutional arrangements that would benefit all three countries and the region. This implies that in order for China, Japan, and Korea to work together, something must be done on the basis of regional cooperation, and this is derived from a common sense of history, mutual trust, and "voting weight" (or voice) proportional to their national power. All of these elements are difficult to find in the relationship between these three countries.

It is a cliché to say that history offers invaluable insights for the study of international relations. However, it is necessary to examine the long history between China, Japan, and Korea to ascertain the root of the mistrust between them and the way forward for regional cooperation.

The Sino-centric Imperial Tributary System and its Effect

In ancient Asia, China was the leader of the tributary system for many years. The imperial tributary system, lasting from the Han Dynasty to the late Qing Dynasty,[3] was the system through which ancient China conducted foreign relations with other nations. The system is premised upon the basic assumption that Chinese civilization, particularly its Confucian ethics and writing system, was superior to that of the "barbarians" outside its borders. Therefore, barbarians who wished to join the Chinese civilization were required to recognize the Chinese emperor as the supreme ruler of all mankind. Representatives of foreign countries acknowledged this relationship by bringing local produce as a tribute, and in turn receiving an official seal, recognition, and gifts from the emperor.

It is worth mentioning that the imperial tributary system is not built on the principle of equality of countries in the Westphalian sense, but rather it is one premised upon a hierarchical China-centered framework. The

---

[2] G. Rozman, "Post Cold War Evolution of Chinese Thinking on Regional Institutions in Northeast Asia," *Journal of Contemporary China* 19, no. 66 (2010): 605–620.

[3] F. He, "A Study on 'Imperial Tributary System,'" *Journal of Peking University (Humanities and Social Sciences)*, no. 6 (1998): 30–45.

elements of Chinese civilization were introduced to Japan through Korea; thus, Korea played a bridge role in this process. That is to say, ancient China was at the core of this system, Korea occupied a semiperipheral position, and Japan was on the periphery or sometimes considered "out" of the system altogether.

The Chinese hold a positive view of the tributary system in general. Most are very proud of the leadership role played by ancient China. Historically, the successive Chinese dynasties paid very little attention to the sentiments of the states bordering China. The Chinese often took for granted that the neighboring countries held similar views on the tributary system and were simply grateful to be part of the civilizing influence of China. This, unfortunately, is a wrong view. According to research in Korea conducted in 2009 and 2010, although the Koreans recognize the positive civilizing influence of the tributary system, they mainly believe that Korea was oppressed, and even invaded, by ancient China and they hold a negative view on Sino–Korean relations.[4] It is unclear to what extent contemporary Koreans hold such a view. What is certain is that such a view is totally different from the Chinese point of view. This may help us to understand why the neighboring countries have been so cautious in accepting China's rise to becoming a regional power over recent decades.

The tributary system has left a negative legacy for international relations in Northeast Asia, which in turn has caused severe mistrust between Korea, Japan, and China. The Koreans and Japanese, as well as the neighboring countries in Southeast Asia, are apprehensive of China's perceived ambition to rebuild the tributary system. China's foreign policy towards neighboring countries in the twenty-first century is described officially as *Mulin Anlin Fulin*, which means to "build an amicable, tranquil, and prosperous neighborhood." China's main purpose is to preserve peace and stability in her "near abroad" so that economic development can proceed. This should, in theory, give no cause for criticism if coming from a smaller country. However, the articulation of such a thought is often perceived and understood to be a call for the re-emergence of the imperial tributary system. According to Eric Teo Chu Cheow, a Singaporean scholar:

> There are echoes of the ancient tributary system in certain geopolitical trends in Asia. The stabilization of China's immediate external environment is proceeding at an impressive pace … ASEAN–China free

[4] X. Dong, X. Wang, and Y. Li, *How the Koreans View China* (Beijing: Social Sciences Academic Press).

> trade project could be perceived as a continuation of China's tributary system across Southeast Asia … China has conceded trade surpluses to its smaller Asian neighbors—including Japan since 2003—in line with the tributary principle of "give more, take less." These trade surpluses are funneling economic growth to the smaller countries, thus confirming China as the heart of the Asian economic system today.[5]

Historical conflicts, such as the controversial claim regarding the ancient warrior kingdom of *Gaogouli* (Koguryo, 37 BC–688 DC), can also block regional trust-building in Northeast Asia. The kingdom encompassed modern-day North Korea, part of South Korea, and northeastern China. Some Chinese scholars have insisted that *Gaogouli* was a local minority of the ancient Chinese empire, while Korean scholars have strongly opposed this view and argue that Koguryo is an integral part of Korea's history. This is one of the more negative issues in the dispute between China and Korea over the last decade, causing damage to their civil relationship.

Being on the edge of the Sino-centric world order, the Japanese people were traditionally and dismissively treated as "eastern barbarians" or "dwarf bandits" by ancient China. Japan, for her part, understood herself to be part of the Sinic-cultural zone, but never saw herself as part of China's traditional world order, nor did she perceive herself to be part of the tributary system. This has caused misunderstanding and conflict between these two nations.

Japan-centric "Greater East Asia Co-Prosperity Sphere" and its Legacy

While China declined, during the late Qing Dynasty, Japan rose and played a leading role in the region. Japan defeated China in 1895 and annexed Korea in 1910, initiating thirty-five years of colonial rule on the Korean Peninsula. The Japanese rule experienced resistance and revolt from the Korean people. Japan embarked on an invasion of China in 1931, and it was not until Japan came to face the military pressure of the United States and the Soviet Union that Japan was forced to surrender in August 1945. This period of Japanese imperialism brought disaster and suffering to the Chinese and Korean people, and although Japanese politicians have expressed regret over the past decades concerning their actions, the Chinese and the Koreans are far from satisfied.

---

[5] C. C. E. Teo, "Paying Tribute to Beijing: An Ancient Model for China's New Power," *New York Times*, January 21, 2004.

Today, it is evident from Chinese and Korean hostility that many people have not forgiven Japan for her past misdeeds, regardless of the fact that Japan has a more developed economy and shows advanced technological progress. The thirty-five years of colonial rule brought an obvious division to Korean society: the conservative Japanophiles are extremely friendly to Japan, while the progressive elements hold strong nationalistic sentiments and are both hostile to and sensitive about Japan. Such sentiments affect Korea–Japan relations and domestic politics in Korea.

Even though there were many traitors in China during the Sino–Japanese War, China is probably not as polarized as Korea and most of the Chinese people do not possess a friendly view of Japan. At the core of the problems Japan has with China and Korea is Japan's inability to sincerely apologize to China and Korea for her past misdeeds, and this stems from a conviction on the part of the Japanese that she was defeated neither by the Koreans nor by the Chinese. Expressions of such resentment and discontent on the part of the Chinese, Japanese, and Koreans can now be found on the Internet.

Japan and the United States officially signed the San Francisco Peace Treaty in 1951, while Korea and China were excluded from the outset of the process. The United States parted company with the United Kingdom in the decision to invite representatives from mainland China or Taiwan, and eventually neither of them were invited. Korea was asked to attend the meeting; however, Korea was not treated as a member of the alliance, but rather as a colony of Japan.[6] Shortly after the conclusion of the San Francisco Peace Treaty, Japan was asked to rejoin the Western community led by the United States. Her participation and integration into the US-led bloc came without first dealing with the war legacy. Thus, Japan was unable to improve its bilateral relations with its most important neighbors, Korea and China, for a long time. When Korea normalized relations with Japan in 1965, with China following suit in 1972, the historical issues were treated with ambiguity and later became a hindrance to building trust between the three countries.

The Focus of Controversy: The Yasukuni Shrine

The Yasukuni Shrine was established to commemorate and honor the achievements of those who sacrificed their lives for the Japanese Empire during national crises, such as the Sino–Japanese and Russo–Japanese

---

[6] Jeffrey N. Wasserstrom, *The Contemporary and Modern History of Three East Asian Countries* (Beijing: Social Sciences Academic Press, 2005).

wars, World War I, and the Greater East Asian War (World War II), amongst others.[7] These people, regardless of their rank or social standing, are considered to be completely equal to, and worshipped as, venerable divinities of Yasukuni.[8] This is the case according to the inscription on the shrine, and from the perspective of the Japanese people.

However, to Japan's neighbors, especially Korea and China, such a belief is an outright offense. Class-A war criminals of World War II are honored in the shrine, and this has turned Yasukuni into a symbol of Japanese militarism, and of the wartime atrocities committed against the Chinese and Koreans. Therefore, any Japanese politician who visits the shrine is perceived to lack an appropriate degree of reflection upon history, and such behavior is interpreted as a sign of rising militarism.

To the Koreans, the Yasukuni Shrine commemorates the Japanese soldiers and civilian workers who spearheaded the invasion and colonization of Korea, as well recalling the approximately 21,000 Koreans who were forcibly mobilized and sacrificed for Japan's war of aggression.[9]

The Chinese show a much stronger antipathy toward the shrine than the Koreans. After Japanese Premier Koizumi's visit to the shrine on the first day of 2004, the then Chinese Deputy Foreign Minister, Wang Yi, lodged solemn representations over Koizumi's visit and condemned the act immediately. Wang stressed that the shrine honors Class-A war criminals whose hands were smeared with the blood of the people of China and other Asian countries. Prime Minister Koizumi's visit to the shrine not only went back on his promise to reflect upon history, but also impaired the political basis of Sino–Japanese relations. The Chinese people cannot accept such actions by a Japanese leader.[10] Wang's arguments

---

[7] "The origin of the Yasukuni Shrine was the Shokonsha established at Kudan in Tokyo in the second year of the Meiji era (1869) by the will of the Emperor Meiji. In 1879, it was renamed the 'Yasukuni Shrine.' When the Emperor Meiji visited the Tokyo Shokonsha for the first time on January 27 in 1874, he composed a poem: 'I assure those of you who fought and died for your country that your names will live forever at this shrine in Musashino.' As can be seen in this poem, the name 'Yasukuni,' given by the Emperor Meiji, represents wishes for preserving peace for the nation. Currently, more than 2,466,000 divinities are enshrined at Yasukuni Shrine. These are the souls of men who made the ultimate sacrifice for their nation since 1853. See Yasukuni Shrine: http://www.yasukuni.or.jp/english/about/index.html.

[8] Ibid.

[9] The Northeast Asian History Foundation: http://english.historyfoundation.or.kr/?sub_num=81&state=02_J04.

[10] "Koizumi's Shrine Visit Criticized," *Xinhua News Agency*, January 2, 2004. http://www.china.org.cn/english/2004/Jan/83755.htm.

reflect not only China's official standpoint but also the voices of ordinary people in China.

Are there any methods to resolve the Yasukuni Shrine issue? Would it be acceptable to the Chinese and Koreans for the Japanese Prime Minister to visit the shrine if the Class-A war criminals were removed? Would the Chinese and Koreans be satisfied if Japanese officials sincerely apologized for Japan's war crimes? The answer is possibly no; at the core of this issue is neither the Class-A war criminals nor the apologies, but rather it is about who "won" the war. In Japan, it is very common to hear the expression "it was neither China nor Korea, but the United States that defeated us in the war." This view, however, is only partly true. Although China and Korea strived vigorously in their campaign against Japan, Japan only surrendered when faced with direct pressure from the United States and the Soviet Union. In doing so, the regional leadership was not transferred from Japan to China and Korea, but to a country that lies outside the geographical scope of this region, the United States. China and Korea did not defeat Japan in the war, and had no opportunity to exact "an eye for an eye, a tooth for a tooth," i.e., to vanquish Japan. Therefore, the resultant tensions and dissatisfaction amongst the Korean and Chinese civilians can hardly be ameliorated.

Cold War and After: The United States-centric Order in Northeast Asia

There is no doubt that the United States has been the hegemonic power in Northeast Asia since the end of World War II. During the Cold War, neither China nor Japan played a leading role in this region's security arrangements. From a military and security point of view, it was the United States that played the leading role, mainly through her respective alliances with Japan and Korea. The Security Treaty between the United States and Japan was signed in 1951, and subsequently revised as The Treaty of Mutual Cooperation and Security (1960), and again revised in 1996 when President Clinton met with Prime Minister Hashimoto. The 1953 Mutual Defense Treaty between South Korea and the United States is the second pillar of US strategy in Asia. Even though Korea and Japan have had many contradictions and conflicts, they belong to the same camp. What this essentially means is that, in *de facto* terms, China is not dealing with two individual countries, but rather with a quasi-alliance. The term "quasi-alliance" was coined by Victor Cha, and characterizes the relationship of South Korea and Japan as two unallied countries, which are related to each other as quasi-allies through their alliance with the United

States.[11] After the end of the Cold War between the United States and the former Soviet Union, Northeast Asia has possibly become the last Cold War frontier in the world, where millions of North and South Korean soldiers still confront each other along the thirty-eighth parallel. The essence of the Korea–Japan quasi-alliance has not changed that much; in the case of military conflict in Northeast Asia, Japan, together with South Korea, will follow the United States against China.

In analyzing the economic development of Eastern Asia during the Cold War, scholars have used the "Flying Geese Pattern" led by Japan. I would call this a development echelon rather than a regional regime. Japan is deemed to head the flying formation, leading the second tier of newly industrialized economies consisting of South Korea, Taiwan, Singapore, and Hong Kong. After these two groups come the main ASEAN countries: the Philippines, Indonesia, Thailand, and Malaysia. The third tier consists of the least developed major nations in the region: China, Vietnam, etc. Therefore, if we look at this region in terms of economic linkages, it is also plausible to attribute the economic rise of these countries to the technology and market access of the United States. Even though this is the case, both Sino–Japanese and Sino–Korean relations have much improved since the establishment of diplomatic relations in 1972 and 1992, respectively.

The two decades after 1972 seemed like the "heyday" of Sino–Japanese re-engagement.[12] During this time, Japan gave China considerable aid and transferred much-needed technology in lieu of reparations for Tokyo's aggression in the 1930s and 1940s. Also during this period, Japanese cultural products, such as movies, dramas, and cartoons, were imported to China. Beijing's larger strategic agenda, at home and abroad, resulted in cooperation and the minimization of "history" as an issue between the two countries. However, Sino–Japanese relations experienced a downward spiral after the mid-1990s, when Japan began to shift its official development assistance (ODA) from China to Southeast Asia, and a resurgence in Japanese nationalism began to surface. The Chinese public's perception of Japan's purported lack of remorse over the atrocities committed by the Imperial Armed Forces—created by revisionism in textbooks, the Yasukuni Shrine visits, and disputes over the facts and

---

[11] V. Cha, "Abandonment, Entrapment, and Neoclassical Realism in Asia," *International Studies Quarterly* 44 (2000): 261–291.

[12] M. McDevitt, "China's Role in the World: Is China a Responsible Stakeholder?" Hearing before the US–China Economic and Security Review Commission, Panel VI: China's Relationship with Northeast Asian Neighbors, August 3/4, 2006 (revised final) http://www.uscc.gov/.

figures of the Nanjing massacre—led to a rapid deterioration of bilateral relations. The Chinese leadership had to postpone, reduce the frequency of, or even cancel, their visits to Japan on different occasions. From the Japanese perspective, China has failed to adequately express her thanks to Japan for the huge amount of ODA received, and has persisted in what appears to be an incessant demand for the Japanese to apologize for past war crimes; and many Japanese are growing weary of this.[13] Since then, Sino–Japanese relations have been characterized by "hot economics and cold politics." Yet perhaps China and Japan have experienced such a prolonged period of dispute not only because of arguments over "history" but, more importantly, because of the competition between them over leadership in East Asia.

China and Korea also experienced a decade of warm relations after they established diplomatic relations in 1992. The decision to normalize relations with Seoul was not an easy one for China, as China had to persuade her traditional friend, North Korea, to accept this situation. Since then, Sino–Korean trade has grown at an annual rate of over 20 percent, and by 2003 Beijing had supplanted the United States as Seoul's number one trading partner. China and Korea issued a joint statement in May 2008 upgrading their "comprehensive and cooperative partnership" to a "strategic cooperative partnership," which implies stronger ties in foreign affairs, security, economy, society, culture, and personnel exchanges. At the same time, political and economic interactions have generated cultural and social interactions between China and Korea. There are reportedly more than 700,000 Koreans living in mainland China in recent years and forming increasingly numerous Korean communities in Beijing, Shanghai, Qingdao, and other cities in Eastern China. At the same time, there are approximately 600,000 Chinese working or studying in South Korea.

Regardless of these improvements, the Sino–Korean relationship has also suffered a downward spiral similar to that experienced in Sino–Japanese relations over the last decade or so. These two countries have had some trade issues, such as the short-lived "Garlic war" of 2000 and the "Kimchi war" of 2005. Even more so, the *Gaogouli* dispute has cast a shadow over the bilateral relationship since 2003. These episodes are symptomatic of a larger fear, on the part of the Koreans, of the rise in power of the Chinese, even though the ROK also stands to gain from Chinese economic development.

---

[13] Satoshi Amako, *China in Japanese Eyes* (Beijing: Social Sciences Academic Press, 2003), 22–41.

Crisis-driven Cooperation in Northeast Asia

Even though the United States is still the most influential power in Northeast Asia, China and Japan appear to have become embroiled in a rivalry over being recognized as Asia's leading power. It would appear that neither Tokyo nor Beijing is content to be the number two regional power in East Asia, and it could be decades before one of them emerges as the recognized number one. The reality is, therefore, that both China and Japan seek to ignore each other's leadership claims, while at the same time trying their best to coexist.

Negative historical legacies have caused civilian hostilities and national rivalry between China and Japan, and this has had a spillover effect into their competition for regional leadership. After the 1997 financial crisis, Asian governments have been considering strengthening regional monetary and financial cooperation. Ironically, it turns out that ASEAN played a crucial role in regional cooperation, while the big three (Japan, China, and Korea—the three economic giants—account for more than three-quarters of the region's economic activity) have been relatively marginalized under the "10+3" framework. This is partly due to mistrust between these three countries caused by historical disputes, as mentioned above. In other words, ASEAN's driver seat in the regional cooperation framework is the by-product of the leadership rivalry between China and Japan.

It would appear that the only possible way for cooperation in Northeast Asia is "crisis-driven" cooperation. By this I mean that leaders in these three countries can only be pushed into economic and security cooperation in a big way whilst ignoring civilian mistrust and negative sentiments and other domestic political factors—and this can only happen when crises occur, such as during the 1997 and 2008 financial crises, and so on. There is an ancient Chinese aphorism, *Tongzhou Gongji* (同舟共济), which essentially means: "When on a common boat crossing the river, everyone must pull their weight and cooperate peacefully to perform the task at hand."[14] This is a metaphor for the situation in which China, Japan, and Korea now find themselves, faced with nuclear threats and financial crises.

The historic China–Japan–Korea Summit, held on December 13, 2008, in Fukuoka, was a good case for such crisis-driven cooperation. It is a milestone for regional cooperation in Northeast Asia. The summit, which

---

[14] This alludes to an ancient episode in which soldiers from the warring states of Wu and Yue found themselves on the same boat on a river in a storm and agreed to put down their arms to make a common passage.

was very different from previous summits held under the "10+3 framework," was the first time that leaders of China, Japan, and South Korea had held independent summits in order to handle the recent financial tsunami. Yet it must be highlighted that such a summit would most likely have been impossible had it not been for the financial crisis.

Why was China happy to go to Fukuoka to attend such a triangular summit? Gilbert Rozman lists three of the "many advantages" of a summit outside the confines of the ASEAN+3 framework: it puts the states on a level playing field where values will not be the decisive factor in influencing decisions; it opens the door to a three-way free-trade agreement; and it establishes a co-existence which may undercut the alliance triangle led by the United States.[15] This analysis sounds reasonable; however, from my point of view, the most important reason is that Chinese leaders believe that the triangular framework is the core of regional cooperation in East Asia. It is common sense to say that there will be no real cooperation in Asia without the institutionalized cooperation of the big three.

The Chiang Mai Initiative is another example of how China and Japan can cooperate peacefully with each other, driven by economic crisis. During the ASEAN+3 Finance Ministers' Meeting, held in Bali in May 2009, the countries involved signed an agreement on the multilateralization of the Chiang Mai Initiatives (CMIM), allowing the members to tap into a regional pool of foreign exchange reserves to better fend off an attack during any given financial crisis. What is interesting is that both Japan and China obtained their wish in a miraculous way: Japan will contribute 32 percent of the total to the CMIM, or US $38.4 billion of the US $120 billion pool. The PRC will also contribute US $38.4 billion in total: US $34.2 billion from the mainland and US $4.2 billion from Hong Kong, China. Thus, Japan is the "single largest contributor" and at the same time the PRC (including Hong Kong) and Japan are the "largest co-equal contributors." To observers, the CMIM is symbolic of China's rise, and the consequent eclipsing of Japanese power. When one looks at the other regional institutions that China had joined earlier, such as the Asian Development Bank, China's presence (and potentially its formal voting weight) as a ratio of Japan's has increased from under one-half to near parity.[16]

As for the security sphere, the most important issue on the agenda for these three countries is the nuclear threat posed by North Korea. China,

---

[15] Rozman, "Post Cold War Evolution of Chinese Thinking."

[16] J. Rathus, "The Chiang Mai Initiative: China, Japan, and Financial Regionalism," May 11, 2009: www.eastasiaforum.org.

Japan, and South Korea have to find a resolution within the framework of the Six-Party Talks for a peaceful settlement of the Korean Peninsula nuclear issue. So the formation of the Six-Party Talks can be seen as a regional regime driven by the nuclear crisis.

With regards to the Six-Party Talks, Gilbert Rozman argues that it shows China is a "driving force in Asia," and that "the Six-Party Talks were not China's idea in 2003, but lately it has taken the lead in promoting their revival with a much broader agenda for regional security."[17] Actually, China's role in the Six-party Talks is as coordinator rather than as leader. The reason China became so actively involved in coordinating the peaceful negotiations is to prevent a war on the Korean Peninsula. China's intention was not to become the leader of the regional security cooperation, but to prevent disaster happening to Northeast Asia and China itself. China was happy to see the United States and North Korea negotiate bilaterally within the Six-Party Talks framework if they were able to achieve the denuclearization of the Korean Peninsula. As a Korean scholar has argued, China and South Korea share "common aversions," not "common interests," as both countries want to avoid any kind of military conflict on the Korean Peninsula and prevent North Korea's nuclearization.[18] If war happens, China and South Korea will suffer much more than any of the other countries. This is why China and South Korea cooperated much more smoothly than other countries during the first period of the Six-Party Talks.

Denuclearization of the Korean Peninsula in a peaceful manner has been the objective of the Six-Party Talks right from the beginning. Yet the problems on the Peninsula are much more intricate and difficult. Peaceful negotiations failed to prevent North Korea's two nuclear tests in 2006 and 2009. From the very beginning, it appeared that none of the major players held denuclearization as the top priority objective for the talks. For the United States, the top priority goal was nonproliferation, as the United States was eager to prevent Pyongyang from sharing nuclear weapons with Islamic terrorists. China and South Korea would like to end North Korea's nuclear program more than the other parties because they are wary of the consequences of nuclear testing. China and South Korea are careful not to force North Korea into a war, and at the same time, neither of them wants to apply serious economic pressure that could cause the Kim regime to

---

[17] G. Rozman, "East Asian Regionalism and Sinocentrism," *Japanese Journal of Political Science* 13, no. 1 (2012): 143–153.

[18] T. Kim, "China's Ascendancy and the Future of the Korean Peninsula," in *Korea in the New Asia: East Asian Integration and the China Factor*, edited by Francoise Nicolas (London: Routledge, 2007).

collapse. Japan's top priority, it would appear, was the kidnapping issue rather than nuclear disarmament. Even though Russia is involved in the talks, it is not very clear what the Russians want out of them. To sum up, from the beginning of the talks, it would almost appear that, to some extent, the nuclearization of North Korea is not so unacceptable to the United States, China, South Korea, Russia, and Japan as one might expect. This is the main reason why the Six-Party Talks have not been successful.[19]

Conclusion

From a macro perspective, it would appear that relations between China, Japan, and Korea are rather more complex than a first glance would suggest. The tributary system, centered on ancient China, and the Japan-centric "Greater East Asia Co-Prosperity Sphere" were both, in a sense, hierarchical structures that placed China and Japan at their respective centers. Their difference lies in the fact that the former was based on political and cultural tributary relations, and the latter on military power. Disputes over "history" amongst these three countries are direct manifestations of the contestations for regime legitimacy and regional political leadership. Japan and Korea have, until today, maintained a close alliance with the United States, so what China has been facing is, essentially, not just two individual countries, but rather an alliance or quasi-alliance. As such, we can hardly say that the relations between China, Japan, and Korea have been "ordinary" triangular relations.[20] In the last decade, it appears that China and Japan have embarked on another round of rivalry for leadership in the region. This rivalry, along with negative historical legacies, has become the main obstacle to regional cooperation. Owing to negative historical legacies and leadership rivalry, initiative cooperation is difficult and rarely found in Northeast Asia. Regional cooperation has moved several steps forward, driven mainly by

---

[19] Other reasons which render the denuclearization negotiations impotent relate to the essential nature of nuclear weapons. First, to most of the powers involved, the nuclear threat is a potential threat, not a real one, and when faced with more pressing immediate threats, such as war, it is unlikely that parties would assign it a high priority. Second, the nuclear capability of North Korea is comparatively limited, and is insufficient to threaten the interests of the United States and so to become a major issue in the Oval Office.

[20] S. Tang and X. Cao, "Seeking the Base Point of Mutual Security between China, the United States and Japan," *Strategy and Management*, no. 1 (2002): 99–109.

the 1997 and 2008 economic financial crises and the 2003 nuclear crisis in the Korean Peninsula.

The rise of China and South Korea, and the comparable stagnation of Japan, has changed the regional structure since the 1990s. China has, in some ways, overtaken Japan as the main engine for regional economic growth over the last two decades, but from an economic and technical perspective, China still lacks the ability to lead Asia by itself. For the foreseeable future, China has to respect Japan's achievements and, in return, Japan has to accept the rise of China, no matter how reluctant they both might feel. As the Chiang Mai Initiatives has shown, China and Japan are the largest, co-equal contributors, and neither of them is able to play the leading role. This may mark the balance period of China–Japan leadership rivalry. Under such an arrangement, although South Korea's part would not be as big as that of China and Japan in absolute terms, it could have an important role in balancing the ambitions and rivalry between China and Japan.

It is not controversial to say that every power in East Asia is trying to be the leader of regional cooperation. As an old Napoleonic saying has it, "those soldiers who are not willing to be a general are not good soldiers." Nonetheless, China is not so eager to be the leader in the foreseeable future. As Zhang Yunling, the famous and influential expert on Asian cooperation, has argued, although China is acknowledged to be the leader of East Asian regional cooperation, the fact remains that China cannot play such a role; from China's perspective, she is still a developing country, and thus to become a top-ranking decision maker is beyond her. From another point of view, China's leadership is always linked to China's potential monopoly, which inspires fear.[21] If China can keep moving forwards, a leadership position is natural for her. However, if China does not continue to develop, it is useless for her to compete for the role of leadership. To date, China has chosen to eschew this leadership rivalry competition by emphasizing the lead role of ASEAN. In addition, she promotes functional cooperation step by step and avoids the dilemmas of leadership. This means, at least at present, that "China does not aim towards a self-centered East Asian regionalism, although giving up the leadership totally is also unacceptable."[22] Time is somewhat on China's side.

---

[21] Y. Zhang, "Searching the Road to Push East Asian Cooperation Forward," *Foreign Affairs Review* 6 (2011): 7–11.

[22] Wang Yuzhu, "China, Economic Regionalism, and East Asian Integration," *Japanese Journal of Political Science* 12 (2011): 195–212.

CHAPTER THREE

HISTORIOGRAPHICAL CONFLICTS AND RECONCILIATION IN EAST ASIA: KOREA AT THE CENTER

LEONID A. PETROV

Controversies over history in East Asia are not a recent phenomenon. In modern times, Japanese colonialists and nationalist historians in China and Korea have clashed over the origins of their respective nations. After the 1945 Liberation, North and South Korea fiercely competed for the right of national unification based on historical legitimacy. In the 1980s, a highly publicized controversy over Japan's textbook screening process flared in the region. The issue of "comfort women," the cultural heritage of the *Koguryŏ/Gaogouli* kingdom, and official visits by Japanese politicians to the Yasukuni Shrine continue to cause tensions between the neighbors.

Due to its central geographical position and nationalistic cultural policies, Korea is entangled in territorial, historiographical, and cultural disputes. The legacy of colonialism, the unfinished Cold War, and the ongoing nuclear confrontation have turned the Korean Peninsula into the hub of regional conflicts. The genuine reasons for confrontation with China and Japan are economic competition and security concerns. What helps Korea to successfully pursue its national interests is its unique location and strategic alliances. However, to achieve internal reconciliation and to advance regionalism, many unresolved issues of the neighboring countries' common past should be properly addressed and closed.

The Troubled Region

Looking at the map of East Asia, where China, Japan, and the Russian Far East occupy by far the most space, one cannot help but notice that Korea is at the center. The Korean Peninsula has always been a natural bridge for migration, trade missions, and culture waves between the continent and the islands of the northern Pacific. It used to be the conduit linking ancient China and Japan, and became the terminating point of Mongolian military expansion eastward, the springboard for Japanese colonization plans in Asia, and the Cold War's hottest and most long-lasting frontier. Policy makers and strategists of all periods have seen Korea as an important place, worthy of control and protection from potential enemies.

Relations with its neighbors, the dominating powers in the region, have been fateful for Korea. Even a minor political event occurring on the Peninsula would attract their attention and incur a swift reaction. For this reason, Korea has an exceptionally rich and dramatic political history. Time and again, the ruling dynasties of China attempted to incorporate Korea into their empires but could hardly secure anything more than its vassal status, which in modern terms would mean a security treaty. Military regimes on the Japanese islands, when planning to expand their sphere of influence towards the continent, would first have to win a war against Korea before being able to go any further.

More recently, in the late nineteenth century, China, Russia, and Japan all expected Korea to be friendly, or neutral and equidistant. The modern expansion of Japanese power and influence over the rest of East Asia started with the Sino–Japanese War (1894/95). Fought between Qing Dynasty China and Meiji Japan, this conflict's main argument was related to the question as to which country would control Korea. As a rising power, Japan wished to protect its own interests and security by either annexing Korea or by ensuring Korea's independence from other competitors. China was weak, but had strong allies who were quick to intervene on its behalf. As the result of this "First Korean War," in 1897 the *Taehan Cheguk* (Great Korean Empire) was proclaimed, only to start falling under the influence of Imperial Russia shortly after.

The piecemeal reforms and sluggish administration once again made Korea an easy target for imperialist contest. The temporary agreement over the influence on Korea was once again challenged in the course of the Russo–Japanese War (1904/05). This "Second Korean War" gave Japan a free hand to annex its closest neighbor and then to turn it into a colony. Korea lost control of its foreign policy and was managed by Japan, who tried to extend its influence in Manchuria.

To expand its proper control in China and to extract more concessions, Japan took advantage of the existing border dispute between the Qing government and the Lee Dynasty of Korea concerning the Kando/Jiandao territory in southern Manchuria. The 1909 Kando Convention recognized the Chinese claim to Kando in exchange for Japan attaining railroad rights in Manchuria.[1] The colonized Korea found itself deprived of political independence and other attributes of a sovereign nation, and was forced to serve the military needs of Tokyo, which was geared for the colonization of the entirety of East Asia and the Pacific. For the long thirty-six years of colonial rule, radical Korean partisan groups pursued anti-Japanese military resistance, while Korean intellectuals struggled against the colonial distortions of history.

With the fall of Japan and the end of World War II, Korea was suddenly liberated by the Soviet Union and the United States, who divided the Korean Peninsula into two temporary zones of occupation. At that time, when the new global conflict known as the Cold War had already been brewing, this "temporary" division of Korea became consolidated and ideologically cemented. Soon after the "liberators" left the Peninsula, a new Korean War broke out. Starting in June 1950 as a civil war, this conflict in Korea soon escalated to the level of a surrogate World War III, where sixteen nations under the UN flag were fighting the Communist Bloc countries. The hostilities halted in July 1953 with an Armistice Agreement, but the "Third Korean War" has never really ended.

For decades the region remained an active conflict zone dominated by the unresolved issues and legacies of colonialism, World War II, and the Cold War conflict. Korea was divided politically, economically, and ideologically, where both the Democratic People's Republic of Korea (DPRK) and the Republic of Korea (ROK) were supported by their respective international camps, which were hostile towards each other. The civil war in China also ended inconclusively in 1949, leaving the country divided into the People's Republic of China (PRC) and the Republic of China (ROC). And after Moscow and Tokyo failed to agree on the terms of the Peace Treaty, signed by forty-nine other nations in San Francisco in September 1951, Japan remains divided, with its Northern Territories controlled by Russia.

Tensions between South Korea and Japan are rising due to their claims for administrative rights over the tiny islets of Dokdo/Takeshima. These islets, also known as the Liancourt Rocks, were not mentioned in the 1951 San Francisco Treaty. Existing historical documents fail to provide sufficient evidence to support the claims by one side or another. Even the name of the sea that surrounds the disputed islets is controversial. The

---

[1] Under the 1951 San Francisco Treaty this agreement became null and void. D. Kang, "The 100 Years of Kando Convention… 'Returning our Lost Land' is Spreading," *Hankook Ilbo* 2 (September 2009): http://economy.hankooki.com/lpage/worldecono/200909/e2009090217445969820.htm.

Koreans insist that the Sea of Japan should be universally called the "East Sea," as it was known before the colonial expansion of Japan in the late nineteenth century. However, the Japanese, on principle, refuse to use this name in relation to the sea that lies west of their islands.

These days, Korea and China struggle over the ownership title for the cultural relics left behind from the ancient kingdoms of *Chosŏn/Chaoxian*, *Koguryŏ/Gaogouli*, and *Parhae/Bohai*. Despite contentious evidence provided by archaeologists and linguists, these kingdoms are revered by Koreans as the earliest states in their national history. The fact that their territories once occupied the plains of Manchuria and the Liaodong Peninsula makes this issue particularly sensitive for China. The defunct 1909 Kando Convention is not forgotten by ultra-nationalists, and one day may spark irredentism in the areas heavily populated by ethnic Koreans.

What makes East Asian affairs even more troubled and complicated is the old system of block alliances that has been inherited from the times of the Cold War. Japan and South Korea are still firmly on the side of the United States, who built this regional alliance in the early days of the communism-containment strategy. Despite the collapse of the Communist Bloc (in which North Korea is a rare survivor) and the dwindling economic aid from China and Russia, Pyongyang's security alliance with Moscow and Beijing is still in force.[2] In other words, we still observe the existence of remnants of the old system within the region which has long since disappeared elsewhere. The bloc mentality in international affairs, the level of inter-governmental distrust, and mutual animosity make East Asia highly volatile.

The region remains deeply divided, and the front line lies right across the Korean Peninsula. However, it is not only the unresolved issues of the Cold War that keep the countries of East Asia tense and paranoid. The toxic legacies of Japanese colonialism and the earlier Western imperial competition in China have left deep scars across this troubled region. In short, East Asian politics are deeply entangled in a multilayer pile of problems. Without resolving them, the trauma left from colonial and imperial domination will never be healed, and the badly needed reconciliation will remain unaccomplished.

---

[2] J. D. Pollack, "The Major Powers and the Two Koreas: An Uneasy Transition," *The Korean Journal of Defense Analysis* 21, no. 1 (2009): 1–9.

Historiographical Conflicts

History studies and education, in such complex circumstances, resemble a minefield replete with dangers and traps. The natural relativity of history opens numerous avenues for politicizing this academic discipline. As Michael Oakeshott noted in *Experience and its Modes* (1933): "History is a product of historians whose writings create it."[3] The rewriting of history in accordance with political necessity is normally initiated by policy makers. According to Benedetto Croce, "all histories are contemporary histories" (1941).[4] That leaves the business of interpretations of the past to the discretion of people with vested interests. Ultimately, history research and education become highly politicized and ideological. This was also noted by Robin Collingwood, who argued in 1946 that "all histories are the histories of ideas."[5]

It is also important to remember that "history" and "past" are not the same. Max Weber (1977) understood the "past" as events which existed before and cannot be changed. On the contrary, "history" for him was a constellation of facts assembled from the infinite material provided by the past.[6] Here the "perception of history"—the standard that historians use when they pick certain facts from an available assortment—comes into play, where "history" becomes a product of "historical perceptions" determined by people's current interests.

Thus, the selection of facts from the past is discretional and motivated by the changing necessity of the present. Edward H. Carr in his *What is History?* (1961) believed that history is a continuous dialogue between the past and the present, and an everlasting interaction between the historian and his facts.[7] The subjectivity of views and hidden political agendas are always present even in the most innocuous investigations of the past. Historians are often hired by governments or partisan groups to exaggerate or, alternatively, to whitewash historical records. As a result, History as an academic discipline conceals inconvenient truths and creates new myths.

---

[3] M. Okeshott, *Experience and Its Modes* (Cambridge: Cambridge University Press), 99.

[4] B. Croce, *History as the Story of Liberty* (London: George Allen & Unwin, 1941), 19.

[5] R. G. Collingwood, *The Idea of History* (Oxford: Oxford University Press, 1946), 215, 317.

[6] M. Weber, "Interpretive Sociology, and the Sense of Historical Science: A Positivistic Conception of Verstehen," *The Sociological Quarterly* 18, no. 2 (1977): 165–175.

[7] E. H. Carr, *What is History?* (New York: Alfred A. Knopf, 1961).

An infinite variety of facts continue to nurture conflicting views and stimulate debates between the different schools of historiography. Among the most incompatible are those of China and Taiwan, Japan and Russia, Sino–Korean and Japanese, colonial and nationalist, and leftist and conservative. Contrasting historical narratives include the "Japanese version," "Korean version," and "Chinese version" of East Asian history, where the same events can be viewed from completely different perspectives, depending on whether their authors were motivated by the "national autonomy concept" (*Juch'esŏng*) or "modernization concept" (*Kŭndaehwa*).

No historiographical tradition is perfect. The Positivist School is concentrated on fact-finding and verification. However, in circumstances where obvious facts were not properly documented (i.e., Dokdo/Takeshima, "comfort women") this method is deficient. The Constructivist School challenges this lack of records by utilizing the alternative available sources (oral histories, mirror statistics, etc.) but the objectivity of utilized sources can be questioned. The Nationalist School of historiography concentrates on the acute needs of a nation, but is prone to myth-building and appealing to people's emotions, while the Marxist School of historiography tends to view history only from the perspective of class struggle and does not take into account any "subjective" factors, such as the role of personality in history.

History research in East Asia is particularly susceptible to a number of specific problems. The legitimacy of wars, colonization, and national boundaries are still vehemently contested. Competing nationalist conceptions and interpretations of history encourage states to lay claims and deny the claims of others. History generates controversies, and hinders regional reconciliation and integration. In this context, the Nationalist approach to contested history seems to be the most problematic and echoes Ernest Renan's famous adage: "getting history wrong is an essential part of being a nation" (1882).[8]

Current conflicts in East Asia can be divided into three categories. The first category of disputes involves the possession of cultural assets (physical, spiritual, and territorial) of long-extinct civilizations. Debates over the cultural affinity of ancient kingdoms (i.e., *Koguryŏ/Gaogouli, Parhae/Bohai, Imna/Mimana*) fall into this category, as well as territorial disputes over the Dokdo/Takeshima islets, the Diayou/Senkaku islands, the South Kuril/Northern Territories, and geographical names of the East

[8] E. Renan, "What is a Nation?" in *Nation and Narration*, edited by Homi K. Bhabha, 8–22 (London: Routledge, 1990).

Sea/Sea of Japan. Disputes about the origins of traditional Oriental medicine, calligraphy, the *Tano/Duanwu* Festival, and the family lineage of Confucius and the poet Qu Yuan can also be included.

The second category of conflicts pertains to the ways in which certain militaries colonized and maltreated the peoples of neighboring countries. An example would be Japan's notion of the "Greater East Asia Co-Prosperity Sphere," developmental colonialism in Korea and Taiwan, and wartime atrocities. The Nanking Massacre, Unit 731 in Manchuria, "comfort women," and forced labor camps provide a plethora of evidence to support such claims. The liberation, occupation, and division of Korea by the Allied Powers (1945–48) must be included in this category.

The third category of conflicts relates to those caused by the contemporary accounts on, and debates about, the issues outlined above. The ongoing discussions about the timeline and location of ancient civilizations, reactions to Japanese government apology and compensation for war crimes, history textbooks controversies, changing geographic maps, administrative borders, and names create political issues. Reexamination of the Tokyo Trial, the San Francisco Peace Treaty, and post-war repatriations also belong here.

Sharp generational divides in Japan, Korea, and China can also deeply affect their societies and instigate fierce political debates within and without these countries. According to the former ROK President Kim Dae-jung, the silence of the old generation on the problems that had haunted them for half a century increased the shock of the new generation upon their discovery of newly learnt facts.[9] The issues of "historical perceptions," which the old generation avoided challenging, led to a number of heated disputes between the regional governments. Interestingly, recent generational change does not seem to have solved the problem.

Many historiographical controversies continue to result from the anxieties generated by competition. Cold War confrontation was the first of its kind where suspicions about each other's motives were particularly troubling. Then the intense economic competition between the regional "Tigers" and "Dragons" came into play. The regional export-oriented economies of Taiwan and South Korea engaged in a cut-throat struggle for resources and markets with Japan. Under such circumstances, History was utilized by the export-encouraging governments as an additional mobilizing factor in domestic politics.

---

[9] D. J. Kim, *Together with History: Kim Dae-jung's Autobiography* (Japan NHK Chowijaeban kusŏng); trans. Y. Kim (Seoul: Indong, 1999).

Ultimately, the slowing of economic growth in the 1990s and the recurring financial crises continue to feed the distrust in economic structures and political elites in East Asia. Universities and research centers became actively engaged in the race for popularity, desperately needed by young and inexperienced leaders. The loss of popular support by well-established political parties and long-standing governments pushed their leaders closer to nationalistic populism, which often leads to history revision.

Nationalists and National History in Korea

Nationalist historians in East Asia appeal to common tradition, history, and culture by relying on the commonality of biology, psychology, and spirituality. Their insistence on the exclusive uniqueness of national history helps them legitimize claims over territories and grants them the power to eradicate or minimize disputes. From a nationalist perspective, democracy is unable to provide a single criterion for deciding which people and territories are to be included in a political community and which are not. Most decisions are made under the influence and in the name of the mystical "national spirit" that is not always rational.

One more specific factor complicates regional affairs. In East Asia, collecting, editing, and publishing national history has always been controlled by the state. This millennia-long tradition has found its way into the twenty-first century and does not seem to be dissipating. History as an academic discipline continued to be a tool for constructing a linearity of collective memory, where the state monopolizes debate and sets a national meta-narrative with the purpose of turning subjects into citizens. The final determinant is not reason but national interest and power. Plurality and local reporting are suppressed while new, convenient "facts" are often fabricated. With such facts at hand, local historians start rewriting their national history. Nationalists usually write history for a specific audience which is not necessarily residing within the national borders but which is definitely associating itself with the particular nation-state. Historical events and issues that involve numerous countries (i.e., wars, colonization, border incidents, etc.) cannot be easily recounted without offending the perpetrator.

Also, wars and anti-colonial struggle represent the birth (or re-birth) of independent nation-states. Collective memories affected by trauma are particularly strong and replicated in school textbooks. Thus, the rewriting of history helps to construct cohesive national identities but harms the prospects for regional integration. Such a situation also makes it difficult to share a common "historical perception" between the nationalists in Korea, China, and Japan who continue to claim supremacy in regional affairs of the past.[10]

The continuing ideological conflict between liberal democracy and self-reliant Communism, and the clash of national identities, make history an especially politicized topic which can easily disrupt positive developments on the regional-political stage. Korea is still suffering from the tragedy of national division that makes the North and the South particularly susceptible to conflicts. In this connection, the temporary improvement of inter-Korean relations during the last decade (1998–2008) created a momentum for consolidation of divided historiographies. Korea, in this sense, provides a good example for its neighbors.

History in Korea has always been a sacrosanct subject. As a nation with an overinflated sense of pride in its national past, the Koreans support every argument that presents their history as long and glorious. While boasting about their 5,000 year-long history, rich culture, and the "economic miracle" that occurred in the second half of the twentieth century, the Koreans never tire of emphasizing the unique nature of their history. They put much effort and resources into studying and propagating it around the world.

When the leaders of North and South Korea met in Pyongyang in June 2000, a Joint Declaration promoting peace and reconciliation was adopted. This move, above many other positive developments, created a solid ground for reconciliation of differing national history views. Research centers and universities in the DPRK and ROK began cooperating for the first time. Academic delegations from the North and South exchanged visits to Seoul and Pyongyang. Since then, a number of history seminars, conferences, and congresses have been jointly held in both Koreas. An attempt to co-host the Second World Congress of Korean Studies was undertaken by the ROK Academy of Korean Studies and the DPRK Academy of Social Sciences in 2004. The exhibition of an ancient Korean art collection from the North was displayed in Seoul at the National Museum of Korea in 2006.

Resumed academic cooperation demonstrated that the general understanding of the national past in North and South Korea is much closer than many would expect. Scholars of history on both sides of the divided country have few disagreements about ancient kingdoms and medieval wars with foreign invaders. What sparks conflicts are the issues

---

[10] K. Kimura, "Historical Perceptions and South Korea's Changing Identity," *Japan Echo* 32, no. 5 (2005): 11–15.

which might affect their legitimacy for leadership in the future unification of the country, and which concern the interpretations of post-1945 events. To avoid disagreement, North and South Korean scholars prefer not to bring these topics forward when they meet.

North Korean historians, while assessing the national past as an inexorable process inspired by class struggle and nationalistic drive, depict the history of Korea as an orderly continuum of self-reliant shifts in socio-economic formations leading from primitive communal society through slave-owning, feudalism, and capitalism to the victory of Korean-style socialism. No foreign influences are admitted, while the influence of Korean culture on the neighboring nations is especially emphasized.[11]

Contrary to the theories which used to dominate the DPRK historical scholarship in the 1960s, when the site of the former capital of Old Chosŏn was expected to be found somewhere on the Liaodong Peninsula, the current views of North Korean historians are concentrated on the Taedong River Basin near contemporary Pyongyang.[12] In 2002, North Koreans officially celebrated the 1,575th anniversary of Pyongyang, but *The Pyongyang Times* was quick to proclaim that this city had been the capital of ancient Korea since the early thirtieth century BC.

> Pyongyang, that boasts a time-honored history as a cradle of human civilization and the old capital of the first ancient and feudal states, adds brilliance to its history as the capital of the DPRK, playing the role of political, economic, and cultural centre.[13]

South Korean historians cannot fully agree with this claim. They have a different perspective, methodology, and political agenda, which leads them to different conclusions. The Emeritus Professor of Seoul National University, Sin Yong-ha, argues that Koreans—the "Hanjok people"—actually came from the banks of the Han River, the area of contemporary Seoul. It is natural that South Korean scholars prefer the south-centered hypotheses of national inception. However, these days, there are many reconciliatory themes in such hypotheses. Sin believes that there were three ancient tribes (Han, Ye, and Maek) who equally contributed to the creation of the first Korean kingdom of Old Chosŏn.

---

[11] L. Petrov, "Restoring the Glorious Past: North Korean *Juch'e* Historiography and Koguryŏ," *Review of Korean Studies* 7, no. 3 (2004): 231–252.

[12] C. Ku, "Uncovering Korea's Past," *The Pyongyang Times*, September 22, 2002.

[13] H. Cha, "Pyongyang, 1,575 years," *The Pyongyang Times*, November 16, 2002, 8.

> The Han had settled on both sides of the Han River; the Maek had lived south along the Songhua River; and the Ye had inhabited the Liaodong Peninsula before establishing the confederation of Old Chosŏn, a tribal state called in Korean "*Asanara*" with its capital at "*Asadal*" in the basin of the Taedong River, contemporary P'yŏng'an Province.[14]

Analyzing the development of socio-cultural evolution in the region, historians in the North and South both emphasize Korea's progressive role in the development of East Asian civilization. Sin is not claiming that Korea was the "cradle of human civilization," as many of his colleagues in the North do, but argues that his discoveries concerning the history of Old Chosŏn warrant a total reconsideration of world history. The implication of his research is that Korean culture has some historical links with the cultures of Turkey, France, and Finland.

Nowadays, it has become trendy in the South to argue that the birthplace of the Korean nation was not on the Korean Peninsula but in the wilds of Manchuria and Siberia. Some hypotheses are based merely on personal impressions and cursory analysis. For example, journalist Kim Chong-rok, in the pages of the popular magazine *Exploration of History* (2003), declared the shores of Lake Baikal to be the cradle of the Korean nation and culture. "This area is the birth-place of Siberian shamanism and the local people look very much like Koreans," concluded Kim.[15] The proto-Koreans, according to the author, continued moving southeast until their descendants settled down in, and around, the Korean Peninsula, and established their first state of Old Chosŏn.

Historians in the North and South often seem obsessed with the issue of national origins and use every opportunity to present such origins as exceptionally ancient and glorious. Any supporting evidence, regardless of how dubious it may be, is grist to the mill. The claims that some ancient Korean territory was the cradle of human or regional civilization are increasingly common for both Seoul and Pyongyang. The recent reappearance of historical romanticism must be a subconscious way of displacing fears associated with pending Korean unification.

Finding a common origin somewhere outside the Peninsula can disguise the legitimacy contest between the North and the South. Interpreting Old Chosŏn as a multicultural society composed of various

---

[14] Y. Sin, "Tracking the History of Old Chosŏn Warrants the Reconsideration of World History," *Yŏksa T'amhŏm*, no. 1, Supplement to *Wŏlgan Chungang* (June 2003): 6–9.

[15] C. Kim, "Finding the Baikal Lake, the Symbol of Korean National Origins," *Yŏksa T'amhŏm*, no. 1, Supplement to *Wŏlgan Chungang* (June 2003): 36–46.

tribes can appeal to tolerance of the differences that have arisen since 1945. The only obstacle in the way of historiographical reconciliation in Korea remains the ideological schism. Thus, the separation of history from ideology and from politics forms the main task for all historians working on issues of Korean history.

Resolving History Conflicts

As can be seen from the Korean example, contrasting national narratives can and should be overcome. In the Northeast Asia of the twenty-first century, there are many people for whom colonialism and war are not past history but realities that still shape their everyday lives. As proposed by Tessa Morris-Suzuki, the history wars in the region can be ended through the creation of a "historiography of reconciliation," a "geography of reconciliation," and a "media of reconciliation."[16] These three important initiatives should ultimately bring about political reconciliation and economic synergy by soothing the bad memories of the past and alleviating anxieties about the future.

"Historiography of reconciliation" can be represented by a single historical narrative for all countries of the region. Alternatively, it can be formed by multiple historical narratives created by stimulation of an open-ended dialogue and by promoting mutual understanding without generating consensus. Also, what is important is that the righting of past wrongs must be done not by "contesting over-responsibility," but through "celebration of once-silent protagonists."[17]

Under "geographies of reconciliation," bilateral, multilateral, and cross-regional research and educational projects are considered. Special focus in such projects should be placed on frontier areas (islands, seas, borders, the Demilitarized Zone, etc.) which either link or separate regional neighbors. Cross-border issues (i.e., "comfort women," forced labor, migration, and displacement of population) will be of particular significance for such projects since it would literally be "giving voice to the voiceless" across the boundaries.[18]

---

[16] T. Morris-Suzuki, "Lost Memories: Historical Reconciliation and Cross-Border Narratives in Northeast Asia," in *Contested Views of a Common Past: Revisions of History in Contemporary East Asia*, edited by Steffi Richter, 397–422 (Frankfurt: Campus Verlag, 2008).

[17] Morris-Suzuki, "Lost Memories," 405–406.

[18] Morris-Suzuki, "Lost Memories," 407–408.

"Media of reconciliation" is another vital part of the plan aimed at resolving history conflicts. It includes both conventional and innovative methods of communication. The written word (articles, books), face-to-face dialogue (seminars, conferences), mass media and new media (vernacular and multi-lingual), and museums and exhibitions (images and documents) are considered. Films play an important role in making narratives of historical events more accessible for audiences who are unlikely to read complex history texts.

Still, the lingering ideological confrontation and persistent security dilemmas are likely to continue to beset the troubled region of Northeast Asia for many years to come. Under such circumstances, an approach based on the democratic principle of deliberation would be needed to create the ethics of difference and tolerance. The so-called "Deliberative Approach" method of conflict resolution was analyzed and proposed by Baogang He and David Hundt. They encourage a pluralist, rather than a nationalist, reading of history, and presume broad involvement of civil groups, NGOs, and school teachers. This method departs from the simplistic historical dichotomies of "liberation–invasion," "oppressor–victim," etc.[19]

The Deliberative Approach has already been successfully tested in the form of the China–Japan Intellectual Community Dialogue (1997), East Asia Historical Forum for Critique and Solidarity (2000), Korea–Japan Joint History Research Committee (2002), Forum for Historical Consciousness and East Asian Peace (2003), Korea–Japan Solidarity 21 (2004), and the Trilateral Joint History Editorial Committee (2005). The latter project came to fruition with the publication of a sub-textbook, *A History that Opens the Future: The Contemporary and Modern History of Three East Asian Countries* (2005), in three regional languages—Chinese, Japanese, and Korean.[20]

The most important result of this new approach was that the conflicting nation-states started losing their monopoly on history writing. They have not yet been excluded completely from this process, but the first step in this direction has already been made. Democratization and liberalization of access to historical records will permit subaltern and handicapped groups

---

[19] B. He and D. Hundt, "A Deliberative Approach to East Asia's Contested History," *Annual Meeting, Boston, Massachusetts*, The American Political Science Association, NW, Washington DC, 2008.

[20] Trilateral Joint History Editorial Committee, *A History that Opens the Future: The Contemporary and Modern History of Three East Asian Countries* (Seoul: Hankyoreh Sinmunsa, 2005).

of people to seek recognition. Globalization and trans-nationalization of trade and capital will help cultural narratives cross borders easily.

Conclusion

In order to correctly interpret the present and to predict the future, we must know and understand the past—objectively, as well as how it is popularly perceived. The problem, however, exists in the variety of interpretations of regional history that stem from divergent attitudes toward the origins of colonialism and the results of the Cold War. These conflicting views create misunderstandings and often lead to "history wars." Such wars polarize public opinion, halt regional cooperation, and aggravate international relations. The continuing marketization of societies leads to increased competition and growing uncertainty in the region and results in the search for cultural identity and resurgence of nationalistic anxieties.

Korea has always occupied an important geostrategic position in East Asia. The target of imperial contest, the subject of colonial exploitation, and the scene of hostilities in the Cold War, Korea was left deeply divided. These days, every change in the country's local affairs greatly resonates in the actions and policies of its powerful neighbors, who genuinely fear the prospects of Korea's unification.

The place and time of the nation's inception, the cultural affinity of ancient kingdoms, the problem of unification, and even the chronology of basic historical events are vehemently debated among Koreans themselves. Significant differences in the methodology of history research and the issue of political motivation also remain afoot. North Korea continues to regard national history as a useful tool for political indoctrination and domestic mobilization, while South Korea brings up the issues of the national past predominantly when it deals with its neighbors.

However, the ten years of the "Sunshine Policy," which was pursued by the liberal government in South Korea, prompted the beginning of cooperation between the two Korean states in many areas, including research on national history. Some of the developed hypotheses looked promising for the process of national unification. In the face of aggressive academic maneuvers in China and Japan, historians of North and South Korea managed to unite their positions and iron out their differences.

Through the prism of this short cooperation, historians across East Asia received an opportunity to have another look at some controversial issues of regional history and learned to overcome the existing differences and conflicts inside their own camps. In developing the new understanding of the common past, a solid foundation for the peaceful future of this region can be laid. Nevertheless, the remaining ideological schism, the militant nationalism, and increased economic competition continue to cultivate phobias and anxieties which spoil the prospects for regional integration.

CHAPTER FOUR

NORMALIZATION AND JAPAN'S KOREA POLICY, 1972–75*

KIM SUNG-CHULL

Introduction

It is true to say that the policy of the United States during the Cold War determined the overall contours of international relations in Asia. However, the Guam Doctrine (later called the "Nixon Doctrine") in July 1969 and the US–China rapprochement in July 1971, beginning with Henry Kissinger's secret mission to Beijing, brought about a seismic change in interstate relations in the region. The US engagement with the People's Republic of China (henceforth PRC) entailed Sino–Japanese normalization in September 1972. These dramatic changes impacted inter-Korean relations substantially. Tension and confrontation on the Peninsula—exemplified in 1968 by the North Korean abduction of the *Pueblo*, a US intelligence ship, and by the North Korean armed infiltration near the South Korean presidential residence—suddenly thawed in the beginning of the 1970s, and in turn the two Koreas entered into competition for peace initiatives.

In this chapter, I will show that the impact of Sino–Japanese normalization on the Korean Peninsula was greater than that of US–China rapprochement. Both the US role in the division of Korea in 1948 and US participation in the Korean War in 1950–53, were related to her strategy of containing the Soviet Union. In this containment strategy, the United States incorporated Japan as a "strong point," to use George Kennan's

* This work was supported by the Academy of Korean Studies Grant (AKS-09, 10-R59) and National Research Foundation of Korea-Grant funded by the Korean Government (NRF-2010-361-A00017).

term.[1] Japan played this role faithfully, for instance by providing supplies and logistical support to US forces during the Korean War, while at the same time she was able to take advantage of the wartime procurement for her own economic growth.[2] Sino–Japanese normalization *per se* was a reflection of Japan's extended scope of diplomacy, and it had a direct and unprecedented impact on the Korean Peninsula. The core element of this impact was Japan's letting go of diplomatic relations with Taiwan, officially the Republic of China (henceforth ROC). Right after US President Richard Nixon's July 1971 announcement of his planned Beijing visit, Japanese "fever" concerning China developed into another fever over North Korea (Democratic People's Republic of Korea, henceforth DPRK), which then led South Korea (Republic of Korea, henceforth ROK) to fear a possible expansion of Japanese–North Korean relations. Sino–Japanese normalization, and Japan's severing of diplomatic relations with Taiwan, not only forced South Korea to accept the reality of the *de facto* existence of two Koreas but also encouraged North Korea to launch peace initiatives towards Japan and the United States, as well as towards the South.

Japan's policy of "two Koreas" was gaining some momentum in this context. Once again, it was seen that Japan's policy towards the Korean Peninsula (hereafter Japan's Korea policy) was held independently of the ROK government's demand, wish, or protest, despite the fact that the Japan–ROK quasi-alliance anchored by the United States remained intact, particularly in the security sector.

In the following discussion, I will be examining, first, Sino–Japanese normalization and its implications for the Korean Peninsula; second, the ensuing changes in inter-Korean relations and the transformation of Japan's Korea policy; third, expanded economic relations between Japan and North Korea and the subsequent debt problem; and finally, points of interest arising from this analysis. This chapter covers the period from 1972 to 1975, the years when the fever of Japan–DPRK economic relations abated and Vietnam united under socialist rule.

---

[1] J. L. Gaddis, *Strategic Containment: A Critical Appraisal of American National Security Policy during the Cold War*, revised and expanded edition (Oxford: Oxford University Press, 2005), 54–64.

[2] The US procurement orders during the Korean War amounted to close to half a billion dollars. A. Iriye, "Chinese–Japanese Relations," *China Quarterly* 124 (December 1990): 631.

Sino–Japanese Normalization and the Taiwan Issue at the Core

US President Nixon's July 1971 announcement of his plan to visit Beijing shocked the Japanese people (the Japanese called it "*shokku*"). The announcement, particularly the manner of its delivery in Tokyo, was a tremendous surprise; then Japanese Prime Minister Sato Eisaku was informed of the announcement only a few minutes in advance, via a telephone call from the Japanese ambassador in Washington, Ushiba Nobuhiko.

Considering the cautious but gradual US approach to the PRC taken even before Kissinger's clandestine visit to Beijing, in reality Nixon's July announcement was not only a political shock but also a diplomatic opportunity for Tokyo.[3] As to the issue of Chinese representation in the United Nations, in 1969 the United States witnessed that the "Albanian Resolution" supporting the PRC's representation was gradually gaining support in the UN General Assembly (48 votes for and 56 against) and that the US position, which tried to maintain the ROC's representation in the United Nations, was losing support. In response, in 1970 the United States arranged for a mandatory two-thirds majority vote of the General Assembly before any country could be expelled from the United Nations (known as the "Important Question"), and there is no doubt that this was a last-ditch effort to protect Taiwan on the diplomatic front. However, in 1970 the Albanian Resolution succeeded in gaining more support than in the previous year; it received, for the first time, an affirmative simple majority at the UNGA (51 votes for and 49 against). Should this trend continue, it seemed obvious that the Important Question also would be overcome in 1971.[4] The Japanese government, in consultation with the United States on UN issues, particularly the issue of Chinese representation, might have noticed a subtle change in US policy towards the PRC as early as 1970.

The Japanese government responded to the ongoing situational change by allowing a certain latitude when dealing with the issue of Chinese representation. To the US request for Japan's cooperation with the dual representation proposal (representation of both PRC and ROC in the UN) in 1971, the Japanese government's initial reaction was negative. For

---

[3] See J. Mann, *About Face: A History of America's Curious Relationship with China, from Nixon to Clinton* (New York: Vintage Books, 2000).

[4] A. H. Meyer, *Assignment: Tokyo* (Indianapolis and New York: Bobbs-Merrill, 1974), 138.

Japan, the dual representation proposal seemed to satisfy neither the mainland nor Taiwan. Nonetheless, Japan eventually had to accept the US proposal and go along with it at the General Assembly vote held on October 25. The result of the voting was disastrous for both Japan and the United States. The Important Question eventually succeeded in getting a majority vote (61 for and 53 against), whereas the Albanian Resolution received surprisingly high support, greater than a two-thirds majority (76 votes for and 35 against). In fact, many countries that supported the Important Question defected later to support the Albanian Resolution for PRC representation.[5] This voting result reflected a bandwagon effect regarding the PRC's rise to international status. Taiwan was theoretically able to maintain its UN membership, regardless of the replacement of the representation of "China" in the UN. However, at the behest of Taipei, the ROC's UN ambassador walked out just before the Albanian Resolution vote, and gave up his country's membership.

In view of the development described above, Nixon's announcement in 1971 of his plan to visit Mainland China must have been an opportunity for Japan. Indeed, Japan waited for the chance to turn the prevalent "China fever" into something more fruitful; that is, she deepened economic relations based on normalization. Owing to this China fever, the volume of trade between Japan and China in 1970 had already reached US $826 million, which was approximately 30% of Japan's total trade and brought Japan a black-ink balance of US $318 million.[6] In the absence of diplomatic normalization, however, most Japanese firms (except Nippon Steel) had to accept Zhou Enlai's Four Principles—the PRC's unilateral conditionality that prohibited Japanese firms with economic activities in Taiwan from engaging in trade with China. Given this situation, the political circle prepared the development of Japan–China relations by establishing the League of Diet Members for the Restoration of Japan–China Normalization in December 1970, whereas the business circle raised its voice as early as 1971 with demands for a normalized relationship with China.[7]

From the end of 1971, Japan's official position regarding China, particularly Sato's viewpoint over the Taiwan Strait, changed drastically. Sato had opposed the scrapping of the Japan–ROC peace treaty, even though he had endorsed that Taiwan was a part of China. However, as

---

[5] Meyer, *Assignment: Tokyo*, 142–143.

[6] C. Howe, "China, Japan, and Economic Interdependence in the Asia Pacific Region," *China Quarterly* 124 (December 1990): 678.

[7] T. Akihiko, *Nicchu kankei, 1949–1990* [Japan–China relations, 1949–1990] (Tokyo: University of Tokyo Press, 1991), 68–69.

China's UN representation changed in favor of the PRC, Sato reversed his previous views on the Taiwan issue, disregarding the "Taiwan clause" in particular. The Taiwan clause, which was one of the points that appeared in the Joint Communiqué of the Nixon–Sato summit on November 21, 1969, affirmed that "The Prime Minister said that the maintenance of peace and security in the Taiwan area was also important for the peace and security of Japan." At a news conference held straight after the second Nixon–Sato summit on January 7, 1972, however, the prime minister subsequently stated that "I do not believe that the expression [Taiwan clause] used at that time is still applicable today … The Taiwan clause has disappeared." Foreign Minister Fukuda tried to extinguish the fire ignited by Sato's abrupt statement and the ensuing fallout, by saying that Sato misunderstood the "Taiwan clause" for the "Taiwan situation."[8] The logical implication behind Sato's statement, even if corrected later by his foreign minister, was that the United States, but not Japan, was obliged to militarily defend Taiwan and that the 1969 Joint Communiqué, if not scrapped, was applicable only to the United States. At any rate, Sato's statement perfectly reflected Japan's changed position regarding the China issue in early 1972.

As the Taiwan issue seemed to become a focal point for Sino–Japanese relations, in late 1971 at the earliest, or in early 1972 at the latest, the ROK government became nervous about the perceived change in Japan's Korea policy. In the 1969 Nixon–Sato Joint Communiqué, the so-called "Korea clause," along with the Taiwan clause, had been a critical component, reflecting the mounting tension centered around the Pueblo incident and North Korean armed infiltration into the South in 1968. The clause read that "The President and the Prime Minister specifically noted the continuing tension over the Korean Peninsula. The Prime Minister … stated that the security of the Republic of Korea was essential to Japan's own security." However, if the Japanese government, in early 1972, did not consider Taiwan to be an obligatory partner, then what would become of the Korea clause? For South Koreans, throwing out the Korea clause would mean undermining Japan's commitment to Korea, particularly in the arena of economic aid. Snowballing South Korean anxiety occurred amidst emboldened North Korean overtures. This was happening while Pyongyang accepted a flurry of visits from Japanese politicians, both ruling Liberal Democratic Party (LDP) members and opposition parties'

---

[8] Report from the Ministry of Foreign Affairs to the President, Abuk 700–11, January 12, 1972, in *Sato Eisaku Ilbon susang Miguk pangmun* [Japanese Prime Minister Sato Eisaku's visit to the United States], January 6/7, 1972, 722.12JA/US, 1971-72, C-0052 (ROK diplomatic archive).

members. The Japanese visits to Pyongyang did not follow, but paralleled, if not preceded, their visits to Beijing.

Nixon's visit to China in February 1972 was an historic event, enough to warrant Japanese concern: "we have been left behind."[9] However, the change of prime minister from Sato Esisaku to Tanaka Kakuei changed the sense of being "left behind" to one of high expectations regarding the development of Japan–China diplomatic relations. Indeed, Prime Minister Tanaka expressed a strong desire for normalized relations with the PRC at his first press conference, where an abnormally large number of foreign correspondents were in attendance. Tanaka, right after his inauguration as prime minister, made an "unusual political determination" by which he started preparing for a normalized relationship with the PRC, bypassing the foreign ministry's high-ranking officials who had stuck to the two-China formula.[10]

The subsequent Nixon–Tanaka summit, held in Hawaii on August 31/September 1, 1972, focused on two issues: trade-imbalance adjustment and Tanaka's planned visit to Beijing. Regarding the Beijing visit, Tanaka used the Hawaii summit to make the United States understand that Japanese policy towards the PRC had changed.[11] Whereas the summit was a chance for Japan to be relatively independent regarding the China issue, the United States could hardly avoid experiencing the "Tanaka shock," which was comparable to the Japanese *shokku* at Nixon's July 1971 announcement of his plan to visit China. Inasmuch as there was a subtle difference between Nixon's China policy and Tanaka's audacious overture, particularly in relation to the Taiwan issue, the joint statement publicized after the summit perfectly reflected American vigilance and precaution. For instance, the allies differed with each other over the wording of the joint statement's draft, particularly in interpreting the

---

[9] Meyer, *Assignment: Tokyo*, 164.

[10] I. Naotaka, *Nichi-Bei kankei to hutatsu no chugoku* [Japan–US relations and two Chinas] (Tokyo: Bokutakusha, 2004), 409.

[11] Before the Hawaii summit, the Japanese government articulated its own China policy on the occasion of Kissinger's Tokyo visit on August 19. Then Prime Minister Tanaka and Foreign Minister Ohira raised the point that due to the changes in the regional situation, there would be little possibility of military conflict; they went on to say that the US–Japanese security alliance would be compatible with the Japan–PRC normalization. It is noteworthy that Tanaka expressed that Japan was ready to sever relations with the ROC if Japan made its trade with, and invested in, Taiwan. See "Kissinger pojwagwan nongil chongnyo" [Completion of National Security Advisor Kissinger's visit to Japan], telegram from the Ambassador in Tokyo to the Minister of Foreign Affairs, JAW-08369, August 21, 1972 (ROK diplomatic archive).

implications of Tanaka's planned visit to China on the regional situation. The joint statement finally read that: "… they [the Prime Minister and the President] *shared the hope* that the forthcoming visit of the Prime Minister to the People's Republic of China would also serve to further the trend for the relaxation of tension in Asia" (my emphasis). It is noteworthy that the Japanese draft was worded "*shared the view*," but with US insistence the joint statement finally adopted the wording "*shared the hope*."[12]

In this rapidly changing environment, North Korea became more daring than ever before and South Korea had to act quickly, particularly in view of Japan's seemingly imminent abandonment of Taiwan. As a result, the North and the South reached an historic agreement, called the "July 4 Joint Statement," after several rounds of Red Cross meetings as a preliminary means of rapprochement between the two sworn adversaries. Notably, South Korea accepted the three concepts for national unification—independence, peaceful unification, and national unity—concepts with which North Korea had justified its long insistence on withdrawal of US forces.

As a result of Tanaka's visit to China, from September 25 to 30, 1972, Japan and the PRC achieved their own objectives. Of the many points adopted at the Zhou–Tanaka Joint Communiqué on September 29, the following issues called for special attention: the Japanese government recognized the PRC government as the "sole" legal government of China, and it "fully understands and respects" that Taiwan is an inalienable part of the territory of the PRC; the PRC renounced its demand for war reparations from Japan; and the two governments agreed to establish a renewal of diplomatic relations immediately, putting an end to their abnormal relations.[13] As for the Taiwan issue, the two governments did not formally nullify the Japan–ROC peace treaty, as China desired.[14]

For the ROK government, the Zhou–Tanaka Joint Communiqué meant, more than anything else, Japan's abandonment of Taiwan. Only two weeks after Tanaka's visit to China and the Joint Communiqué, South Korean president Park Chung-hee declared the launching of the Yushin regime in

---

[12] Mi-Il sunoe hoedam ui p'yong'ga pogoso [Analysis Report on US–Japan Summit], from the Embassy in Tokyo to the Minister of Foreign Affairs, Iljong 700-5157, September 18, 1972, in Tanaka Kakuei Ilbon susang Miguk pangmun [Japanese Prime Minister Tanaka Kakuei's visit to the United States], August 31/September 1, 1972, C-0052 (ROK diplomatic archive).

[13] Joint Communiqué of the Government of Japan and the Government of the People's Republic of China, September 29, 1972. See http://www.mofa.go.jp/region/asia-paci/china/joint72.html.

[14] Memorandum for the President, October 2, 1972, POL 7 JAPAN (US archive).

Korea, allegedly naming it after the Japanese Meiji Ishin in 1867. The Yushin regime was a clear departure from the existing procedural democracy. With a presidential special statement, the constitution lost a part of its function, owing to the dissolution of the National Assembly, there was a ban on all party and political activities, and the declaration of nationwide emergency martial law. It remains a controversial question as to why Park chose a new authoritarian model at this particular juncture. But the key point is that Park Chung-hee viewed the rapid change in international relations surrounding the Peninsula as a break from the balance of power on the Peninsula and as a move favoring North Korea.

Japan's Two Koreas Scheme: Emboldened North and Nervous South

Alongside the development of Sino–Japanese relations, the improvement of Japan–DPRK relations seemed to be only a matter of time. In Japan, a kind of "North Korea fever"—which followed the "China fever"—suddenly emerged. In North Korea, the painful memory of the 1965 ROK–Japan normalization was still lingering, but changes in the Japanese attitude towards North Korea were experienced as encouraging news. Convergence between Japanese society's interest in China extending to North Korea, on the one hand, and North Korea's dream of having a new relationship with Japan, on the other, seemed to be becoming a reality.

As early as the beginning of 1972, Japanese politicians' visits to North Korea flourished. One of the most important visits was the Diet members' trip to Pyongyang from January 16 to 29, 1972. Kuno Chuji, an LDP member, led a group of Japan–North Korea Friendship Promotion League members to visit Pyongyang. From an early stage, particularly in the formation of the visitors' group, there was controversy in the LDP over the visit. Faced with strong opposition from top LDP leaders who were concerned about Japan–ROK relations, LDP members, except Kuno, had to give up their trip. Moreover, Kuno was warned by the top party leaders that he would be turned over to a disciplinary session upon returning to Tokyo. No doubt this warning was also aimed at South Korean audiences.[15]

Kuno and the Japan–North Korea Friendship Promotion League's visit to Pyongyang was not a courtesy one but had tangible consequences. At the meeting with North Korean leader Kim Il-sung, Kuno's group

[15] Telegram from the Embassy in Tokyo to the State Secretary, January 17, 1972, POL 7 JAPAN (US archive).

expressed remorse about Japan's past wrongdoings in the colonial period and apologized for them, and Kuno expressed a desire for establishing Japan–DPRK normalization.[16] This was the first time that Japanese politicians in office, although not part of the government, had openly expressed apologies to Kim Il-sung. The most noteworthy achievement that Kuno and North Korea achieved, on this occasion, was the Agreement on Japan–North Korea Trade Promotion, which would be effective until December 31, 1976. This document set a target of total trade volume at the end of 1976 at 150 to 200 million pounds. According to this agreement, Japan was expected to export manufacturing plants related to weeding machines, automobiles, and oil refining, whereas Japan was to import tools, pig iron, compound metals, and nonferrous metals. Opposition parties and the business circle in Japan welcomed the agreement; in particular, business firms rushed to request that their own government should allow North Korean technicians to enter Japan, which was considered a necessary measure for exporting the plants.[17] Major Japanese newspaper editorials unanimously requested that the Japanese government pursue a more open approach to North Korea, on the one hand, and "persuade South Koreans" to understand the changed situation, on the other.[18]

Kuno and the Japan–North Korea Friendship Promotion League's visit to Pyongyang coincided with another visit by Kawasaki Kanji, the director of the International Affairs Bureau in the Japan Socialist Party. Using this opportunity of a visit by such a high-ranking official of a progressive party in Japan, Kim Il-sung professed his new peace initiatives to Japan and the world. He stated that previously unfriendly relations would end as soon as the two countries' relations were normalized; that US forces should be withdrawn and the UN Commission for the Unification and Rehabilitation of Korea (UNCURK) be dissolved; that the North and the South should establish a peace treaty; and finally, that the two Koreas should achieve

---

[16] Telegram from the Embassy in Tokyo to the Minister of Foreign Affairs, JAW-01266, January 20, 1972, in Ilbon Il-Cho uhochokjin uiwonyonmaeng taepyodan Pukhan pangmun [Visit to North Korea by the representatives of the Japan–North Korea Friendship Promotion League], 725.32JA, 1971/72, D-0021 (ROK diplomatic archive).

[17] Telegram from the Ambassador in Tokyo to the Minister of Foreign Affairs, JAW-01331, January 24, 1972, in Ilbon Il-Cho uhochokjin uiwonyonmaeng taepyodan Pukhan pangmun [Visit to North Korea by the representatives of the Japan–North Korea Friendship Promotion League], 725.32JA, 1971/72, D-0021 (ROK diplomatic archive).

[18] *Asahi Shimbun*, January 25, 1972; *Sankei Shimbun*.

arms reduction on condition of US troop withdrawal. It is apparent that Kim intended to demonstrate the DPRK's posture of "reasonableness" and "flexibility" with regards to the reunification and tension reduction.[19]

In mid-1972, Japanese politicians engaged in a kind of race to visit Pyongyang. The Komeito representatives led by Takeiri Yoshikatsu visited Pyongyang from May 30 to June 7 and concluded the trip with a joint statement. The statement requested withdrawal of foreign forces from the Peninsula, establishment of a trade representative office, and normalization based on mutual interests and equality.[20] The Pyongyang trip of July 18–28 by members of the Socialist Party's Special Committee for the Korean Problem marked the first visit after the July 4 North–South Joint Statement and occurred right after the inauguration of the Tanaka Cabinet on July 7. It is noteworthy that at the meeting with the visitors, Kim Il-sung evaluated that the Tanaka Cabinet's forthcoming attitude towards the North would be positive, compared with the attitude of previous cabinets; furthermore, Kim expressed North Korea's changed attitude towards the United Nations, stating his willingness to send a representative, if invited, to the discussion about Korean affairs at the General Assembly in the coming Fall.[21]

Also worthy of note is that the Japanese government's position was indeed in accordance with the viewpoints of the Pyongyang visitors, such as the Komeito and the Socialist Party's representatives, as well as the unusually progressive LDP member Kuno. For example, in response to the ROK embassy official's protest in January 1972 against the Japanese government's refusal to give permission to Kuno in particular, Sunobe, the bureau director of Asian affairs in the Foreign Ministry, made it clear that the Japanese government would "diversify" its diplomatic efforts, attempting to persuade the Korean government also to be "flexible."[22]

---

[19] Telegram from the Embassy in Tokyo to the State Secretary, February 8, 1972, POL 15-1 KOR N (US archive); Telegram from the Ambassador in Tokyo to the Minister of Foreign Affairs, JAW-01309, January 24, 1972, in Ilbon Il-Cho uhochokjin uiwonyonmaeng taepyodan Pukhan pangmun [Visit to North Korea by the representatives of the Japan–North Korea Friendship Promotion League], 725.32JA, 1971/72 (ROK diplomatic archive).

[20] Telegram from the Ambassador in Tokyo to the Minister of Foreign Affairs, JAW-06068, June 5, 1972, in Ilbon chuyo taepyodan Pukhan pangmun [Japanese representatives' visit to North Korea], 725.32JA, 1972, D-0012 (ROK diplomatic archive).

[21] *Asahi Shimbun*, July 28, 1972; *Yomiuri Shimbun*.

[22] Kang kongsa wa Sunobe asea kukjang kwaui myondamrok [Memorandum of conversation between the Minister at the Embassy in Tokyo Kang Young-kyu and the Director of Asian Affairs Bureau Sunobe], JAW-01025, January 4, 1972, in

In February 1972, a high-level official in the Ministry of International Trade and Industry (MITI), on behalf of the minister, participated in the ceremony of the establishment of the Japan–North Korea Export and Import Corporation and had a meeting with Chongryon's president Han Dok-su. In view of the fact that Chongryon (the General Association of Korean Residents in Japan) is a North Korea–controlled Korean organization in Japan, the meeting between Han and the government official meant a green light from the Japanese government in relation to direct economic exchanges between two countries with no diplomatic relations. Furthermore, Foreign Minister Fukuda, in responding to the ROK ambassador's complaint over the meeting, stood in defense of the establishment of the Japan–North Korea Export and Import Corporation; Fukuda said that the corporation followed Japanese domestic law and that it was similar to Mitsui & Co., which was a window to Japan–South Korea trade.[23]

The government's approval of extended business relations with North Korea became further apparent in subsequent months. It approved the opening of *de facto* regular shipping lines between Japan and North Korea in March, even if they were officially registered as irregular shipping lines. The three shipping companies in Tokyo—Tokai, Seiwa, and Eiwa—originally intended to submit their registrations as regular lines, but the government advised them to register as irregular lines, in order to avoid criticism from the ROK government. Whereas the companies had to submit a shipping report after each journey, the reporting was a formality only. With regards to this development, the ROK ambassador in Tokyo sent a telegram to Seoul stating that "the development of Japan–North Korea relations would be inevitable," owing to Japan's improved relations with communist China.[24] That is, as a consequence of the expanded Japan–North Korea economic exchanges, South Korea ostensibly became more defensive, nervous, and anxious.

The expanded Japan–North Korea relations contributed to the competitive peace initiatives of the two Koreas, which were essentially a competition for legitimacy. Given this situation, the Japanese government

---

Han-Il jongmu ilban [Korea–Japan Political Affairs], 722.1JA, C-0051 (ROK diplomatic archive).

[23] Telegram from the Ambassador in Tokyo to the Minister of Foreign Affairs, JAW-02406, February 23, 1972, in Han-Il jongmu ilban [Korea–Japan political affairs], 722.1JA, C-0051 (ROK diplomatic archive).

[24] Telegram from the Ambassador in Tokyo to the Minister of Foreign Affairs, JAW-03297, March 17, 1972, in Han-Il jongmu ilban [Korea–Japan political affairs], 722.1JA, C-0051 (ROK diplomatic archive).

came to launch its "two Koreas" policy and to further develop Japan–North Korea relations, if not normalization itself.

The competitive peace initiatives were related to the unification issue. One clash between the two Koreas occurred on June 23, 1973. South Korean President Park Chung-hee announced the Special Declaration for Peaceful Unification, whereby the ROK government would admit the existence of two Koreas at an international level. In this declaration, Park stated that his government would not oppose simultaneous entry of the North and the South to the United Nations.[25] Before the declaration was made, legal experts carefully scrutinized it to make sure there was no logical contradiction between the internationally recognized two Koreas and the domestically legitimized one Korea.[26] The declaration was intended to allow international organizations and foreign countries to recognize the two Koreas, while reserving the open recognition of the North by the ROK government. The declaration realized, for the first time, the possibility of ending, or at least reducing, the twenty-five-year-old tension between the two Koreas.

Park's adventurous peace initiative was immediately followed, on the same day, by North Korean leader Kim Il-sung's declaration of the Five Points for Peaceful Unification. The main points of Kim's declaration were the establishment of a Korea Confederation and the opposition to Park's proposal for the entry of two Koreas into the United Nations. North Korea renewed its own proposal for the building of a Korea Confederation as a precondition to UN membership; in other words, North Korea maintained that Korean membership in the United Nations should consist of a single seat, rather than two.[27] Kim Il-sung's peace initiative was mainly intended to reiterate the DPRK's determination for national unification without foreign influence, projecting Park's idea as leading to the prolongation of Korean division. Kim's peace initiative was followed by some concrete actions. North Korea entered the WHO and made efforts to open UN observer offices, both in New York and Geneva, and to

---

[25] Y. Yang, *Tong'il chongch'aengnon* [A study on unification policy] (Seoul: Pakyongsa, 1997), 176–178.

[26] 6.23 p'yonghwa t'ong'il oegyo sonon, 1973–74 [June 23 Declaration of Peaceful Unification Diplomacy, 1973–74], 726.11, 1973/74, Vol. 1, D-0015 (ROK diplomatic archive).

[27] The North Korean opposition to the ROK proposal of simultaneous entrance to the UN was a reversal of its previous position regarding UN membership. On February 9, 1949, North Korea submitted a membership application to the UN General Secretary; legally speaking, the application was still alive in 1973. See 6.23 p'yonghwa t'ong'il oegyo sonon.

actively access the countries that already had diplomatic relations with the ROK.

The Japanese government welcomed both Park Chung-hee's declaration and Kim Il-sung's proposal. Foreign Minister Ohira Masayoshi appraised Park's declaration as "practical, constructive foreign policy" at a news conference on June 23. Likewise, Ohira stated at the Committee for Foreign Affairs of the Upper House on June 28 that the Japanese government would carefully pursue the development of Japan–DPRK relations without damaging existing Japan–ROK relations. In a similar vein, major Japanese newspapers welcomed Park's practical approach to the international recognition of two Koreas. *Asahi Shimbun* published an editorial on June 24 entitled "Two Koreas and Japan's Diplomacy," which interpreted the South Korean declaration as a recognition of two Koreas and the pursuit of peaceful coexistence. A *Yomiuri Shimbun* editorial, entitled "South Korea's Policy Shift Reflecting the Reality," interpreted the North's and South's declarations in a unique way: "South Korea's internationalization of the Korean issue, and North Korea's intra-nationalization of the Korean issue."[28]

For both Japanese politicians and the media, Park's declaration provided the Japanese government with an opportunity to embark upon the "two Koreas" policy. That is, opening the possibility of two UN memberships would mean legitimizing the Japanese wish for freer access to the North than before.

Meanwhile, on August 8, 1973, there occurred an incident, the abduction of Kim Dae-jung, which further damaged the image of Park Chung-hee's authoritarian regime, on the one hand, and strengthened the pro–North Korean atmosphere in Japanese society, on the other. Kim, who had been the opponent of Park in the 1971 presidential race, was kidnapped at the Grand Palace Hotel in Tokyo by members of the Korea Central Intelligence Agency (KCIA) and their associates. According to a truth-finding report recently published in Korea, the KCIA director ordered the abduction, and President Park might have either ordered or at least implicitly approved of the operation. After the abduction, the ROK government established a special investigation into the kidnapping, but such an action was only seen as a response to Japan's mounting criticism of the ROK government's non-cooperation with the Tokyo police's investigation. The ROK government strenuously searched for a resolution to the incident through negotiation rather than legal procedures; with the

[28] The US media also welcomed the South Korean proposal. The *Washington Post* on June 23 referred to Park's declaration with the headline "Seoul alters on North Korea in UN."

ROK Prime Minister Kim Jong-il's visit to the Japanese Prime Minister Tanaka on November 2, 1973, the abduction incident was settled politically.[29]

The impact of this kidnapping on both Japan–ROK relations and Japanese society was enormous, not only because of the nature of the incident—South Korean agents' infringement of the law within Japanese jurisdiction—but also because of the significance of Kim Dae-jung's status as the leading opponent of Park's authoritarian regime. Both the strain on Japan–ROK relations and anti-authoritarian sentiment in Japan further promoted the pro–North Korea attitude. Opposition parties quickly moved to use this chance to promote a campaign for gearing up Japan–DPRK relations, with the Socialist Party taking the lead. The Socialist Party initiated the establishment of the National People's Assembly for Japan–DPRK Normalization and held the first meeting in Tokyo on September 8, 1973. At this meeting, the party chairman Narita Tomomi underscored in his speech that the Japanese government's intimacy and collusion with Park Chung-hee's authoritarian regime, represented by the political resolution of the abduction incident, was hampering unification of the Korean Peninsula.[30]

The pro–North Korea attitude, counterbalanced by the critical views towards the South Korean authoritarian regime, coincided with, and was strengthened by, Japan–North Vietnam normalization on September 21. Japan became the sixty-second country to normalize relations with socialist Vietnam. The following morning, major Japanese newspapers included articles reporting that Japan–DPRK normalization was the last issue to be resolved. The newspapers reported that the Japanese government was examining the possibility of providing an Export and Import Bank loan to North Korea for exporting manufacturing plants. As the Export and Import Bank was completely government-subsidized, the bank loan to the exporters, from the point of view of the ROK government, meant the Japanese government's involvement in economic exchanges with the DPRK. A more delicate issue for the ROK government was that within the Japanese Foreign Ministry, there were officials who openly argued that the effect of the 1965 Japan–Korea Treaty (on Basic Relations between Japan and the Republic of Korea) would amount to nothing, legally speaking, in the northern part of the Peninsula where the

---

[29] The Committee for the Development through Truth Finding, National Intelligence Agency, ed., *Kwago wa taehwa, mirae ui songchal: chuyo uihok sagon pyon* [Dialogue with the past, reflections for the future: Main mysterious incidents], Vol. 2 (Seoul: National Intelligence Agency, 2007), 548–550.

[30] *Asahi Shimbun*, September 9, 1973.

ROK's jurisdiction was unable to reach. In reply, the South Korean ambassador in Tokyo hurriedly sent a telegram to Seoul concerning the changed atmosphere in the Japanese Foreign Ministry, as well as the cooling public attitude towards Park's non-democratic practices, exemplified by the Kim Dae-jung abduction incident.[31]

Among the Japanese political arena's pro–North Korea approaches, Diet member Utsunomiya Tokuma's Pyongyang visit of August 5–15, 1974 was probably the most troubling case for the ROK, on the one hand, and one of the most encouraging cases for the DPRK, on the other. Utsunomiya was a member of the liberal faction under the leadership of Miki Takeo in the LDP; he was a career Diet member, having been elected seven times since 1942; his progressive tendency had first appeared in his visit to mainland China in 1959 as an envoy for Sino–Japanese normalization. At the time of the Pyongyang visit in 1974, he was leading the Asia–Africa Alliance, a leftist organization composed of Diet members of the ruling LDP and the opposition parties. At the press conference in Beijing on the way home, Utsunomiya delivered Kim Il-sung's idea of the Korean unification model, particularly the Korea Confederation under which two different systems might coexist. He went on to note that Kim had told him that "the Japan–Korea Treaty's Article 3 that defines the ROK a sole legal government is unreasonable, but if DPRK–Japan normalized, the DPRK would not stick to that article."[32] Utsunomiya's press conference appeared to resemble a North Korean spokesman's speech. Considering his status in the LDP and his lengthy political career, his visit to Pyongyang and the ensuing press conference caused a great sensation both domestically and on Japan–ROK relations.

Utsunomiya's visit had larger ramifications than Kuno's 1972 visit; it rendered Kim Il-sung more emboldened than before and made Article 3 of the 1965 ROK–Japan Treaty a controversial one in political discourses in Japan. Regarding its relations with Japan, North Korea became proactive, cornering the South. Owing to both the changed Japanese attitude and Japan's "two Koreas" policy, ROK–Japan relations underwent their worst period ever until the unification of Vietnam in the Spring of 1975.

---

[31] Telegram from the Ambassador in Tokyo to the Minister of Foreign Affairs, JAW-09521, September 24, 1973, in Pukhan-Ilbon kwan'gye, 1973 [North Korea–Japan Relations, 1973], 725.1JA, D-0014 (ROK diplomatic archive).

[32] Utsunomiya Ilbon chamindang uiwon Pukhan pangmun, 1974.8.5–15 [LDP Diet member Utsunomiya's visit to North Korea, August 5–15, 1974], 725.32JA, D-0018 (ROK diplomatic archive).

"Fever" in Economic Affairs

The changed Japanese attitude toward North Korea and the ensuing shift in Korean policy coincided with "North Korea fever" in economic affairs. The LDP Diet member Kuno's visit to Pyongyang in early 1972 paved the way for expanded trade between the two countries. The Agreement on Japan–North Korea Trade Promotion, adopted at the time of Kuno's visit, was not a governmental-level agreement, and for this reason any legal protection in trade with, and investment in, the risky country was not guaranteed. But the agreement was a kind of political substitute for a governmental guarantee, in view of the tacit approval by the Japanese government at that time.

Table 1: Japan's Trade with North Korea (thousand US dollars)

	Export	Import	Total	Balance
1970	23,344	34,414	57,758	-11,070
1971	28,907	30,059	58,966	-1,152
1972	93,443	38,311	131,754	55,132
1973	100,160	72,318	172,478	27,842
1974	251,914	108,824	360,738	143,090
1975	180,630	64,839	245,469	115,791
1976	96,056	71,627	167,683	24,429
1977	125,097	66,618	191,715	58,479
1978	183,347	106,862	290,209	76,485
1979	283,848	152,027	435,875	131,821

Source: Ilcho muyokhoe [Japan–Korea Trade Association], *Niccho Boeki* [Japan–Korea Trade], No. 305 (March 1985), 16–17.

The July 4 North–South Joint Statement, which was a landmark agreement for reconciliation between the confronting Koreas, provided the Japanese business circle with further confidence. As seen in Table 1, the trade volume in 1972 doubled from that of the previous year; in particular, a sudden jump in exports (more than tripling) changed Japan's trade with North Korea into a black-ink balance during the same period.

On the other hand, there were two controversial issues in Japan and in Japan–ROK relations with regards to Japan's economic exchange with North Korea: one was the export of manufacturing plants, and the other was the use of the government-owned Export-Import Exchange Bank loans.

Indeed, the rapid increase in trade largely relied on the export of manufacturing plants, and for this reason the ROK government registered protests to the Japanese government. To South Koreans, the export of manufacturing plants would strengthen the "war potential" of North Korea, whether or not the plants were directly related to the military industry in the North. South Koreans believed that the introduction of new facilities, accompanied by advanced technology the North did not possess, would facilitate economic growth and technological improvement, and in turn would contribute to the modernization of the existing military industry. This might be theoretically true, but South Korea could not obstruct Japanese firms' growing interest in business with North Korea.

Fourteen plants were exported to the North during the Japanese fiscal year 1972 (from April to March of the following calendar year); the total amount reached US $45 million. During the fiscal year 1973, a lesser number of plants were exported to the North (decreased to eleven plants), but the total amount quadrupled in comparison to the previous year, reaching US $188 million. It is notable that this amount in 1973 was almost three times that of Japan's plant exports to South Korea; also, North Korea ranked third in importing Japanese manufacturing plants, after the PRC and Brazil. The plants and facilities that Japan exported, or attempted to export, included a cement plant (US $120 million) and a towel plant (US $2 million) in 1973, a bolt-nut plant (US $2.4 million) in 1974, and a vinylon weaving plant (US $6.4 million), a newspaper intaglio rotation machine (US $5 million dollars), and a standard weighing system related to physics and chemistry (US $2.6 million) in 1975.[33]

In response, the ROK Foreign Ministry repeatedly instructed its embassy in Tokyo to make the utmost effort to prevent the increased plant exports from occurring; one of the main tasks of the embassy officials in the first half of the 1970s was to meet and persuade the Japanese foreign ministry officials and business leaders sympathizing with South Korea that the export of manufacturing plants would improve North Korean "war potential" particularly during the upbeat Six-Year Economic Plan from 1971 to 1976.

The most troubling issue, in relation to the export of manufacturing plants, was the use of Export-Import Bank loans. The exporters of plants expected firms to experience capital mobility problems; for exporters, the

---

[33] Kugoe Iril Jeongbo [Daily Foreign Information], No. 159, July 11, 1974, in Ilbon ui tae Pukhan plant suchul mit suchurip unhaeng chagum sayong sung'in munje, 1974 [Japanese export of manufacturing plants to North Korea and the controversy over the approval of the use of Export-Import Bank Loans, 1974], 725.6JA, D-0018 (ROK diplomatic archive).

exportation of manufacturing plants was not followed by immediate payment from importers, because long-term deferred payment was the usual practice for their export. For this reason, Japanese exporters attempted to receive low-interest loans (lower than commercial banks) from the Export-Import Bank, a procedure that was administered by the Ministry of International Trade and Industry.

Table 2: North Korea's debt problem (as of December 31, 1976; million US dollars)

	Total Amount	Payment Delay
Japan	300	100
France	162	55
West Germany	125	29
Sweden	130	4.3
Austria	90	Unknown
United Kingdom	60	51
Netherland	70	Agreement on delay
Finland	19	3.8
Swiss	32	10
Italy	20	2.7
Denmark	7	Agreement on delay
Belgium	4	Agreement on delay
Socialist block	900	-
Others	80	-
Total	1,999	255.8

Source: Pukgoe ui oechae hyonhwang mit sanghwan kyosop hwaldong [North Korea's debt and its negotiation activities with regard to repayment], in Pukhan ui tae sobang oechae munje, 1976–77 [North Korea's debt to western countries, 1976–77], 725.6XG, 2007-24 (ROK diplomatic archive).

The suspension of the Export-Import Bank's loans had originated from the so-called "Yoshida Letter," dated May 7, 1964, in which the then prime minister pledged to Taiwan that Japan would not approve Nichibo's chemical fiber plant export to mainland China through the Export-Import Bank.[34] No doubt the letter was considered equally applicable to North Korea. The Japanese government, however, suggested an end to the Yoshida

[34] Y. Soeya, *Japan's Economic Diplomacy with China, 1945–1978* (Oxford: Clarendon Press, 1998), 98.

Letter effect in the fall of 1971, when the US–China rapprochement continued and the development of Japan–China relations was expected. At the Diet session of October 28, Minister of Finance Matsuda stated that the considerations pertaining to the Yoshida Letter had ended, suggesting approval of Export-Import Bank loans for plant exports to China.[35] Foreign Minister Ohira confirmed the change in the government's policy at a press conference by stating that "there was no reason to discriminate against China" and that "if there was application, the government would accept it."[36]

As the Japanese government's policy to provide exporters with Export-Import Bank loans seemed imminent, the ROK government became panicky. An internal document of the ROK government, dated October 11, 1972, analyzed the trend of Japan's trade with the North, including plant exports, and practical difficulties in differentiating between the CoCom-listed strategic materials and non-strategic materials. The document reached the conclusion that to stop the Export-Import Bank loans would be the best strategy to undercut the existing trend and to prevent the export of large plants.[37] Since then, the South Korean strategy has focused on obstructing the Export-Import Bank loans, not simply opposing the export of manufacturing plants.

Japanese fever regarding economic relations with North Korea deflated from around 1975. One may attribute the loss of Japanese business interest in the North to the impact of the unification of Vietnam in 1975, and the Japanese government's heightened security concerns. But this observation is not true. The loss of Japanese business interest in North Korea was largely due to the debt problem, which became an issue from 1974. The volume of trade between Japan and North Korea dropped after reaching a peak in 1974; a sharp decline in exports was visible from 1974 to 1976 (see Table 1). Furthermore, North Korea owed a large debt to Japan (see Table 2), and it is noteworthy that one-third of North Korea's Japanese-

[35] Ilbon ui tae Pukhan plant suchul mit suchurip unhaeng chagum sayong sung'in munje, 1974 [Japanese export of manufacturing plants to North Korea and the controversy over the approval of the use of Export-Import Bank loans, 1974], 725.6JA, D-0018 (ROK diplomatic archive).

[36] *Nihon Keizai Shimbun*, July 23, 1972.

[37] Ilbon ui tae Pukhan kyongje kwan'gye chuyo hyonan munui e taehan hoesin [Reply to the inquiry into the main issues related to Japan's economic relations with North Korea], from Korea Central Intelligence Agency to the Minister of Foreign Affairs, Chungjaehaeng 150, in Ilbon-Pukhan kyongje kwan'gye, 1972 [Japan–North Korea Economic Relations, 1972], 725.6JA, 1972, D-0012 (ROK diplomatic archive).

owned debt suffered from payment delay from 1974, and that Pyongyang was unable to pay the principal and interest from December 1975.[38] Aside from the European countries' debt negotiations with North Korea, Japanese business groups, represented by the Japan–North Korea Trade Association, frequently visited Pyongyang in 1976 to negotiate the debt issue, and not to expand their businesses. The result of the negotiations was delayed repayments and lowered interest, but no payment has actually been made until now.

It is fair to say that South Vietnam's fall and the loss of Japanese business interest in North Korea happened simultaneously; however, the two events did not have a cause-and-effect relationship. Japan's gradual severing of economic relations with North Korea in the mid-1970s originated from the debt problem, rather than from a change in the security issue.

Conclusion

Sino–Japanese normalization, in comparison to US–China rapprochement, had a more direct, immediate impact on the Korean Peninsula in the first half of the 1970s. The Taiwan issue was at the heart of the affair for all those countries involved: the PRC, Japan, the United States, and the two Koreas. Only by doing away with its diplomatic relationship with Taiwan was Japan able to achieve its objective of normalization with the PRC. On the other hand, the development of Sino–Japanese relations and their eventual normalization rendered South Korea nervous and emboldened North Korea. Japan's "two Koreas" policy was consolidated and entrenched in this context. The ROK government, witnessing the Japanese abandonment of Taiwan, became concerned about her own fate, whereas the DPRK not only became audacious in launching peace initiatives, but also demonstrated flexibility and reasonableness in her policy towards Japan and the United States.

There are two noteworthy points arising from this discussion. First, Japan's Korea policy was not responsive to South Korean demand, request, wish, or complaint; the policy was relatively independent of the Japan–ROK quasi-alliance anchored by the United States. This independence became more evident after US–China rapprochement and Sino–Japanese

---

[38] Pukgoe ui oechae hyonhwang mit sanghwan kyosop hwaldong [North Korea's debt and its negotiation activities with regard to repayment], in Pukhan ui tae sobang oechae munje, 1976–77 [North Korea's debt to western countries, 1976–77], 725.6XG, 2007-24 (ROK diplomatic archive).

normalization. Japan secured a certain degree of autonomy in the early 1970s and afterwards in its foreign policy and, particularly, in its Korean policy. Second, Japan's foreign policy in general, and the Korean policy in particular, did not depend on political leadership—for example, who the prime minister was—but relied on Japan's national interest and consensus politics. No doubt, Sato Eisaku was a pro-American conservative politician, but he swiftly adapted in early 1972 to the changing international environment at that particular juncture of US–China rapprochement. Tanaka Kakuei was certainly an audacious politician, but he could neither achieve Sino–Japanese normalization nor improve Japan–DPRK relations without increasing China fever and domestic pressure for new relations with the two communist countries.

CHAPTER FIVE

THE ROLE OF SOUTH KOREA IN ASIAN REGIONAL POLITICS: BALANCING OR COLLABORATION?

LEE SANG-HYUN

Introduction

Under the Lee Myung-bak administration, South Korea (Republic of Korea, ROK) has endeavored to play a constructive role in Northeast Asian regional politics. The Lee administration vowed to pursue the foreign policy of a "Global Korea" and a "New Asian Diplomatic Initiative." Global Korea and the New Asian Diplomatic Initiative have required South Korea to seek a bigger role in both global and Asian regional affairs. For instance, Korea sought a calibrating role in creating complex cooperative networks among East Asian nations—particularly among the United States, China, Japan, and Korea. A broader regional framework—such as a multilateral security cooperation mechanism—was another issue in which South Korea has played a creative role. South Korea has also sought a more active role in the peaceful resolution of the North Korean nuclear crisis. In all cases, South Korea is pursuing a national strategy that will maximize the benefit of future complex interdependent networks among East Asian nations.

The Lee Myung-bak government's foreign and security policy has been referred to as "pragmatic diplomacy." Pragmatic diplomacy includes many things. Lee has announced an "MB [Myung-bak] Doctrine" that covers the following themes and principles for foreign policy:

1. Promote strategic policies that will induce North Korea to abandon its nuclear program and that will bring real change in the North;
2. Practice a utilitarian foreign policy based upon the national interest rather than on ideology;

3. Find a way to strengthen and improve the US alliance based on a long tradition of friendly relations, common values, and mutual benefit, and develop a new US–ROK "strategic master plan";
4. Increase cooperation and expand the South's diplomacy in East Asia to create a "great Asian era in the twenty-first century";
5. Strengthen the South's contribution to international society so that it can take a responsible international role commensurate with its position as a major world economy;
6. Maximize the South's "energy diplomacy" so it can join the world's most advanced economies, and build a national "energy cooperative belt" through a new "energy silk road";
7. Aim to create a "cultural Korea" based on mutual exchange and openness, practicing cultural diplomacy and the globalization of Korean culture.[1]

Among the items on this agenda, President Lee Myung-bak has placed the highest priority on revitalizing the ROK–US alliance and peacefully solving the North Korean nuclear crisis. Korea's diplomatic tasks have not only been restricted to the points mentioned above. Since the launch of the new administration in 2008, South Korea's MOFAT (Ministry of Foreign Affairs and Trade) has been undertaking a "creative and pragmatic" approach in its diplomatic efforts to realize the ROK's vision of becoming a truly "Global Korea." Although the ROK's foreign policy has prioritized revitalizing the domestic economy, developing the ROK–US strategic alliance, and making substantial progress on the North Korean nuclear issue, South Korea has also been turning its attention to other regions of the world. Naturally, Asia comes first, not simply because Asia is where South Korea belongs geographically, but also because the region is becoming strategically important to South Korea's national interests.

Asian Regional Order: What is it and where is it going?

In considering the future of the Asian Regional Order, I will begin by examining current global trends. By 2025, the international system will be a global multipolar one with gaps in national power continuing to narrow between developed and developing countries. Concurrent with the shift in power among nation-states, the relative power of various non-state actors—including businesses, tribes, religious organizations, and criminal networks—is increasing. The players are changing, but so too are the scope and breadth of transnational issues important for continued global

---

[1] "GNP (Grand National Party) North Korea policy," GNP Policy Committee. See GNP website: http://www.hannara.or.kr.

prosperity. Growth projections for Brazil, Russia, India, and China (BRIC) indicate they will collectively match the original G-7's share of global GDP by 2040–50. The trend towards greater diffusion of authority and power, both economically and militarily, that has been occurring for several decades is likely to accelerate because of the emergence of new global players, the worsening institutional deficit, the potential expansion of regional blocs, and the enhanced strength of non-state actors and networks. With this change, greater Asian regionalism—possibly by 2025—would have global implications, sparking or reinforcing a trend towards three trade and financial clusters that could become quasi-blocs: North America, Europe, and East Asia.[2]

Although it might sound slightly premature to assume such a multipolar international order, the trend is already quite obvious, and Asia is no exception. For the past ten years, East Asia has been witnessing a series of inexorable changes.[3] Four developments in particular deserve to be mentioned.

The first is Asia's growing economic and political weight. Currently, the region generates approximately 30 percent of global exports and its two-way trade with the United States exceeds $1 trillion annually. It holds two-thirds of global foreign exchange reserves. The second factor is China's rise, a trajectory that has introduced an increasingly self-assured, rich, and powerful actor into the Asian strategic landscape. To its credit, China understands that it needs a peaceful security environment in order to realize its transformation. Yet this rise creates certain dilemmas: the growing strength of China's military has alarmed its neighbors, who also depend on China for their own economic growth. China's military strategy is a concern to neighboring countries, as they perceive Beijing's quest for security as creating an insecure environment. Improving cross-Strait ties in recent months has helped assuage some regional concerns.

The third factor is the emergence of an increasing number of nuclear-weapon states and the attendant threat of proliferation. India and Pakistan have conducted nuclear tests, as has North Korea. China continues to modernize its nuclear and ballistic missile capabilities. Russia is embarking on a strategic modernization program of its own. The United States has withdrawn from the Anti-Ballistic Missile (ABM) treaty and is deploying missile defense systems in the region. There are fears of an arms

[2] US National Intelligence Council, *Global Trends 2025: A Transformed World* (Washington, DC: Government Printing Office, 2008), vi–xi.

[3] In this paper, "East Asia" refers to the region composed of the nation-states of Northeast Asia and Southeast Asia, including China, Japan, the two Koreas, Taiwan, and ASEAN member states.

race. At the same time, there are rising concerns about the proliferation of weapons of mass destruction (WMD) technology, materials, and know-how to states and non-state actors.

The fourth factor is an increasing interest in multilateral cooperation. Once a laggard, the region now hosts a veritable "noodle bowl" of multilateral political, economic, and security mechanisms. These institutions are incomplete and imperfect, but they have inculcated habits of cooperation and built mutual understanding. Regular political dialogue, economic integration, and other aspects of globalization have created a new atmosphere in which countries are exploring cooperative approaches to a wide range of security challenges.[4]

East Asia, apparently, lacks a more or less enduring multilateral mechanism like the Organization for Security and Cooperation in Europe (OSCE). East Asia's lack of integration grows largely out of the high level of attention given to the actions of the region's governments and to the cooperative or conflictual interactions of nation-states. However, a strikingly contrasting view of the East Asian region emerges when one looks at linkages beneath the level of state-to-state actions. East Asia has in recent years become considerably more independent, connected, and cohesive. This increased cohesiveness has been driven by developments, among other things, in trade and investment, cross-border production, banking, technology sharing, popular culture, transportation, communication, and environmental cooperation, as well as in crime, drug, and disease control. Reflecting upon such developments, there have emerged a burgeoning number of formal institutional arrangements linking various geographical regions together.

In order to appreciate the linkage mechanisms operating across East Asia, it is useful to recognize that at least three discrete drivers have been spinning webs across East Asia: governments, corporations, and *ad hoc* problem-oriented coalitions. To focus exclusively on one of these, while ignoring the others, is to miss the greater multiplicity and complexity of the ties that are emerging in this region. The processes are two-fold: regionalism and regionalization. Regionalism is a top-down process of government-to-government formation of institutions such as ASEAN or the ASEAN Regional Forum (ARF). Regionalization refers to a bottom-up process of cross-border cooperation driven primarily by nongovernmental

[4] R. A. Cossa, B. Glosserman, M. A. McDevitt, N. Patel, J. Przystup, and B. Roberts, "The United States and the Asia–Pacific Region: Security Strategy for the Obama Administration" (co-published by IDA, Pacific Forum CSIS, INSS, CNA, and CNAS; February 2009), 3–4: http://csis.org/files/media/csis/pubs/ issues insights_v09n01.pdf.

Figure 1: Existing web of multilateral arrangements in Asia–Pacific[5]

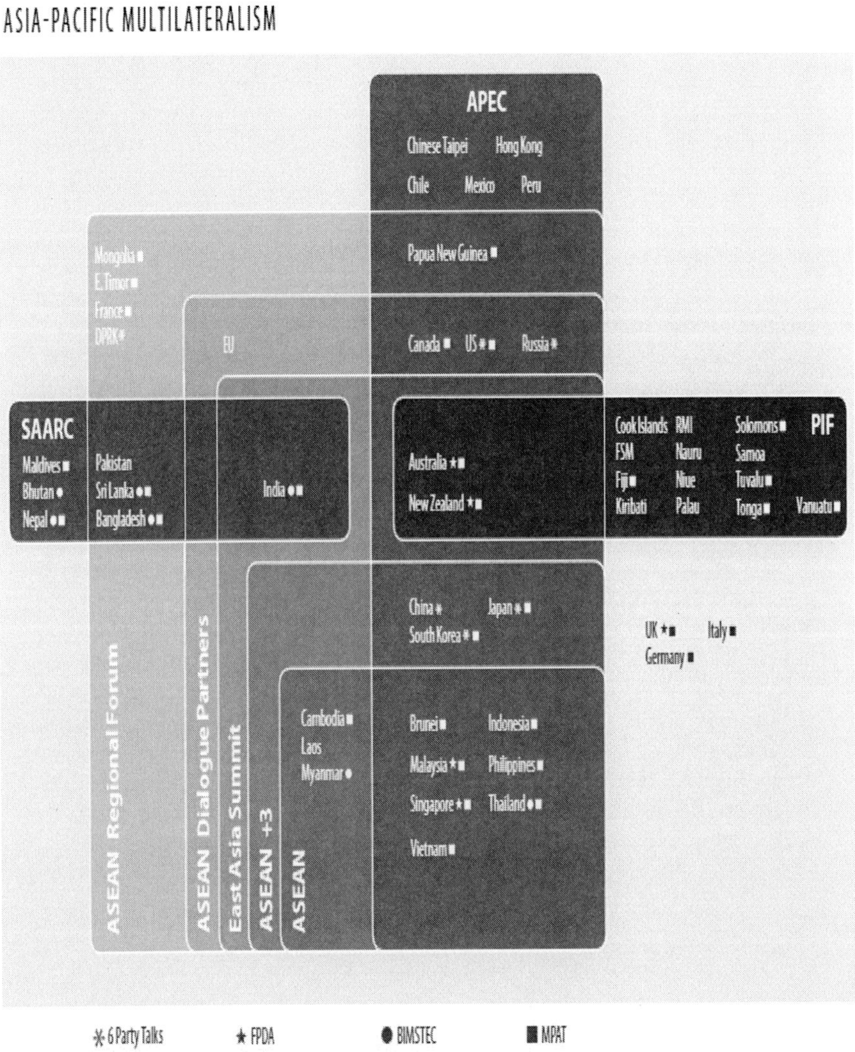

[5] Cossa et al., "The United States and the Asia-Pacific Region," 27.

actors such as corporations or NGOs. In either case, the important point is that a host of overlapping and reinforcing regional ties are being built in East Asia.[6]

Another recent study described East Asia's emerging identity as "iAsia." The study characterized the Asia-Pacific region as dynamic and integrating, calling this emerging reality in the region, "iAsia." "iAsia" comprises the notion of an integrated, innovative, and investing Asia. It is also characterized by insecurity, instability, and inequality. According to the analysis, Asians are shaping a world that is ever more integrated, both politically and economically. New regional forums are reshaping cooperation and fostering deeper ties. Some are governmental, and some are more focused on the private sector. Amidst this integration, innovation defines twenty-first-century Asia.

Obviously, Asia is not yet a theater at peace. Throughout the region, many people die every day from causes related to conflict, and suspicions rooted in rivalry and nationalism run deep. The region harbors every traditional and non-traditional challenge of our age: ethnic tension, terror and extremism, and conflicts over energy, to name but a few. Despite challenges and risks of regional insecurity, instability, and inequality, Asia will be integrating, innovating, and investing for years to come.[7]

To sum up, East Asia is, indeed, experiencing a burgeoning network of governments, corporations, and both formal and informal institutions across the region. Such a rich and thick web of interactions will surely be beneficial for most nations in the region. Despite such optimism, however, Asian unity is still a long way off. Unlike Europe, there is no shared philosophy about government and economics to align Asian powers. Despite growing prosperity, Asia suffers from the greatest degree of inequality in the world, both across the region and within nations like China and India. For example, in Asia real GDP growth rates per capita ranged from a low of $1,100 in Nepal to $48,900 in Singapore in 2007.[8]

---

[6] T. J. Pempel, ed., *Remapping East Asia: The Construction of a Region* (Ithaca: Cornell University Press, 2005), 2–6.

[7] K. M. Campbell, N. Patel, and V. J. Singh, *The Power of Balance: America in Asia*, Center for New American Security, June 2008: http://www.cnas.org/files/documents/publications/CampbellPatelSingh_iAsia_June08.pdf.

[8] CIA World Fact Book: https://www.cia.gov/library/publications/the-world-factbook/rankorder/2004rank.html.

Korea's Strategic Choice: Balancing versus Collaboration

With tectonic changes, a new landscape has opened up remarkable opportunities for the nations of the Asia-Pacific to develop their economies and build more hopeful futures for their peoples. However, it also poses two new kinds of danger for the region.

The first is the risk that Asia will fail to develop the structures of cooperation that are necessary both to seize the opportunities and to master the threats that come with globalization and interdependence. The second is that the emergence of new, more powerful economic and military actors will generate rivalry and even conflict, manifesting itself in the classic security dilemma that has characterized much of Asian history.

To avoid such dangers, it is imperative for Asian nations to develop a rich and thick web of cooperative networks throughout the region. The reason is quite obvious. Simply put, we live in a world of networks. War is networked; the power of terrorists and the militaries that would defeat them depend on small, mobile groups of warriors connected to one another and to intelligence, communications, and support networks. Diplomacy is networked; managing international crises—from SARS to climate change—requires mobilizing international networks of public and private actors. Business, media, and society are networked, linking hundreds of millions of individuals all over the world.

Anne-Marie Slaughter, former Director of Policy Planning in the US State Department, claimed that in this world, the measure of power is connectedness. The twentieth-century world was, at least in terms of geopolitics, a billiard-ball world, described by mainstream political scientists as a system of self-contained states colliding with one another. The results of these collisions were determined by military and economic power. This world still exists today. For example, Russia invades Georgia, Iran seeks nuclear weapons, and the United States strengthens its ties with India as a hedge against a rising China. This is what Fareed Zakaria, editor of *Newsweek International*, has dubbed "the post-American world," in which the rise of new global powers inevitably means the relative decline of US influence and hegemony.[9] The emerging networked world of the twenty-first century, however, exists above the state, below the state, and through the state. In this world, the state with the most connections will be

[9] F. Zakaria, *The Post-American World* (New York: W. W. Norton & Company, 2008); see also F. Zakaria, "The Rise of the Rest," *Newsweek*, May 12, 2008:.

the central player, able to set the global agenda and unlock innovation and sustainable growth.[10]

East Asia is not the exception. The future dynamism in East Asia will very much depend on how Asian nations create and utilize such connectivity among themselves and across the region. Luckily, the current situation is quite favorable to carving out a cooperative regional network because the United States strongly supports a regional framework that goes beyond existing bilateral relations in East Asia. Actually, one of the key elements of the Obama administration's Asian policy is the building of structures of cooperation both in the region and across the world that link Asia to the wider global order. Washington recognizes that the emerging regional architecture is an important part of how Asians see themselves and how the nations of the Asia-Pacific must set the norms for cooperation for decades to come. For this reason, during Secretary Clinton's trip to Asia, she visited the secretariat of ASEAN and pledged to attend the ASEAN Regional Forum in July 2009. In addition to using existing groupings to work collaboratively with the region, the United States will continue to explore ways to better coordinate multilaterally with nations in the Asia-Pacific region.[11]

Although it is true that the United States has a clear and sustainable edge in this regard, the networked order does not exclude any player. China, Japan, and Korea can also create a network, and be central players in specific areas. If power is indeed derived from connectivity, then East Asian nations must cooperate to create mutually beneficial connections. In this century, both regional and global power will increasingly be defined by connections—who is connected with whom and for what purpose. Some networks can be malicious and intend to exclude others. Nevertheless, on the whole, the positive effects of networks will greatly outweigh the negative.

South Korea, indeed, wants to contribute to the creation of a thick web of networks among China, Japan, and Korea. A perennial South Korean foreign policy objective has been the successful management of ties with each of the four major powers surrounding the Korean Peninsula—the United States, Japan, China, and Russia. Although the Lee government had also prioritized good relations with China and Russia by sending

---

[10] A. Slaughter, "America's Edge: Power in the Networked Century," *Foreign Affairs*, January/February 2009.

[11] "Engaging Asia 2009: Strategies for Success," James B. Steinberg, Deputy Secretary of State, Bureau of Deputy Secretary, Remarks at the National Bureau of Asian Research Conference, Washington, DC, April 1, 2009: http://www.state.gov/s/d/2009/121564.htm).

special envoys to Beijing and Moscow, there were early signs that President Lee's emphasis on the United States and Japan was making China uneasy. Such unexpected negative effects should be remedied.

Both the ROK and the United States must work to reduce the negative connotations associated with the term "strategic alliance." Many Chinese people understand the concept of "value-based partnership" as intended to exclude countries with different values, particularly China. The ROK–US strategic alliance does not aim to contain the rising China; it intends to cope with the comprehensive security threats of the twenty-first century. The Obama administration and the Lee Myung-bak government must work together to reduce such grave misunderstandings of the Chinese people.

In addition, South Korea must focus on creating networks among China, Japan, and Korea whenever possible. South Korea can contribute in many of the areas discussed below.

First, a breakthrough can be found on the North Korean nuclear crisis in cooperative networks among Asian nations—particularly among China, Japan, and Korea. North Korea's nuclear ambition is more than a decade old. One of the key objectives of North Korea in the recent nuclear brinkmanship is to gain the status of a nuclear weapon state. Some analysts even argue that the North wants negotiations, not about denuclearization, but about arms control. Their model is to turn the Six-Party Talks into a bilateral US–DPRK nuclear arms reduction negotiation in which the North is accorded a status as a nuclear weapon state that agrees to mutual nuclear-arms reductions (not elimination) and confidence-building measures. They frequently refer to the US–Soviet strategic arms-control negotiations as their empirical referent. The outcome of these negotiations, in the North's view, is a situation similar to that of India: an agreement in which the North is assured of a civilian nuclear energy element and the carving off of a portion of its nuclear programs outside international inspection, which can then serve as a nuclear deterrent. In short, they want the rules of the Nuclear Nonproliferation Treaty regime rewritten for them as they were for India.[12] To persuade North Korea to voluntarily get off the nuclear track, concerted efforts among China, Japan, and Korea are essential.

Second, South Korea can play a mitigating role in the case of a potential rivalry between China and Japan. The rise of China is a reality of the twenty-first century. China has had continued economic growth at a remarkable rate for the past decade. Based on such economic confidence,

[12] V. D. Cha, "What Do They Want?" *PacNet Newsletter*, no. 36, May 18, 2009.

China has recently invested heavily on its military modernization programs. Due to such trends, and although China's rise is dubbed as "peaceful," China is viewed with awe, rather than with respect, by most Asian nations. If Japan further proceeds along the path towards becoming a "Normal State," the possibility of a clash between China and Japan will increase. In such a case, a cooperative network among the three nations—preferably created by South Korea's initiative—will prove quite useful.

Conclusion

For peace, stability, and prosperity in East Asia, nations in the region should foster the vision of a "networked Asia" as a guiding principle. Such a vision encompasses a change from a "balance of power" to a "power of balance" perspective, characterized by an overlapping web of networks among Asia-Pacific nations. The relationship will also shift from "zero-sum" relations to that of "win-win" for all nations. Diversifying issue areas for cooperation—trade, transnational security issues, energy and environmental cooperation—are always better than narrowing the scope.

In order to proceed in this direction, East Asian nations must share a common perception about the future of Asia. They must share the vision that engaging, not antagonizing, is the way forward. They should proclaim less nationalism, and more emphasis on cooperative-security perspectives. They must support multilateralism, instead of rivalry, on the nation-state level. Such a development will require a strong leadership of leading East Asian nations—particularly China, Japan, and South Korea.

CHAPTER SIX

SINO–JAPANESE RELATIONS AND DIVERSIFYING KOREA'S NATIONAL INTERESTS

PARK IHN-HWI

Introduction

In post–Cold War international relations, Northeast Asia has come to lie at the heart of global security concerns. With the end of the US–Soviet confrontation, scholars with perspectives rooted mainly in the Western tradition have determined that the underdevelopment of regional institutions, absence of visionary leadership, and aggravation in structural differences among regional states make inter-state conflict in the region a real possibility.[1] With the slow pace of structural change in Northeast Asian international relations, many post–Cold War concerns remain largely unresolved. Irrespective of the different standards and subjects of analysis among scholars, the consequences of the rise of China, the effects of Japan's military build-up, and instability on the Korean Peninsula and in the Taiwan Strait, all seem to endorse such pessimistic views.

The rise of China has been at the center of post–Cold War insecurity in the Northeast Asian region. In particular, future Sino–Japanese relations and any related confrontation(s) between the two countries holds special meaning for Korea's national interest. Of course, there are also theoretical

---

[1] R. K. Betts, "Wealth, Power, and Instability: East Asia and the United States after the Cold War," *International Security* 18, no. 3 (1994): 34–77; A. L. Friedberg, "Ripe for Rivalry: Prospects for Peace in a Multipolar Asia," *International Security* 18, no. 3 (1994): 5–33; B. Buzan and G. Segal, "Rethinking East Asian Security," *Survival* 36, no. 2 (2010): 3–21; T. Christensen, "China, the US–Japan Alliance, and the Security Dilemma," *International Security* 23, no. 4 (1999): 47–98.

discussions associated with possible hegemonic confrontation between the United States and China over the strategic rise of the latter. China may not confront the interests of the United States directly, but may instead choose to target and challenge the interests of the US–Japanese alliance. In this sense, South Korea's national interests could be seriously infringed by the conflict between China and the US–Japanese alliance, since any future conflict among these powers is most likely to erupt around the Korean Peninsula. Being the state most representative of "Northeast Asian regional identity," Korea finds the region's stability to be one of its most important interests.[2] In short, any future confrontation between China and Japan may undermine Korea's national interests. Therefore, in order to avoid the negative consequences of Northeast Asian structural problems, Korea needs to carefully define her national interests and identify strategies to realize them both at the Northeast Asian regional level and beyond. Based on this background, this paper will firstly discuss the structural problem of Northeast Asian security and its significance to Korea's national interests. Secondly, it will discuss how Korea should define her national interests at the global, regional, and peninsular levels to avoid Northeast Asian structural limitations.

Structure of Northeast Asian Security

Theories of Northeast Asian Security

The United States, despite being geographically a non-Asian entity, had established its position as the undisputed hegemon in the Asia-Pacific by the end of the Cold War. With the collapse of the USSR, any decline of US power would become a significant factor in causing instability in Northeast Asia.[3] Despite minor disagreements, security analysts predict that China and Japan would competitively try and fill the power vacuum left behind should there be a decline in US influence in the region. Prior to analysis of Sino–Japanese strategic rivalry, there needs to be theoretical explanations of the conditions of global politics under which rivalry between two states intensifies. A number of important theoretical concepts directly applicable to the subject of this essay will be examined first.

---

[2] I. Park, "The Northeast Asian International Relations and Korea's National Interest: On the Perspective of the US–China–Japan's Power Balance," *The Journal of East Asian Affairs* (2005): 5–32.

[3] K. E. Calder, "US Foreign Policy in Northeast Asia," in *The International Relations of Northeast Asia*, edited by S. Kim (Lanham, MD: Rowman & Littlefield, 2004), 225–248.

First, with regards to the changing regional security environment, and operating under the assumption that the international system is anarchical, a state would try to determine the size of national power and military capability required to secure its sovereignty.[4] States generally consider the following two questions: what kind of power distribution is recognized as acceptable to states as a "safe" international order among different states? What efforts would each state try to undertake in order to secure such an order? More specifically, the ultimate question is whether states should encourage and support an order premised on "balance of power," or rather accommodate a hegemon that dominates the order to produce the stability sought in the desirable international security order. Whether an individual state pursues a balance of power or power maximization is the result of complex foreign policy calculations based upon geopolitical circumstances, its relations with the existing hegemon, the status of power distribution in international politics, and interpretation of a state's own prospects in such changing circumstances.[5] Such elements of consideration in Northeast Asia can be observed in the relationship between the United States, China, and Japan, and each state's status in the region. The United States is a regional stabilizer with geographical distance. Its security alliance with Japan has been strengthened and transformed to suit the twenty-first century international security environment.[6] Maritime territorial disputes and contention over history continue to occur between China and Japan. Considering the circumstantial evidence, regional actors are most likely to find that it is in their best interests to pursue the balance of power approach.

Second, there are contending arguments on continuity and divergences between global and regional hegemonic influences. According to offensive realists, meaningful global hegemony cannot exist without clear superiority in nuclear capability.[7] All hegemonic influence then, in theory, is limited to the regional level. Different analytical perspectives, in contrast, explain that in the contemporary world—characterized by

---

[4] K. N. Waltz, *Theory of International Politics* (New York: Addison-Wesley, 1979), Ch. 6.

[5] R. Gilpin, *War and Change in World Politics* (Cambridge: Cambridge University Press, 1981), Ch. 5.

[6] C. W. Hughes and A. Fukushima, "US–Japan Security Relations: Toward Bilateralism Plus?" in *Beyond Bilateralism: US–Japan Relations in the New Asia-Pacific*, edited by E. S. Krauss and T. J. Pempel, 55–85 (Stanford, CA: Stanford University Press, 2004).

[7] J. J. Mearsheimer, *The Tragedy of Great Power Politics* (New York: Norton, 2001), 145.

globalization, development of information technology, and prevalence of institutionalization—the influence of global and regional hegemony may not be distinctively defined.[8] Such contemporary elements in international relations would sustain the US hegemony at the global level, and thus the status of the United States would cause any pursuit of hegemony by China or Japan to remain regional in character. In the meantime, China and Japan, in order to maximize their national interests, are likely to continue to struggle to determine the direction of foreign policy between two contending predictions: whether they would continue to pursue power expansion relentlessly, or refrain from further power acquisition after a certain level has been achieved.[9]

The third question is related to the availability of regional or global mechanisms that can restrain actors' propensity towards power expansion. Traditional theories explain that states' balancing behavior, or war against the existing hegemon, determines the status of a new power. In most historical cases, however, rising hegemons have chosen the "power maximization strategy" more frequently than the "balance of power strategy." In the pre–World War II period, Germany, Italy, the former Soviet Union, and Japan continued to pursue power maximization over self-restraint, while recognizing themselves as rising powers.[10] In such scenarios, there were both successes and failures of regional mechanisms in restraining states' attempts at power expansion. Despite the two world wars, Europe today has somewhat successfully achieved a regional institutionalization that restrains states' power expansion, a phenomenon which is distinctively different from current East Asian international relations. However, in Northeast Asia, Japan remains the only nation to reach a high level of industrialization. If China's modernization project

---

[8] V. S. Peterson, "Shifting Ground: Epistemological and Territorial Remapping in the Context of Globalization," in *Globalization: Theory and Practice*, edited by E. Kofman and G. Youngs, 11–27 (London: Pinter, 1996); S. Dalby, "Crossing Disciplinary Boundaries: Political Geography and International Relations after the Cold War," in Kofman and Youngs, *Globalization: Theory and Practice*, 29–41.

[9] H. J. Morgenthau, *Politics among Nations: The Struggle for Power and Peace* (New York: Alfred A. Knopf, 1948), Ch. 1; A. Wolfers, *Discord and Collaboration: Essays on International Politics* (Baltimore: The Johns Hopkins Press, 1962), 84; K. N. Waltz, "The Origin of War in Neorealist Theory," in *The Origin and Prevention of Major Wars*, edited by R. I. Rotberg and T. K. Rabb (Cambridge: Cambridge University Press, 1989), 40; J. J. Mearsheimer, "Back to the Future: Instability in Europe after the Cold War," *International Security* 15, no. 1 (1990): 5–56.

[10] J. J. Mearsheimer, *The Tragedy of Great Power Politics* (New York: Norton, 2011).

succeeds, China and Japan will be the two major states in confrontation. This region, characterized by such bipolar rivalry, lacks a mechanism that could constrain the power expansion ambitions of regional states. Considering the structural, cultural, and historical factors that contribute to the underdevelopment of institutionalization, the emergence of any embryonic institutional mechanism would still have many limits in effectively constraining the Sino–Japanese rivalry.[11]

Lastly, it is necessary to consider causal relations between the conditions that lead to war and the structure of international politics, assuming that there is a potential for war to break out between China and Japan. The current distribution of power may be characterized by unstable unipolar-multipolarity with a slight difference in high and low politics. Unipolarity under the US military superiority will continue in "high" politics, while unstable multipolarity among second-rank powers, e.g., Europe, China, and Japan, will continue until approximately 2030.[12] In response to any possible rise of China or Japan, counter-balancing forces among the states will effectively contain each other from rising to a position of relative superiority against the other. However, in the current unstable unipolar-multipolar system, the United States, which possesses military superiority, is likely to take the role of balancer if rivalries resulting from power expansion lead to conflicts in high politics. In this context, the so-called "buck-passing theory" has increasingly prevailed among scholars in recent discussions.[13] More analysis is required in choosing between balancing and buck-passing. For instance, if China pursues a policy of becoming the regional hegemon, Japan will have to find a point of compromise between balancing against China with autonomous capability and buck-passing the role to the United States.

---

[11] E. Solingen, "East Asian Regional Institution: Characteristics, Sources, Distinctiveness," in *Remapping Asia: Competing Patterns of Regional Integration*, edited by T. J. Pempel, 31–52 (Ithaca: Cornell University Press, 2005); J. S. Duffield, "Asia–Pacific Security Institutions in Comparative Perspective," in *International Relations Theory and the Asia–Pacific*, edited by G. J. Ikenberry and M. Mastenduno, 243–269 (New York: Columbia University Press, 2003).

[12] F. Zakaria, *The Post-American World* (New York: W.W. Norton and Company, 2008).

[13] J. M. Lind, "Pacifism or Passing the Buck," *International Security* 29, no. 1 (2004): 92–121; G. Snyder, "Mearsheimer's World—Offensive Realism and the Struggle for Security: A Review Essay," *International Security* 27, no. 1 (2002): 149–173; T. J. Christensen, "Fostering Stability or Creating Monster?: The Rise of China and US Policy toward East Asia," *International Security* 31, no. 1 (2006): 81–126.

The Third Stage of Sino–Japanese Relations

The beginning of the Cold War in the Northeast Asian region, marked by the United States's "reverse course" in her plans to disarm Japan, was the beginning of the so-called first stage of Northeast Asian international relations.[14] The bilateral alliance structure that applied to Korea, Japan, Taiwan, and parts of Southeast Asia was significant in the sense that it completely excluded and isolated China.[15] In the mid-sixties, the Cold War structure in the Northeast Asian region was modified with the normalization of relations between South Korea and Japan. The relationship between Japan and China during this period was tense, and marked by the severing of any diplomatic interaction between the two countries.[16] Japan's complete dependence on the US Cold War containment policy made diplomatic relations between China and Japan impossible.

The first stage of Northeast Asian international relations met its turning point in 1969 with the announcement of President Nixon's Guam Doctrine. More specifically, Northeast Asian international relations underwent a structural change in 1972 when China and Japan normalized relations, marking the point where China began to gradually participate in international relations in the region. Although it cannot be said that Northeast Asian relations went through a complete change, due to the sharp Cold War situation on the Korean Peninsula, the amelioration of US–China relations and normalization of Japan–China relations showed a definite contrast to the first stage which was characterized by China's isolation.[17] This was especially so after the 1980s as China began to devote herself to the strategy of economic growth and increased diplomatic interactions with countries not only within Northeast Asia but throughout East Asia as well. Thus, China–Japan relations during the second stage can be explained as being focused on securing limited independence in diplomatic relations.

---

[14] T. J. Christensen, *Useful Adversaries: Grand Strategy, Domestic Mobilization, and Sino–American Conflict, 1947–1958* (Princeton: Princeton University Press, 1998).

[15] Christensen, *Useful Adversaries*, 181–193.

[16] Y. F. Khong, "The United States and East Asia: Challenges to the Balance of Power," in *Explaining International Relations since 1945*, edited by N. Woods, 179–196 (Oxford: Oxford University Press, 1996).

[17] M. Schaller, "Détente and the Strategic Triangle: Or, 'Drinking Your Mao Tai and Having Your Vodka, Too,'" in *Re-examining the Cold War*, edited by R. S. Ross and C. Jiang, 361–392 (Massachusetts: Harvard University Press, 1971).

The second stage of Northeast Asian international relations began in the early seventies and lasted until the end of the Cold War. The third stage of Northeast Asian international relations began with the end of the Cold War around 1990. Unlike the previous two stages, the third stage went through a long transition period. With the end of the Cold War, China began to play an active role in international society, and also improved its relations with Korea. However, because the US alliance strategy, which was the center of Northeast Asian international relations, underwent strategic reassessment, the actual establishment of a new goal took place in 1997 with the so-called "New Guidelines" for US–Japan defense cooperation. In short, there was a long transition period between the end of the second stage, around the year 1990, and the beginning of the third stage, the period 1996/97. The reason for setting the period 1996/97 as the beginning of the third stage is rooted in the argument that the Japan–US alliance was to continue even after the Cold War, and also in the common security threat the two countries perceived in the rise of China, a fact stated in the Japan–US defense guidelines.[18] Thus, China–Japan relations came to face a new phase with the start of the third stage of Northeast Asian international relations. As for the characteristics of the third stage, the economic relations between the two countries are seen to develop into intimate diplomatic ties. However, in traditional security relations there has been no development of mutual trust.

As observed, when looking retrospectively at China–Japan relations, today's China–Japan relationship would fall under the third stage. It shows, characteristically, the coexistence of strategic conflict and realistic cooperation. From the perspective of South Korea's national interest, Korea–China socio-economic relations have seen revolutionary progress since the third stage of Northeast Asian international relations. As for Korea–Japan relations, although relatively weakened, there is no question that the diplomatic partnership between the two countries will continue. As a relatively weak country, it is difficult for South Korea to change the framework of Northeast Asia's security structure. However, because the conflict between China and Japan has not yet reached critical levels, now would be an appropriate time to maximize South Korea's national interest, especially over issues concerning North Korea.

---

[18] Hughes and Fukushima, "US–Japan Security Relations," 73–77; M. Mochizuki, "Terms of Engagement: The US–Japan Alliance and the Rise of China," in *Beyond Bilateralism: US–Japan Relations in the New Asia-Pacific*, edited by E. Krauss and T. J. Pempel, 88–95 (Stanford: Stanford University Press, 2004).

Korea's National Identity and National Interests

Korea's National Identity

All nations have their own national identity, in the same way that individuals do. Consequently, in order to explain Korea's national interest in relation to the prospects of Sino–Japanese relations, an explanation of Korea's national identity is necessary. Two main characteristics of Korea's national identity can be identified. First, Korea's most important national identity is its identity as a "Northeast Asian state." We often use the expression "Northeast Asian region," but it is difficult to pinpoint a specific country as a Northeast Asian state. For instance, China, Japan, Russia, as well as the United States, each has its own interests in Northeast Asia, but in terms of national identity it may not be possible to categorize these countries as Northeast Asian countries. From this point of view, Korea is the country with the strongest Northeast Asian identity, and such an explanation means that the regional stability of Northeast Asia is the most important issue for South Korea's conception of national interest. Northeast Asia is one of the Eurasian continent's main strategic points, and a rare place where the world's two largest continental powers, China and Russia, interact with the other two major maritime powers, the United States and Japan. As the region stands at the intersection of international politics, it follows that the struggle for political, economic, and security interests is extremely intense. The Korean Peninsula, being positioned at the center of such an area, is extremely sensitive to the stability and balance of the geopolitics of the region. The region's stability is a life-and-death precondition for Korea's national interest and destiny. This requires Korea to have the diplomatic power to continuously and effectively engage the great powers at both the regional and global levels, rather than be confined to regional politics alone.

Second, another main component of Korea's national identity is the complex characteristic of the security situation that the Korean Peninsula faces. It is impossible to guarantee Korea's security and national interest without achieving a balance between the "peninsular factors" and the "international factors," because these two categories of factors are intricately intertwined. Neighboring great powers such as China, Japan, and the United States each have their own interests on the Korean Peninsula, and a future unified government on the Korean Peninsula under any particular country's exclusive influence would be something everyone would wish to avoid. Accordingly, Korea's diplomatic strategy must be very intricately established from a perspective of seeking a harmonious combination of the "peninsular factors" and "international factors" on the Korean Peninsula.

In this regard, China and Japan are both key actors of the Northeast Asian region and are pursuing their own advantages with respect to the peninsular problem. As mentioned above, if any form of conflict in Sino–Japanese relations is to occur, history's lessons suggest that it will most likely be manifested on the Korean Peninsula. Consequently, it will always be extremely important for Korea to have the ability to strategically analyze changes in the power structure between China and Japan and understand how that change affects the Korean Peninsula.

Korea's National Interests

Based on the notion of national identity outlined above, the following section will specify the constraints and opportunities facing South Korea's pursuit of national interests. South Korea has experienced the furthest development of political democratization, and this experience could well be a unique East Asian model. South Korea's national interest at the peninsular level would, therefore, be to achieve a consolidation of democracy, continued economic growth, and to propel cultural pluralism on top of this. If and when unification happens, the unified North–South Korean government should exist with the aim of realizing such national interests as outlined.

There is no question that South Korea lags behind China and Japan in terms of military and economic power. At the same time, North Korea appears to be determined to pursue a diplomatic strategy of defying the international norms and behavior of international society. The greater the relative power of the states surrounding the Korean Peninsula is, the more South Korea must focus on cultivating the universal principles, such as democracy and rule of law, free-market economic principles and multiculturalism. Only when South Korea can establish a democracy and a market economy to a sufficient level will it be respected by the international society. Such efforts will allow South Korea to maintain its integrity on the peninsular level and guarantee a relative superiority vis-à-vis neighboring states. Korea's democratization came as a consequence of industrialization and the expansion of civil society. This is something South Korea could be proud of when compared to China, a socialist state, or Japan, where a single party has held a monopoly on power. The prolonging of the nuclear crisis on the Korean peninsula means that this goal of promoting a peaceful and democratic environment in preparation for a unified government in the long run is, therefore, more important than ever.

Second, South Korea's national interest at the Northeast Asian regional level is to acquire a certain degree of deterrence capability so that states surrounding the Korean Peninsula cannot infringe upon South Korea's sovereignty. As such, one of the most pressing initiatives South Korea should undertake should be the "institutionalized security framework" in the region, taking into account Korea's national capacity, to employ a diplomatic strategy so that the great powers can balance each other. It is widely considered that, compared to the level of institutionalization of Europe, institutionalization in East Asia is underdeveloped. South Korea is in a more advantageous position to lead regional institutionalization than China or Japan. Particularly when considering the historical animosity between China and Japan, we can see that Korea is the country most suited to play the role of a diplomatic mediator between China and Japan.

In terms of Korea's regional interest, the Korea–US alliance still remains an extremely valuable diplomatic asset. In case conflict between China and Japan becomes so severe that military force is used, Korea could request the help of a non-regional superpower, the United States, to ensure her security. Korea has even maintained an alliance with China, although during pre-modern times that alliance was formed on the basis of unequal relations between the two countries. In terms of the diplomatic relationship with Japan, Japan has made attempts to invade the territory of Korea, and even to gain imperialistic control over the Peninsula. Thus, utilizing the capacity of a superpower which does not have a territorial interest in the Peninsula to diplomatically counter China and Japan and, at the same time, seeking institutional stability in the Northeast Asian region, are very important to Korea's national interest.

Third, our interest at a global level is to adopt universal values, such as democracy, freedom, fair competition, human rights, etc., and incorporate these values into our national interest. In doing so, South Korea would always aim to preserve access to the most advanced capitalist regions represented by the United States and Western Europe, and to inaugurate a national image that contributes to world peace. In particular, we will have to bear in mind the fact that our Northeast Asian identity requires a continued understanding of balanced diplomatic strategies between the regional level and beyond. Even though Korea's national identity can be defined as that of a Northeast Asian state, it is essential for Korea to develop amicable diplomatic relations with superpowers beyond Northeast Asia.

Militarily, Korea should dispatch peace-keeping troops to conflict areas and free itself from the image of a divided country, and assume a positive image as a contributor to world peace. Economically, by expanding commercial exchanges at various levels, Korea must continuously build up its economy and enhance its technological and scientific prowess. Culturally, South Korea must attempt to enhance her cultural diplomacy so that a greater level of global recognition can be attained for Korean culture, beyond the current level achieved by the Korean Wave, *Hallyu*. Lastly, overseas development aid (ODA) diplomacy, to which the Korean government has lately been paying great attention, is a desirable national strategy that should be continued. Korea is the prime example of a country which was once a recipient of international support that has grown into a very strong economic power. Thus, by converting such an experience into its own national diplomatic strategy, Korea could create a national image as a positive contributor to international peace.

Diversifying Korea's National Interests

In relation to the subject of this paper, the future of relations between China and Japan will have a great influence on Korea's national interest at both the regional (Northeast Asian) level and the global level. Korea will have to consider the following three main points in relation to the strategy of separating our national interests as regards the Northeast Asian dimension from that of the global dimension. Major powers, such as China, Japan, and the United States, can realize their national interests even if their diplomatic resources and attention are divided through the pursuit of their core national interests and their interests in Northeast Asia. However, in Korea's case, if the national interest is "buried" under Northeast Asian regional matters, or if global-level interests are unintentionally neglected, it could fatally damage Korea's entire national interest.

Second, there are very different images about Korea. This is most unfortunate. Most notably, the terms "Korea in a global context" and "Korea in a regional context" have different meanings for viewers in the international community as well as for Koreans themselves. "Korea in a global context" is evaluated as a country that has achieved unprecedented success in industrialization and democratization and is now casting an eye on attaining the status of the tenth to fifteenth largest economy in the world. On top of such legacies, Korea has recently been building the image of a country that is actively trying to contribute to global peace. However, "Korea in a regional context," in contrast, is relatively negatively portrayed. On a regional scale, Korea is surrounded by the superpowers of the world—the United States, China, Japan, and Russia—and finds herself to be one of the weakest countries. Especially in the post–Cold War era, North Korea has been continuously causing instability in the region, and for this reason the so-called "Korean Peninsula problem" has become a symbol of a pending Northeast Asian question. Therefore, in order to maximize South Korea's diplomatic interest, it is important that Seoul prepares a diplomatic grand strategy to connect our regional and global strategies in a way that that is mutually reinforcing.

Third, traditionally, China has been regarded as a continental power and Japan a maritime power. Over the course of history, whenever China and Japan clashed, Korea has always found herself in a difficult spot. This position, however, also yields opportunities for Korea today. Precisely because of her size and clout, Korea might be able to play a greater role in regional affairs. For example, in the case of Northeast Asian multilateralism, Japan has traditionally been deploying diplomacy toward Asia, focusing on its alliance with the United States, which makes it difficult for Japan to exercise its leadership in relation to regionalism. China is also in a difficult position as regards exercising its leadership due to its socialist political system, human rights problems, and environmental policies that do not meet global standards. Korea can overcome these limits of China and Japan and lead the regionalization efforts in East Asia. Korea will continue to enjoy the unlimited possibilities of China's export market, will work through the free trade area (FTA) arrangements with Japan, and will enjoy the benefits of the Korea–Japan–US coalition.

It is difficult to judge the kinds of consequences the competition between China and Japan will have for Korea. History tells us that intense military conflict between China and Japan has always brought about severe damage on the Peninsula. That is, only when diplomatic relations between China and Japan are established, and Northeast Asia's security is assured, will Korea's national interest and security be guaranteed. Most Northeast Asian issues that have a significant impact on the national interest of Korea are related to China or Japan. South Korea, thus, must have the diplomatic wisdom to categorize its national interests into various levels and tend to them with special care.

Sino–Japan Relations and Korea's Place: Key Subjects

As has been observed, Korea needs to form a concept of national interest based on a "Northeast Asian identity" and, in pursuing this national interest, must know how to strategically distinguish between pursuing it on the Northeast Asian regional level and on the global level. Following are pointers towards key subjects that Korea should be aware of regarding China–Japan relations, and in particular the Sino–Japanese rivalry.

The North Korea Problem

With the beginning of the post–Cold War era, the North Korea issue became the center of Northeast Asia's security concerns. The slightest escalation in the Sino–Japanese rivalry, let alone a physical clash, may negatively impact the North Korea issue. This is because North Korea, having chosen nuclear diplomacy as its strategy for regime survival, is now an international security concern. This has, in turn, drawn the intervention and engagement of neighboring countries, such as Japan and China, as well as the United States.[19] Therefore, whether achieved forcibly or amicably, negotiations between China and Japan and a mutual assistance structure are critical preconditions for solving the North Korea problem.

Interestingly, whenever North Korea has had an opportunity to discuss her nuclear plans, Pyongyang has always emphasized two facts. First, with regards to the question of proliferation, the DPRK has always stressed that no nuclear capability, nuclear material, or nuclear equipment will be allowed to proliferate from the Korean Peninsula. The second point is that the denuclearization of the Korean Peninsula is also the wish of the former leader Kim Il-sung. In other words, North Korea is, on its own, trying to limit the significance of its nuclear program on the Northeast Asian region. This is because North Korea is aware that the moment its nuclear ambition is internationalized, it will be prone to severe criticisms from the international community and the United States. The continued survival of the ruling regime—this being the real goal of North Korea behind Pyongyang's nuclear strategy—will be impossible to achieve. In short, the North Korea issue represents a typical Northeast Asian security concern in character and deeply involves the national interests of China and Japan.

The South Korea–US Alliance

Historically, whenever there has been a major political change in China or Japan, Korea's destiny has always hung in the balance. Moreover, when there was a major clash between China and Japan, in most instances it took place on the Korean Peninsula.[20] This historical truth did not change in the pre-modern era, nor even after the modern development of Northeast Asia. Needless to say, history may not repeat

[19] J. Wit, "Enhancing US Engagement with North Korea," *The Washington Quarterly* 30, no. 2 (2007): 53–69.
[20] G. Hensley, "Asia–Pacific Security: Paradox and Riddle," *New Zealand International Review* 23, no. 1 (1998): 33–37.

itself, and even if the reality of post-modern international relations of the twenty-first century is too different from the international relations of previous eras for China and Japan to resort to military conflict, the possibility still exists.

Under such circumstances, it is easy to understand why Korea has the United States, a global hegemonic state outside the Northeast Asian region, as her alliance partner. The Korea–US alliance has a history of slightly more than fifty years. Compared to the unique diplomatic alliance Korea had with China for thousands of years, the history of the US–Korea alliance is incomparably short; however, the fact that Korea's alliance partner is not a Northeast Asian country is a positive point. Korea might have independently became a strong state after establishing its government in 1948 without forming any alliances, or might have formed an alliance with China or Japan: but neither of these scenarios would have been as beneficial as the current US–Korea alliance, nor would the alliance have been viewed as one of among equal powers. More than anything, the US–Korea alliance is a valuable diplomatic asset because it allows Korea to pursue its national interests separately at both the regional (Northeast Asian) level and also the global level.[21]

"Middle Power" Strategy

Looking retrospectively at Korea's national development since the establishment of the official government in 1948, the significance of diplomatic relations has been crucial. As was briefly mentioned above, Korea is a weak nation in the Northeast Asian region. However, weak as she is, Korea is categorized as a "middle power" state that can assume the initiative in international matters that are too sensitive or impossible for stronger states to engage in.[22] If Korea falls from its relative weakness in relation to China and Japan and neglects developing its diplomatic power, then Korea will become trapped in the power struggle between China and Japan, and will be unable to pursue or preserve her national interests. Korea needs to develop, for instance, its Korean ODA diplomacy or public diplomacy and secure a seat as a diplomatically strong state in international society.

---

[21] S. H. Lee and J. C. Baek, *Korea–US Relations in Transition: Korea–US Alliance in Retrospect and Prospects for a New Strategic Partnership* (Seongnam, Korea: Sejong Institute, 2002).

[22] E. C. Jordaan, "The Concept of a Middle Power in International Relations: Distinguishing between Emerging and Traditional Middle Power," *Politikon: South African Journal of Political Studies* 30, no. 2 (2003): 165–181.

Moreover, Korea has achieved a more dynamic and participatory democracy than China or Japan. Owing to such a democracy, Korea has experienced amazingly rapid economic development, and has developed a highly professional civil society. Korea's diverse and advanced civil society can serve as a driving force for expanding and developing democracy in Northeast Asia and East Asia as well. Furthermore, compared to other regions, Northeast Asia's collective sense of regional identity is underdeveloped. For many reasons, China and Japan are not in a position to initiate the development of Northeast Asia's collective identity. Korea, however, might be relatively better situated to develop the collective identity of the Northeast Asian region.

Conclusion

China and Japan will continue to build up their militaries to maximize their interests. The regional power struggle will take place through a combination of policies based on the traditional balance-of-power concept, combined with Japan's policy based on buck-passing to the US–Japan alliance. In relation to the Korean Peninsula, it is highly probable that the United States, China, and Japan will adhere to policies of maintaining the status quo of the North–South division. If the North Korean nuclear problem is not resolved smoothly, that probability will increase.[23]

It is not an easy task for Korea to remain a meaningful actor in Northeast Asia. The Korean Peninsula is a place of strategic importance, where territorial and maritime powers meet, and Western and non-Western civilizations co-exist. Thus, there should be consistent emphasis that, without the peace and prosperity of the Korean Peninsula, Northeast Asian regional security cannot be guaranteed. After the end of World War II, it was understood that Northeast Asian international relations were characterized by a complex security structure that depended on competing elements: the role of the United States as a balancer, the possibility of hegemonic war along the China–US axis, the US–Japan alliance overcoming cultural differences, and finding resolutions to the Korean Peninsula and the Taiwan Strait problems. The course of history has a definite meaning. The changes in the power balance among the surrounding states require continuous attention from Seoul in order to maintain Korea's national interests.

---

[23] Presidential Committee on Northeast Asian Cooperation Initiative, "Analysis on Neighbouring Four Countries' Mid-term Security Strategy," April 1, 2005.

CHAPTER SEVEN

NORTHEAST ASIAN DEVELOPMENT AND THE KOREAN PENINSULA ISSUE

JIANG LIFENG

Introduction

The Northeast Asian region is one of the current international hotspots. Having received much worldwide attention in the past owing to the Taiwan and Korean Peninsula issues, the region is increasingly in the global limelight due to the important roles played by China and Japan in the recent international financial crisis. The developments in Northeast Asia, as well as the region's ability to overcome unfavorable factors working against its stability, are becoming most crucial not only to the core interests of various countries in the region, but also to those of surrounding countries outside the region, as well as the development of countries whose interests are related to the region. Addressing all these issues requires a detailed analysis of four main factors that influence the developments in Northeast Asia.

Four Factors Influencing Northeast Asia's Development

The role of the United States is, perhaps, the most important among the four factors that influence the stability of the Korean Peninsula. Geographically speaking, the United States is not a part of Northeast Asia. However, given its status as the sole global superpower with its interests spreading to various parts of the world, as well as the interventionist policies that it has been pursuing internationally for a long period of time, the United States remains a force to be reckoned with in Northeast Asia. Ever since the Pacific War, Northeast Asia has remained a major area of US intervention. In view of such a reality, it is unrealistic to expect an American withdrawal from the region and self-management of regional affairs by the various Northeast Asian countries within the next ten years. The current situation indicates that the United States may be able to maintain its status as the sole superpower, although its technological and military strength may be reduced in relative terms vis-à-vis China. While its interventionist policies in Northeast Asia will remain consistent in the years to come, there might be smaller adjustments within such consistency. Nonetheless, a small adjustment may possess the potential for a major change. In the face of continual US presence, the chief concern of countries in the region is how to maintain regional stability under US intervention.

How will US policies towards Northeast Asia change? In mathematical terms, this is a question that requires incessant model-building and painstaking calculations and analysis in order to arrive at a satisfactory answer. Amongst all the factors that should be taken in account, the most crucial factor is how China and Japan might change and develop. In response to changes in China and Japan, would it be best for the United States to make China its strategic partner and forgo its strategic ties with Japan? This might possibly become a dilemma for the United States over the next ten years. However, the United States will certainly consider its options wisely and make suitable choices at suitable times.

China makes up the second important factor. Under the present circumstances, China is developing at a rapid pace. Its foreign exchange reserves are growing significantly. It has been playing a highly visible and critical role in the world's economic recovery after the recent international financial crisis. The livelihood of its people has substantially improved and the level of development of its coastal areas is more or less equivalent to that of mid-level developed nations. Yet, at the same time, we need to be aware that the quality of China's economic development (i.e., the technological dimension) is still at an inadequate level and its progress has been taking place at the huge expense of her environment (both natural and social). Moreover, prevalent social injustices, the ever-growing gap between the rich and the poor (with its Gini index going beyond the critical level of 0.4 in 2000 and reaching 0.496 in 2006), continual population pressures, and the country's increasing energy and natural resource shortages remain major concerns. If these concerns are not addressed in a timely fashion, China's future prospects could be a cause for great anxiety.

In response to the difficulties it faces, the Chinese government has come out with the twin agenda of "scientific development" and "harmonious society." Lying at the core of the agenda are four specific targets: economic growth should be substantial and not superficial, the quality of the country's development should be good rather than bad, the country's military strength should be strong and not weak, and society should be stable and not descend into chaos. In all these matters, China should consistently follow the path that she deems right and suitable for herself. The aspiration of surpassing Japan, and even the United States some day, may serve as a kind of motivation, but it is still crucial for China to maintain a clear and sober mind about her future prospects. Provided that the aforementioned twin agenda could be realized over the next ten years, and that the Taiwan issue could be resolved peacefully, China's international influence would reach a new height, making it not impossible for China to attain the status of the next superpower after the United States. In order to preserve her growth and opportunities for further development, China will continue to pursue persistently and in a concrete manner her peaceful diplomacy agenda of "harmonious surrounding, harmonious world" in coordination with her domestic policies. This is particularly important for the stability and development of Northeast Asia and also for the Korean Peninsula.

Japan constitutes the third factor. The Japanese economy has remained stagnant with low growth rates over the past two decades. Nationalistic conservatism continues to occupy the mainstream in Japanese politics. The Japanese populace's isolationist mindset and expansionist tendencies remain strong and these are manifested in their attitudes towards their history-related issues and the US–Japanese military alliance. At the moment, it is difficult to alter all these characteristics. Over the next decade, even though Japan may be able to maintain its position as a world power (through technologies and finance), the aforementioned factors will contribute to Japan's inadvertent relative marginalization in international affairs. Moreover, the marginalization would be self-inflicted rather than the doing of others. This seems to be Japan's destiny.

Concerning how Japan has been adjusting and fine-tuning its national strategy, the domestic debates on the issue have basically come to form a mainstream consensus. A series of important changes in the legal institutions safeguarding the country's security serves as the manifestation of its national strategy. The double agenda of "Great Welfare Nation" and "Normal State" constitutes the key discourses narrating the national strategy, and the country is now effectively pursuing the goal of becoming a great power in comprehensive terms. All these comprise the strategic consensus reached by the various political factions in Japan. In pursuing such a strategic path, Japan is seeking to rid herself internally of the severe constraints imposed by the post-war institutions and realize the "normalization" of her functions as a state, and externally to play a much greater international role and acquire a permanent seat in the United Nations Security Council. The twin goals of becoming a "Major Economic Power" (in terms of finance and technology) as well as a "Major Political Power" (including the goal of becoming a quasi-military power) correlate to form the substance of Japan's overall national strategy. The essential characteristics of this strategy are as follows. As an economic power, Japan will continue to pursue its policies of nation-building through economic growth and technological advancement, and maintaining its international competitiveness through its superior strengths in technological and financial institutions. Meanwhile, it is not quite possible for Japan to become a military power in the fullest sense of the term. Japan is unlikely to move towards such a goal in a comprehensive manner as a major strand in its overall national strategy. Instead, it is very likely for Japan to seek a breakthrough in its attempts to break free from the various factors constraining its military growth, while continuing at the same time to rely on the paramount military power of the United States, in order to become a "quasi-military power" that possesses premium military strength as well as capabilities in exercising its influence in international security affairs. In other words, Japan will continue to use economic and political strategies as its primary means, and military strategy as a supplementary means, and depend on the US–Japanese military alliance to pursue its ultimate overall strategic goal of becoming a major power in comprehensive terms.

The Korean Peninsula forms the fourth factor. On April 5, 2009, North Korea officially announced the "successful" launch of a rocket and firing of a "satellite" into orbit. However, the United States and Japan insisted that the launch had been a failure, claiming that a "ballistic missile" had been launched instead. Japan expressed a resolve to shoot down and destroy the "missile," while North Korea threatened that any such move would render that country vulnerable to a North Korean attack. Eventually, Japan made no attempt to shoot down the "missile" and the episode turned out to be a melodrama staged by the Liberal Democratic Party government to enflame the emotion of the populace and bolster support for the regime. Given its pathetic record in Iraq, the US measures towards North Korea failed to inspire confidence. The United States and Japan exerted pressure on North Korea through the United Nations. In retaliation, North Korea declared its "withdrawal from the Six-Party Talks and rejection of the constraints imposed by the talks," and attempted to use all available means to boost its nuclear capabilities and revive the nuclear facilities that had previously been disabled. Such moves by North Korea could possibly render all the accomplishments attained in the earlier phases of the Six Party Talks null and void. Meanwhile, tensions have been flaring up between North and South Korea. In January 2009, North Korea declared a state of "total confrontation" against South Korea, terminated all treaties that had been signed between the two sides to end political and military conflicts, and threatened to "deal a blow to South Korea with relentless, unrestrained, and determined actions that are unpredictable by even the most advanced means" and even "fight a nuclear war." North Korea appears determined to follow the examples of India and Pakistan and become a nuclear weapons state. The international community has, so far, been unable to come out with a concerted effort to deal with North Korea due to the differing interests and concerns of the relevant countries. Compared to the other three factors influencing the stability and development of Northeast Asia, the Korean Peninsula is perhaps the most unstable and unpredictable factor, one that deserves our greatest concern.

Over the past decade, there have been scholars who predicted "the coming collapse of North Korea." It seems now that the North Korean regime is quite stable and this fact renders these predictions invalid. However, if the situation in the Korean Peninsula deteriorates further, it remains to be seen what steps the United States would take. Nevertheless, based on the *modus operandi* in international relations, the Korean Peninsula issue should be resolved by the governments and people of North and South Korea. Providing North Korea with a future (and the hope of a future) is perhaps the best long-term solution, rather than the exertion of pressure and containment. The people in North Korea also have the right to the peaceful use of nuclear energy (under effective international supervision).

Resolving the Korean Peninsula Issue: Important Meanings for the Development of Multi-Lateral Relations in Northeast Asia

In general, Sino–US relations will continue on a path of stable development. Whether it has been the Clinton, Bush, or Obama administrations, the Democrats or the Republicans, the general approach of the United States towards the China issue basically follows the principles laid down in the three joint communiqués signed between the two countries. The bombing of the Chinese embassy in Belgrade in 1999, and the collision between US and Chinese military planes over the South China Sea in 2001, had been significant incidents of clash between the two countries, yet these incidents were still unable to affect or alter the overall direction of US–China relations. The United States and China have been consistently pursuing the path of avoiding confrontation and seeking development. This path has been determined according to the mutual core interests and needs of both sides and is, in turn, beneficial to the stability and development of Northeast Asia. The recent international financial crisis also shows how closely related the interests of the United States and China have become. It is, thus, fair to say that China's economic development has been "held hostage" by the United States to a certain extent. China can do very little about this situation, as she does not really possess many options at her disposal.

In 2010, the terms "G2" model and "Chinamerica" were first coined and used in the United States by scholars such as Fred Bergsten, Zbigniew Brzezinski, Niall Ferguson, Robert Zoellick, and Handel Jones. The G2 concept suggests that the United States and China should jointly manage the Pacific Ocean, with the United States assuming responsibility for the Eastern Pacific, and China for the Western Pacific. Notwithstanding how influential and marketable such an idea is in the United States, the thesis itself contains only some symbolic meanings with little practical substance. However, the emergence of the idea at least shows that the degree of US interest in China has undergone a significant change. The Chinese have no need to be sensitive about this and there is also no need to devote too much time and energy on analyzing the intentions behind the idea. What is certain is that China will never form a "G2" with the United States and jointly manage the Pacific Ocean. At most, the United States and China will continue to hold multi-channel and multi-level dialogues over international issues of mutual interest, and work together to realize the consensus reached by both sides. China has no intention of becoming a dominant power and does not possess the capabilities to be one. If it were to pursue such a goal, it would probably end up making too much of a compromise over its own interests. As such, the Chinese do not hope to establish the "G2" framework. Nevertheless, China eventually needs to expand her influence beyond the island chain in the Western Pacific and develop her own interest in the entire Pacific realm. The United States will probably show some understanding towards this.

As for future Sino–Japanese relations, they will be characterized, no doubt, by much complexity. In the next decade, as part of the country's national strategy of becoming a major power in comprehensive terms, Japan's policies towards China will display, most likely, two characteristics, provided that she gradually and rationally accepts the reality of China's rise. First, Japan will seek to benefit from China's economic development and thereby strengthen its power base for becoming a major power. Second, even though Japan will adopt preventive measures against China, she will also try to avert a political standoff in bilateral relations in order to avoid the scenario of China becoming a major negative factor in realizing its "major power" strategy. Junichiro Koizumi's failure in Sino–Japanese relations has been seen as the factor that has hampered Japan's progress towards the goal of becoming a major power. Adopting a more pliant, "reflective" attitude towards the history-related issues (pertaining to the Second World War) between China and Japan, subsequent Japanese governments from the first Abe administration onwards have all been taking a consistent approach towards Sino–Japanese relations. This indicates that Japan will try to emphasize the positives and minimize the negatives in her relationship with China. This was true, at least up until the second coming of Abe as Prime Minister in 2012. Over the next decade, Japan's foreign policy towards China will be determined by how she calibrates her relative position amid the balance between China and the United States.

However, difficulties still abound between both sides in resolving the East China Sea issue (including the demarcation of each side's exclusive economic zone, the delimitation of the East China Sea continental shelf, and respective exploitation of natural resources in the area by China and Japan, as well as the dispute over the Diaoyu Islands) and the history-related issues. The former is an especially difficult issue as it involves each side's current economic conditions, strategic interests, and domestic political situation. As such, we are not able to rule out the likely occurrences of stagnancy or backsliding within the overall progress of Sino–Japanese relations, as well as periods of tensions and confrontations.

Concerning US–Japanese relations, we can expect with certainty that the US–Japanese alliance will be maintained. Over the next decade, strengthening the alliance will be the top priority within Japan's agenda of fine-tuning its foreign-policy strategy. Japan has always perceived her ability to sustain the US–Japan security arrangements as the key to the success or failure of her foreign policy. Both the ruling and opposition parties in Japan are in fundamental agreement that a stronger US–Japanese alliance will form the axis of Japan's international relations in the years to come. As the fundamentals of Japan's foreign-policy strategy, Japan's hopes of overcoming the constraints of a "defeated nation" and becoming a "normal state" still rely very much on the US–Japanese alliance. With this as the basis, Japan seeks to use the alliance as the basic means and strategic pivot of her goal of attaining "major power" status. For example, Japan has been devoting a great deal of effort to strengthening US–Japanese military cooperation and strategic coordination, speeding up joint development and deployment of the anti-ballistic missile defense system, and discussing the issue of rearrangement of US troops stationed in Japan.

Both sides are working closely together to bolster progress towards military integration. Japan has also pushed for the exercising of its right of collective defense by its Self-Defense Force, as well as the passing of the Overseas Permanent Deployment Act, with the partial objective of better serving and collaborating with the missions of US troops. Japan is now seeking to move the alliance in the direction of a more "equal" partnership. Through strengthening the alliance, Japan is also seeking to play a more visible security role in the international arena and fulfill its "major power" strategy. With a stronger alliance as the foundation, Japan is striving to play a leading role in initiating multilateral security dialogue, as well as the role of a vanguard in carrying out the so-called "values diplomacy" in order to bolster her voice and prominence within the international community, particularly in East Asia. At the same time, Japan is trying to lessen the degree of her dependence on the United States and is seeking a breakthrough in gaining a permanent seat in the United Nations Security Council.

Despite the continuity of the US–Japanese alliance, the substance of the alliance and its meaning for China are all undergoing significant changes. China's opposition to the alliance has been due to Japan's persistence in using the alliance as a means to bolster its bargaining power in conducting its foreign policy towards China, as well as in dealing with bilateral issues between Japan and China. However, the triangular relationship between the United States, China, and Japan is now developing in a direction that Japan is reluctant to accept: what has been a scalene triangle with the United States and Japan sharing the two longer sides is now gradually developing into a new equilateral triangle. With the resolution of the Taiwan and Korean Peninsula issues, the US–Japanese military alliance will be replaced by a new framework of relationship between the two sides.

Implications for the Korean Peninsula

Relations between North and South Korea are now mired in uncertainties. No country is currently able to accurately gauge the domestic situation and future direction of North Korea. This is testimony to the effectiveness of Kim Jong-il's ruling methods. Although both North and South Korea are coming to a standoff, an outbreak of war between the two sides is very unlikely. As long as other opportunities exist for North Korea, it will not take the risk of an all-out confrontation. It seems that the possibility of one side taking over the other is not high, and the resolution of the Korean Peninsula issue requires great patience. The Six-Party Talks play an undeniable role and this remains the most viable way of resolving the Korean Peninsula issue.

The relations between North Korea/South Korea and China/Japan will become increasingly complex and unpredictable. How these relations will develop is very much related to the question of how relations will develop between the United States and North Korea. Among these relations, North Korea and China seem to enjoy a "close rapport," yet such a "rapport" exists only in form and is devoid of much substance, with both sides seemingly in harmony yet actually at variance from one another. History and the vicissitudes of current reality make up the reasons that explain such a state of relations. As such, it is highly unlikely that any change will occur between North Korea and China, and the status quo will basically remain in place. Relations between South Korea and China have been quite close, yet with the growth of stronger nationalistic sentiments in both countries, relations have turned lukewarm. In recent years, South Korea has been afflicted by incessant domestic political tensions and a relative weakening of its economic strength. In addition, during the international financial crisis, South Korea haphazardly withdrew its capital and investments from China. All these not only affected the economic relations between the two sides, but overall relations also became stagnant. In sum, China–North Korean relations and China–South Korean relations are unlikely to see significant development in the next decade.

Relations between North Korea and Japan are fraught with tensions and differences that remain difficult to overcome. To make matters worse, North Korea has become a useful target for Japan to divert attention away from its domestic political tensions through presenting herself as a victim of North Korea. There is actually no real reason for Japan not to normalize relations with North Korea. However, Japan is relentlessly holding onto the issue of Japanese abductees in North Korea, and persistently using it as a necessary pre-condition for normalizing bilateral relations. Hence, an improvement in North Korea–Japan relations is something that cannot be expected at least in the near future. As for the relations between South Korea and Japan, despite their belonging to the same alliance system with the United States, both sides are continually at loggerheads over the history issue, as well as territorial disputes. Japan and South Korea are, thus, unable to move forwards in their bilateral relations and this has had a negative impact on the stability of the Korean Peninsula. If North Korea–Japan and South Korea–Japan relations were to develop further, Japan's willingness to change its rigid policies will prove to be crucial.

CHAPTER EIGHT

SAME BED, DIFFERENT DREAMS: WHY CAN'T THE SIX-PARTY TALKS HELP IMPROVE JAPAN–CHINA RELATIONS?

ZHU ZHIQUN

Introduction: The Role of Third Parties in International Conflict

There is a sizable body of literature on the role of third parties in international conflict resolution.[1] Major third parties include qualified nation-states, individuals, groups, and organizations. A trusted third party can talk directly to the disputants as a mediator, hoping to narrow their differences towards ending the conflict. A third party can also offer good offices through which the two quarrelling parties can themselves engage in a meaningful discussion. A third party can occasionally serve as an arbiter, if both disputants agree. States, often represented by incumbent or former government officials and respected individuals, remain the most common third-party mediators in international conflict resolution in today's world politics, which is still dominated by state-to-state relations.

What is lacking in the current literature is discussion of other potential, but less common, forms of third-party facilitators. For example, could an issue in which both conflicting parties have vested interests serve as a facilitator? Could a forum or a platform through which the two parties

---

[1] For more recent works on the topic, see, for example, M. J. Butler, *International Conflict Management: An Introduction* (London and New York: Routledge, 2009); I. W. Zartman, *Negotiation and Conflict Management: Essays on Theory and Practice* (London and New York: Routledge, 2008). For the role of third parties and conflict resolution in East Asia, see J. Bercovitc, K. B. Huang, and C. C. Teng, *Conflict Management, Security, and Intervention in East Asia: Third-Party Mediation in Regional Conflict* (London and New York: Routledge, 2008).

regularly interact with each other also serve as a mediator? This chapter will use the Six-Party Talks as a case study to explore whether, and how, such new forms of third parties can facilitate international conflict resolution.

Ties between China and Japan have always been troubled because of their different interpretations of history, and their territorial disputes and geopolitical rivalry. The two countries do not seem to be able to overcome these difficulties by themselves. One wonders whether a third party might help improve their relations. Major state-level third parties in East Asia that could potentially mediate in China–Japan relations include the United States, the two Koreas, and Taiwan (although, of course, from the People's Republic of China's (PRC) perspective, Taiwan is not a state-level actor). Strictly speaking, none of these parties have played the role of a mediator nor actively pushed for the improvement of China–Japan relations. Oftentimes, these third parties actually perpetuate China–Japan disputes by either taking sides or pursuing their own problems with one or both main actors. Their assistance in promoting China–Japan relations, if any, is mostly indirect. But in addition to these state-level mediators, are there any other forms of third-party mediation between China and Japan?

Potential Mediators between China and Japan

The United States

The biggest question is whether the United States can serve as an impartial mediator due to its military and political alliances with Japan. The United States has taken note of the power shift in Asia today. As a *Financial Times* commentary put it, Japan remains America's closest friend in Asia, but Washington's most important relationship is now with China, especially during the current global economic crisis.[2] Because of America's strong interests in both Japan and China, it could and should help bring the two Asian powers together. However, America's tacit support for Japan in the Japan–China dispute only emboldens the Japanese government to become dismissive of China's legitimate concerns and serves as a reminder that the United States has not been a third party interested in facilitating conflict resolution between China and Japan.

In the Diaoyu/Senkaku Islands dispute, for example, instead of appearing at least neutral, US officials have confirmed that Senkaku was,

---

[2] P. Stephens, "A Diplomatic Feint that Looks to Leave Japan in the Cold," *Financial Times*, February 27, 2009, 11.

indeed, returned to Japan in 1972, together with Okinawa. Japanese Prime Minister Taro Aso said in the Diet in February 2009 that these uninhabited islands were Japanese territory and, thus, covered by the Japan–US security alliance. Since Japan has exercised control over the Senkaku Islands, the US–Japan Security Pact will actually cover the disputed islands if conflict breaks out. A US State Department official reportedly confirmed that the alliance was indeed applicable to the Senkaku Islands. The Chinese government was taken aback by such a comment. After lodging stern representations to Japan, the Chinese foreign ministry immediately asked the US government to clarify the report on the issue.[3]

In a telephone interview with the English-language *Taipei Times*, the American Institute in Taiwan press officer Lawrence Walker said: "The US position on the issue is longstanding and has not changed." Moreover, he added: "The United States does not take a position on the ultimate sovereignty of these islands. We expect the claimants to resolve the issue through peaceful means among themselves." However, apparently contradicting himself, Walker noted that the islands have been under Japanese administrative control since the reversion of Okinawa in 1972. Therefore, Article 5 of the 1960 Treaty of Mutual Cooperation and Security between Japan and the United States, which states that the US–Japanese alliance applies to the territories under the administration of Japan, "does apply" to the islands.[4] By tacitly supporting Japan in the Diaoyu/Senkaku dispute, the United States does not help ease the tensions between China and Japan.

Former President George W. Bush's intimate relationship with former Prime Minister Junichiro Koizumi was another disappointment for those who wished the United States could help mediate between Japan and China. While enjoying much popularity inside Japan, Koizumi had repeatedly irked Japan's Asian neighbors by paying annual visits to the controversial Yasukuni Shrine, despite his disclaimers that he did not go in his official capacity. The shrine honors Japan's war dead, including fourteen Class-A war criminals from World War II. As a victim of Japan's militarism during World War II, the United States should have spoken out against Koizumi's indiscriminate and recalcitrant moves. Yet President Bush treated Koizumi as a close buddy and never pressed him on this key issue in East Asia.[5] During Koizumi's final official visit to the United

[3] "Japan Foreign Minister Flies Into Chinese Storm," *Reuters*, February 28, 2009.

[4] J. W. Hsu, "MOFA Reiterates Claim over Diaoyutai Isles," *Taipei Times*, February 28, 2009, 3.

[5] Only very few high-ranking US politicians openly criticized Japanese leaders' visits to Yasukuni. Two members of the US Congress, Representative Tom Lantos

States as Prime Minster in 2006, President Bush even took time to personally accompany Koizumi to Memphis to visit the memorial museum of Elvis Presley, of whom Koizumi is a fervent fan. In the eyes of many observers, President Bush was supporting a "public enemy" in East Asia at the expense of damaging relations between Japan and its neighbors.

South Korea

In a series of speeches in 2005, former President Roh Moo-hyun of South Korea unveiled a new foreign policy doctrine by declaring that South Korea must play the role of balancer, so that tensions do not escalate in Northeast Asia. President Roh stated that South Korea could serve as an honest broker between China and Japan, and between the United States and China. South Korea and Japan share democratic values. Moreover, China is currently South Korea's most important trading partner. Theoretically, South Korea can play an active role in promoting relations between China and Japan. Unfortunately, South Korea and Japan have their own disputes, especially regarding the Dokdo (Takeshima) Islands and the "comfort women" issue. In the end, President Roh was criticized by his domestic opponents for his unrealistic policy. His successor, Lee Myung-bak, has quietly dropped this ambitious foreign policy agenda.

South Korea and Japan are both US allies. Like Japan, South Korea is also concerned about China's rising military budget. For example, President Lee Myung-bak was the first major leader to raise concerns after China unveiled its 2009 military budget in March 2009: "The Northeast Asia region in particular is a very, very dynamic and volatile region, with North and South Korea [issues] still remaining, and also we have the issue of China building military spending," said President Lee, who also warned of the danger of a Northeast Asian arms race.[6] Given its own problems with Japan, its historical disputes with China, and its suspicion of China, South Korea is unlikely to play a facilitating role between Japan and China.

---

and House International Relations Committee Chairman Henry Hyde, are critics of Koizumi. In a congressional hearing in September 2006, Lantos slammed the Yasukuni visits as "the most egregious example of Japan's historical amnesia." See "US Congress Likely to Boost Pressure on Japan Over Trade, Yasukuni, 2006," *Kyoto News International*, November 13, 2006.

[6] R. Taylor, "China Arms Spend Prompts South Korea Arms Race Warning," *Reuters*, March 5, 2009.

Taiwan

Taiwan is another claimant to the disputed Diaoyu/Senkaku Islands. Though Japan publicly welcomes the easing of tensions across the Taiwan Strait since Ma Ying-jeou came to power in Taipei in May 2008, many believe that Japan does not really wish to see the two Chinese parties become too close. The Ma government has to openly assure Japan that while improving relations with Mainland China, it will not compromise its long-standing ties with Japan. Interestingly, even the United States has not openly squeezed such a statement about PRC–Taiwan–US relations from Taipei.

Having been colonized by Japan for fifty years until 1945, Taiwan has mixed feelings towards Japan. Japan's colonial rule in Taiwan was relatively moderate, and as a result many in Taiwan still hold somewhat favorable feelings toward Japan. On the other hand, Taiwan also has problems with Japan including territorial and historical disputes. Because of its delicate relations with Japan and its longstanding conflict with the PRC, Taiwan, also, is not a good candidate to help improve China–Japan relations.

On May 1, 2009, Masaki Saito, head of the Taipei office of Japan's Interchange Association—Japan's *de facto* embassy in Taiwan—stirred up a controversy in Taiwan. He said, at a meeting at National Chung Cheng University in Chiayi County, that Taiwan's status was still unclear. Taiwan's foreign ministry immediately summoned Saito and objected to his remarks. However, several Democratic Progressive Party legislators and the Friends of Lee Teng-hui, a support group associated with Taiwan's former pro-independence president, defended Saito's remarks, saying that it only reflected the truth. Saito's controversial statement also led to official representations from the PRC government. Tokyo had to clarify that Saito's comments did not reflect the position of the Japanese government, and Saito retracted his remarks later. According to the 1972 Sino–Japanese Joint Statement, the Japanese government fully understands and respects the Chinese government's position on Taiwan as being an inalienable part of the territory of China. After China's protest, the Japanese side had reaffirmed that its position on Taiwan's status remained unchanged and would not change in the future.

The role of these major third parties in promoting Japan–China relations is very limited due to their complex relations with China and/or their own problems with Japan. In fact, none of these third parties has actively helped push for the improvement of Japan–China relations.

How about North Korea? It is hard to imagine that North Korea can be a qualified third party to mediate between China and Japan, since North Korea and Japan have not yet normalized diplomatic relations, and North Korea is perceived to be China's ally, which automatically makes it a biased outsider. In addition, like South Korea, North Korea also has historical and territorial disputes with Japan.

How about North Korea's nuclear issue? This would be a case of less common third-party facilitators, such as issues, forums, and platforms, playing a role in international conflict resolution. What makes the North Korean nuclear issue a potential facilitator in improving Japan–China relations is that the nuclear program is strongly opposed by both Japan and China, thus potentially bringing Japan and China closer together. Handled properly, the North Korean nuclear issue could provide a unique opportunity for China and Japan to improve their relations by focusing on their common interests.

The North Korean Nuclear Issue as a Potential Facilitator

The Korean Peninsula is in a strategic location within Northeast Asia, where the interests of several major powers—the United States, China, Japan, and Russia—are interwoven. The unresolved issue of North Korea's nuclear program, animosity between North Korea and the United States and Japan, and great power competition in the region, have made the Korean Peninsula one of the most unstable and potentially most dangerous flashpoints in the world. Since the Korean War, security on the Korean Peninsula has always been of great concern to countries in the region, as well as to the United States. North Korea's nuclear development program has become the single most challenging issue on the Peninsula since the 1990s. Both Japan and China have a huge stake in ensuring peace and stability on the Korean Peninsula and both have been active participants in the Six-Party Talks aimed at ending North Korea's nuclear program, since August 2003. The Six-Party Talks should have been a chance for China and Japan to enhance cooperation and strengthen relations. It is interesting to explore why the two Asian powers have failed to seize this great opportunity.

Historical Background

The Korean Peninsula has been an object of competition for control and influence between China and Japan at many points in history. The 1876 Treaty of Ganghwa, also known in Japan as the Korea–Japan Treaty of Amity, marked the beginning of the modern-era competition between China and Japan. By coaxing Korea into this treaty, Japan challenged China's dominance on the Peninsula. Competition for influence over the Korean Peninsula led to military conflict between Japan and China in the mid-1890s and the eventual annexation of Korea by Japan at the end of the 1894/95 Sino–Japanese War. Japan's occupation of much of China in the 1930s and 1940s further humiliated China. Although having been a defeated power at the end of World War II, Japan quickly recovered, like a phoenix coming back to life, in the 1950s and 1960s, eventually becoming the second largest economy in the world.[7] Meanwhile, China lost three decades of economic development as a result of various political campaigns launched by Mao Zedong. Deng Xiaoping's reform policies initiated in 1978 fundamentally changed China. Three decades later, China's growing economic and diplomatic influence on the Peninsula has made Japan deeply uncomfortable and jealous.

Since the division of the Peninsula at the end of World War II, South Korea (Republic of Korea, ROK) has developed into a major economic and trading power, as well as a vibrant democracy. North Korea (Democratic People's Republic of Korea, DPRK), on the other hand, at the beginning of the twenty-first century remains isolated and tightly controlled under the Kim family regime. In 1991, the collapse of the Soviet Union and the decision of most of North Korea's allies to normalize relations with South Korea led to a great swing in the balance of power. The two Koreas entered the United Nations simultaneously as separate members on September 17, 1991. Russia and the ROK established diplomatic ties in 1990, followed by China's official recognition of the ROK in 1992. Until today, neither Japan nor the United States has started to seriously discuss establishing diplomatic relations with North Korea.

North Korea's nuclear weapons' program dates back to the 1980s, when it began to operate facilities for uranium fabrication and conversion. In 1985, US officials announced that they had intelligence data proving that a secret nuclear reactor was being built 90 km north of Pyongyang near Yongbyon. In 1985, under international pressure, Pyongyang acceded to the Treaty on the Non-Proliferation of Nuclear Weapons (NPT). However, it refused to sign a safeguards agreement with the International Atomic Energy Agency (IAEA). North Korea significantly improved its nuclear weapons capability in the 1990s. As the 1990s progressed, concern over the North's nuclear program became a major issue in Northeast Asian

---

[7] Japan held the position as the second largest economy in the world until 2010, when China's GDP surpassed Japan's.

security. The 1994 Agreed Framework between the United States and North Korea was not seriously implemented by either side. In August 1998, North Korea test-fired a *Taepodong-1* missile over Japanese airspace, much to Japan's alarm.

In the wake of the September 11, 2001 terrorist attacks on America and the ensuing American invasion of Iraq, North Korea felt more threatened and attempted to enhance its nuclear arsenal. President George W. Bush reversed President Bill Clinton's more moderate policy and adopted a harsher approach toward North Korea. President Bush labeled North Korea a member of the "axis of evil," linking the security issue on the Korean Peninsula to America's global war against terror. Soon afterwards, the United States military listed North Korea as a potential target of a preemptive nuclear strike.

The Six-Party Talks

To jump-start the peace process and resolve the North Korean nuclear issue, China has hosted several rounds of Six-Party Talks since August 2003. The other parties involved are the United States, Japan, South Korea, North Korea, and Russia. After a few rounds of unsuccessful meetings, the Talks stalled in September 2005. On July 5, 2006, North Korea launched seven missiles, including a *Taepodong-2* long-range ballistic missile which failed shortly after taking off, creating another security crisis in Northeast Asia. Before long, on October 9, 2006, North Korea claimed to have successfully conducted a nuclear test, sending shockwaves across the world and generating unanimous condemnations from abroad. The Six-Party Talks resumed in December 2006 and February 2007 in Beijing, and in between the United States and North Korea also met bilaterally in Berlin. After arduous talks, the Six Parties finally reached a landmark agreement in Beijing in February 2007 to dismantle North Korea's nuclear program, the process of which started in July 2007. According to the agreement, North Korea would dismantle its nuclear programs in exchange for aid and political concessions.

In June 2008, North Korea blew up the cooling tower of its Yongbyon nuclear reactor and handed over to the United States a long-awaited declaration of its nuclear activities. In July 2008, US Secretary of State Condoleezza Rice and North Korean Foreign Minister Pak Ui-chun met for the first time at the multilateral disarmament talks in Singapore. However, by August 2008 the United States had not removed North Korea from the State Sponsors of Terrorism List, as it had promised earlier, while insisting that it wanted independent verification of North Korea's nuclear disarmament. Accusing the United States of breaking its promise, North Korea then announced that it had suspended the disablement of its nuclear facilities. Reports about Kim Jong-il's poor health after August 2008 added complexity and uncertainty to the situation. President Bush ultimately removed North Korea from the list of terror-sponsoring countries in October 2008, but the difficult task of verifying North Korea's denuclearization was left for his successor, Barack Obama.

On January 23, 2009, the DPRK leader Kim Jong-il emerged for the first time since August 2008 from a stroke he had reportedly suffered. He told Wang Jiarui, head of the International Department of the Central Committee of the Communist Party of China, that the DPRK was committed to making the Korean Peninsula a nuclear-free zone and wished to live in peace with all the parties concerned. He added that the DPRK did not want the Peninsula to be beset with tension and was ready to cooperate with China in a joint effort to push forwards the Six-Party Talks. Wang said that China was ready to improve relations with the DPRK and work together "to overcome hindrances and ensure the Six-Party Talks would make continuous progress."[8] He did not mention what those "hindrances" were. One wonders whether Japan was one of them.

However, North Korea has continued to defy the international community with its nuclear and missile programs. On April 5, 2009, despite international warnings, North Korea went ahead with a missile launch and subsequently announced its withdrawal from the Six-Party Talks. At the end of May 2009, the DPRK conducted a new nuclear test. In early July 2009 it fired seven more short-range missiles. US–North Korean and Japanese–North Korean relations entered a new stage of stalemate. Displeased with North Korea's recklessness and disrespect of China's national interests, China joined other members at the United Nations in condemning and passing a new resolution against North Korea. Nevertheless, China still emphasized the importance of dialogue, under the framework of the Six-Party Talks, for ending the crisis.

Kim Jong-il died in December 2011 and his youngest son, Kim Jong-un, became the new leader of North Korea. In early 2012, the United States and North Korea reached an agreement, according to which North Korea will freeze its nuclear and missile tests, along with uranium enrichment programs, and allow the return of UN nuclear inspectors; in return, the United States will provide 240,000 metric tons of nutritional assistance to the impoverished country. However, tensions on the Korean Peninsula continue to run high.

---

[8] "Kim Jong-il Meets Chinese Official," *Xinhua*, January 23, 2009.

Same Bed, Different Dreams

Japan and China have important overlapping interests on the North Korean nuclear issue and they have been active participants of the Six-Party Talks. The North Korean issue has failed to bring Japan and China closer largely because of their divergent key objectives and strategies in the Six-Party Talks.

The hosting and resumption of the Six-Party Talks serves China's national interests. First of all, through its role as host and as a facilitator, Beijing has demonstrated itself as a "responsible stakeholder" and boosted its international image and regional influence. Secondly, for its own national security, China does not want North Korea to go nuclear. China already has more nuclear neighbors than any other power. North Korea's nuclearization is likely to propel Japan, South Korea, and Taiwan to seek nuclear weapons, further complicating the security environment for the PRC.

As far as China's objectives are concerned, China finds itself between a rock and a hard place. Many assume that China holds the key to North Korea's survival, but how much pressure should Beijing put on North Korea? If Beijing completely cut its supply line to Pyongyang, the North Korean regime may suddenly collapse. Beijing's primary concern is the stability of the North Korean regime and of Northeast Asia. A sudden collapse of North Korea would create an enormous economic, political, humanitarian, security, and diplomatic challenge for China. The prospect of millions of North Korean refugees crossing into China alone is already intimidating. What if many of the 1.1 million North Korean soldiers, equipped with the weapons and skills to kill, also cross into China? So, while encouraging the DPRK to dismantle its nuclear programs, China wants to ensure that the North Korean government will stay in power and maintain domestic stability. Obviously, Beijing does not want to see Pyongyang fall apart.

The Six-Party Talks' main objective is to ensure Northeast Asia's security through the denuclearization of North Korea, but Japan has complicated the process by linking it to the release of the Japanese citizens abducted by North Korean agents decades ago.[9] After Prime Minister

---

[9] About seventeen, and possibly more, Japanese citizens were kidnapped by North Korean agents in the late 1970s and early 1980s. Five surviving abductees and their immediate families are now back in Japan. Japan insists that at least twelve abductees and their families are still alive and being held against their will in North Korea, while North Korea insists that all the abductees have been accounted for and the case is closed.

Koizumi Junichiro's historic visit to Pyongyang in September 2002, Japan's relationship with North Korea became dominated by a single issue: the plight of Japanese citizens abducted by North Korea. Japan's insistence that the abductees have to be returned or accounted for puts the United States and other parties to the Six-Party Talks in a dilemma. While everybody agrees that it's an important issue for Japan and North Korea to be more responsive to the requests of the abductee families, very few outside Japan would argue that the denuclearization talks should be tied to this completely different issue.

In a telephone conversation with Japanese Foreign Minister Nakasone Hirofumi in January 2009, US Secretary of State Hillary Clinton said that she would "attach importance to the abduction issue, and share the thinking of the Japanese people." She added, "I would like the United States to cooperate with Japan in resolving this issue." Reflecting Tokyo's expectations, Nakasone told Clinton, "The abduction issue is highest on our agenda, and I would like to see its resolution carried out together with the nuclear issue."[10] The Washington DC–based journalist Ayako Doi argued that Mrs Clinton made a mistake by giving the Japanese unrealistic hopes. Doi suggested that Clinton could have told Nakasone that she understood the concerns of the families of the abductees in Japan, but that there were other more important issues to tackle with regards North Korea. She might also have added that the United States and its partners in the Six-Party Talks have no choice but to proceed, even if Japan refuses to participate in an eventual settlement. She should have suggested that the best way to get the kidnapped Japanese back is for Japan to unite with the United States and the other members of the talks to work out an acceptable deal with Pyongyang on its nuclear program, and bring North Korea into the community of nations.[11]

During Hillary Clinton's February 2009 visit to Japan, she met with the families of the abductees, promising, as the Bush administration had before her, that their loved ones would not be forgotten. But she was also very careful not to connect North Korean denuclearization too closely to progress on the abductee issue. Many Japanese feel that President Bush personally "betrayed" them on this issue when Washington removed Pyongyang from the State Sponsors of Terrorism list. Mrs. Clinton wisely avoided getting tied down on this issue. As one commentator put it, at the end of the day, no US administration will sacrifice the opportunity for real

[10] A. Doi, "What Hillary Should Tell Japan," PacNet, no. 8, Pacific Forum, CSIS, February 4, 2009.
[11] Doi, "What Hillary Should Tell Japan."

progress on denuclearization of the Korean Peninsula and the Japanese understand this.[12]

Japan's other major concern is its security under the North Korean nuclear and missile threat. Since North Korea's 1998 *Taepodong-1* missile test over Japan's airspace, Japan has considered North Korea an immediate threat. The fundamental policy of Japan is to ensure that North Korea will not possess nuclear weapons or long-range missiles. China, on the other hand, has suggested that every country is entitled to the right to use nuclear technology for economic purposes, even though she opposes North Korea's possession of nuclear weapons.

The difference between Japan and China at the Six-Party Talks also lies in their strategies. China tends to be more moderate and Japan seems to be the toughest amongst all the powers. In March 2009, North Korea announced its plan to conduct a satellite test. The United States, Japan, and South Korea believed that it would actually be a missile test. Before the North Korean launch, US Defense Secretary Robert M. Gates said that the United States had no plans for military action to preempt the launching of a long-range missile by North Korea and would act only if the missile or its parts appeared to be headed towards American territory. South Korean President Lee Myung-bak said in an interview that his government would also oppose any military response to North Korea's impending rocket launch.[13] Meanwhile, Chinese President Hu Jintao told visiting North Korean premier Kim Yong-il that a question confronting all parties was how to overcome what he termed "the current difficulties" and resume the Six-Party Talks at an early date: "We hope parties concerned will take the overall situation into consideration and properly resolve the differences in a bid to promote the further progress of the talks," Hu said in Beijing on March 19, 2009.[14] China also urged all parties concerned to remain calm and to avoid escalation of the conflict.

While the United States, China, and South Korea were working to diffuse the danger, Japan once again acted differently. North Korea said it would retaliate if its satellite launch was intercepted and the interference would "mean a war." "Shooting our satellite for peaceful purposes will precisely mean a war," a spokesman for the North Korean army said in a statement carried by the state-run Korean Central News Agency (KCNA)

---

[12] R. A. Cossa, "Continuity and Change: US Asia Policy," PacNet, no. 18, CSIS, Washington, DC, March 6, 2009.

[13] "No US Plans to Stop Korea on Missile Test," *New York Times*, March 30, 2009.

[14] "Chinese President Meets DPRK Premier, Urges Resumed Nuclear Talks," *Xinhua*, March 19, 2009.

on March 9, 2009.[15] As if to poke North Korea in the eye, a few days later Japan said it could shoot down the North Korean satellite: "Japan is legally able to shoot down the object to secure safety if it looks like it will fall on to Japan," Chief Cabinet Secretary Takeo Kawamura said during a news conference on March 13, 2009. Clearly, Japan and China prefer different approaches with regard to North Korea.

A UN Security Council resolution in 2006 banned North Korea from conducting ballistic-missile testing, but Japanese officials said they could shoot down the object whether it was a missile or a satellite. "As the UN resolutions prohibit [North Korea] from engaging in ballistic missile activities, we still consider it to be a violation of a technical aspect, even if [the North] claims it is a satellite. We will discuss the matter with related countries based on this view," said Foreign Minister Hirofumi Nakasone in March 2009. Prime Minister Taro Aso added: "No matter what they call it, a satellite or anything else, it will violate the UN Security Council Resolution. We must lodge a stern protest through the UN and strongly demand it be called off."[16] It seems that Japan did not want to leave any doors open. Facing the current economic crisis and the impending political reshuffle, all Japanese politicians wish to appear tough in foreign affairs.

In contrast, China tried hard to persuade North Korea not to go ahead with a planned rocket launch and urged calm among countries in the region, according to a Japanese official after Prime Minister Aso's meeting with the Chinese President in London at the Group of 20 summit in April 2009.[17] President Lee Myung-bak also met with Hu Jintao at the same summit. They expressed concerns about North Korea's impending rocket launch, saying it would have a negative impact on peace and stability in Northeast Asia. Lee and Hu agreed that the Six-Party Talks should not be affected by the missile crisis. "Even if North Korea fires a rocket, the Six-Party Talks should be maintained," Lee was quoted as telling Hu, by his spokesman Lee Dong-kwan.[18] Hu expressed assent, adding that China will continue to try to dissuade Pyongyang from launching the rocket.

China's strategy seems to be "carrots and sticks" while Japan's is all "sticks." For Japan to follow through on its high-profile announcement to consider shooting down the North Korean missile would be counterproductive. A *Financial Times* editorial suggested that if Japan

---

[15] "N. Korea Warns against Intercepting 'Satellite' Launch," *CNN*, March 9, 2009.

[16] "Japan Threat to Shoot Down N. Korean Satellite," *CNN*, March 13, 2009.

[17] S. Biggs, "China Is Trying to Stop North Korea Rocket Launch, AP Reports," *Bloomberg*, April 3, 2009.

[18] J. Hwang, "Lee, Hu Share Concern about N.K. Launch," *Korea Herald*, April 3, 2009.

shot the North Korean missile from the sky, it could "send Pyongyang into a paroxysm of rage, downing any chance of a negotiated settlement for years." Worse still, Japan might miss. That would "reveal the fallibility of missile defense technology and risk emboldening North Korea to try more acts of bravado."[19]

Before the April 5, 2009 North Korean missile test, Tokyo sent two advanced Aegis class destroyers capable of intercepting ballistic missiles to patrol waters near North Korea. The Japanese military also deployed Patriot interceptor missile batteries in Tokyo and Northern Japan. The Japanese government threatened to shoot down the missile or any debris that fell towards Japan, provoking North Korea to declare that any such action would be an act of war. Japan's reaction to North Korea's missile test was considered "hysterical" by an analyst.[20] With his popularity at record lows, Prime Minister Taro Aso probably exaggerated the North Korean "threat," overreacting in order to divert attention from the social and economic crisis at home and boost the case for Japan's military rearmament.

In Akita Prefecture, directly across from North Korea, Governor Sukeshiro Terata acknowledged that the chances of the missile or debris falling towards Japan were "one in a million." Yet the authorities deliberately generated a climate of fear, opening an "emergency centre" with police and rescue workers on standby. Teachers were instructed to keep radios and televisions on at all times from April 4 for any announcement of an "unexpected event."

Eager to capitalize on the "missile crisis" after the DPRK's missile launch, Aso called for a vote in the Diet condemning North Korea's actions. The motion was passed in the lower house with the support of the opposition Democratic Party of Japan (DPJ), which also used the issue to divert public attention from corruption allegations against its leader, Ichiro Ozawa. Japan also pressed the UN Security Council to pass a resolution declaring North Korea in breach of UN resolutions and imposing new sanctions. With China and Russia blocking any punitive action, a non-binding UN presidential statement condemning the missile launch was finally agreed upon on April 13, 2009.

Pyongyang reacted angrily to the UN statement, claiming that it would never return to the Six-Party Talks. It expelled IAEA inspectors and

---

[19] "Caring for Korea: US must be Open to Offering Concessions to Pyongyang," *Financial Times*, March 31, 2009, 10.

[20] J. Chan, "Japan's Alarmist Reaction to North Korean Missile Test," World Socialist Website, April 16, 2009: http://www.wsws.org/articles/2009/apr2009/japa-a16.shtml.

threatened to renew its nuclear facilities. Conservatives in the Liberal Democratic Party (LDP) exploited the missile test to push for more defense spending and less constraints on military action. At an LDP executive meeting, party organizer Goji Sakamoto reportedly argued for Japan to develop its own nuclear weapons, provoking a public uproar. He was forced to withdraw his comments and the government rushed to assure the public that it was not going to build a nuclear arsenal. Previously behind Ozawa in opinion polls, Aso recovered somewhat after the North Korean test. According to a *Mainichi Shimbun* poll, Aso's popularity rose from 16 percent in March to 24 percent in April. Those favoring Aso as prime minister reached 21 percent, compared to 12 percent for Ozawa, reversing the March relationship.[21] To a large extent, domestic politics have driven Japan's thinking in this case. The LDP was defeated by the DPJ in the September 2009 parliamentary election, and Aso was subsequently replaced by DPJ's Yukio Hatoyama as prime minister.

After North Korea's May 2009 nuclear test and its withdrawal from the Six-Party Talks, President Lee Myung-bak flirted with the idea of holding talks amongst the five remaining parties, excluding North Korea. Prime Minister Aso expressed interest in the idea during his meeting with Lee in Tokyo on June 28, 2009. On the other hand, both China and the United States have indicated that the Six-Party Talks remain the most appropriate forum for discussing this issue and resolving the problem.

The North Korean missile threat may have been grossly exaggerated by Japan. After all, Japan has long been within the range of North Korea's *Rodong-1* ballistic missiles. A three-stage *Taepodong-2* rocket with a range of 4,500 kilometers does not constitute a new threat to Japan. Moreover, Japan is under the protection of the US nuclear umbrella. The real concern in Tokyo is probably not impoverished North Korea, but rising China. Once far behind Japan economically and strategically, China is now the second largest economy and military spender after the United States. The Chinese defense budget for 2009 was approximately $70 billion, compared to Japan's $49 billion. The Chinese defense budget is expected to surpass $100 billion in 2012/13, as announced at the March 2012 National People's Congress annual session in Beijing. For Japan, China's military modernization is deeply disturbing. Like the United States, Japan is concerned about China's long-term intentions.

Different expectations from the Six-Party Talks and different approaches to the North Korean nuclear issue are certainly not the only differences

---

[21] Chan, "Japan's Alarmist Reaction."

between China and Japan. Deep-rooted differences lie between the two countries, which often erupt to disrupt the otherwise interdependent relationship. Japan's failure to come to terms with its past by misrepresenting its war conduct in textbooks, and Japanese politicians' high-profile visits to the Yasukuni Shrine serve to perpetuate anti-Japanese sentiments among Japan's neighbors. As one analyst remarked, "it would be a mistake if Tokyo continues to compartmentalize its relations with China, by focusing on economic ties and being oblivious to the larger picture."[22]

After two years of relative calm and improving ties, tensions were stoked again between the two East Asian giants when Japanese Prime Minister Aso said that Tokyo would call on the United States to help it defend the disputed Diaoyu/Senkaku Islands. On February 26, 2009, answering an inquiry from a member of the opposition party, Aso said that since Senkaku is part of Japan's sovereign territory, if invaded by China, Japan would seek help from the United States, which should protect Japan's territory based on the US–Japan security pact.[23] Japanese Foreign Minister Hirofumi Nakasone escalated the war of words when he told *Kyodo News* a day later that the United States recognizes Japanese jurisdiction over the islands. Hence, it was only appropriate for the islands to be covered by the Japan–US security alliance.[24]

Hirofumi Nakasone was scheduled to visit Beijing on February 28 and March 1, 2009, his first visit to China since becoming Japan's foreign minister in September 2008. Before the visit, North Korea was reported to be preparing for a long-range missile launch, which had caused much anxiety in East Asia. Nakasone was supposed to discuss economic recovery and the North Korean nuclear issue with his Chinese counterpart, Yang Jiechi, during his visit. Yet Nakasone's and Prime Minister Aso's comments, either intentional or unintentional, poisoned the political atmosphere and made fruitful talks between the two foreign ministers on these urgent issues almost impossible. The fact that on the eve of Nakasone's scheduled visit to China, the two countries started a fresh row over the Diaoyu/Senkaku Islands is indicative of the delicate and difficult relationship between the two countries. This is a relationship that has to be nurtured by the two countries themselves. The role of third parties is rather

[22] S. M. Tang, "The Future of Japanese Diplomacy: Challenges and Prospects," *Journal e-Bangi*, December 2006.

[23] "Japanese Prime Minister: The US Will Help in Japan–China Conflict," *Voice of America* (Chinese), February 26, 2009.

[24] "China: 'US on Japan's Side' Comments Irk Beijing," *Straits Times* (Singapore), February 27, 2009.

limited if the two countries cannot deal with their historical issues and look to the future. Leaders from both sides must have a strong political will to move the relationship forward.

Conclusion

At the beginning of the twenty-first century, Japan–China relations are still stuck in the past. Japan feels challenged by China's re-emergence as an economic, political, and military power. It is competing with China globally. For example, in the context of China's increasing investment in Africa, in 2005 Japan announced that it would double its financial aid to Africa, in an attempt to win back the lead in the run for popularity among African countries. In May 2006, Japan announced a substantial increase in aid in the South Pacific, in an apparent move to counter Beijing's growing sway in the region.[25]

Historical baggage, opposite approaches, and different expectations have rendered the Six-Party Talks a lost opportunity for Japan and China to move forwards in one area where there is room for improvement. The Six-Party Talks have proved unable to help ameliorate Japan–China relations. It can be argued that this new form of third-party facilitation, like other mediators, can only work if Japan and China themselves have the political will and domestic support for improving bilateral relations.

High-level contacts between China and Japan resumed in 2006 after Prime Minister Junichiro Koizumi left office. Koizumi infuriated China and Korea by visiting the controversial Yasukuni Shrine annually. Bilateral relations have improved, since none of his six successors, as of 2012, have visited the Shrine. To mend ties with China, Prime Minister Shinzo Abe went to Beijing on October 8, 2006, his first overseas visit. Chinese Premier Wen Jiabao returned a visit to Japan in April 2007. Prime Minister Yasuo Fukuda, considered to be very China-friendly, visited Beijing at the end of 2007. Prime Minister Taro Aso, despite his more hawkish tones in the past, paid an official visit to Beijing in April 2009. He called for Tokyo and Beijing to unite in facing the world's environmental and economic challenges whilst playing down concerns over China's military power. In a wide-ranging speech in Beijing, Aso floated the prospect of a bilateral free-trade deal and joint peace-keeping operations, and said that closer ties between the historic rivals were the only way forward: "Cooperation between Japan and China is a pre-condition for taking advantage of Asia's potential as the growth center for

---

[25] "Japan Lavishes Aid on Pacific Islands," *Associated Press*, May 28, 2006.

the twenty-first century," Aso told a gathering of business leaders from both nations.[26] It is indeed up to Japan and China themselves to bury the hatchet and move forwards.

Steadily increasing Chinese influence has fundamentally changed the power structure in East Asia, which has had a significant impact on Japan. Japan will have to discard its "lead goose" mentality and engage in a peaceful and friendly rivalry with China. It is the first time in the past three hundred years that both Japan and China are simultaneously powerful. In the twenty-first century, the two countries are also becoming more interdependent. Japan and China cannot afford to allow historical disputes to interfere with their cooperation. The Chinese have a saying, "One mountain cannot accommodate two tigers." As two great powers in East Asia, can Japan and China defy this conventional wisdom? The Chinese have another saying, "Close neighbors are dearer than distant relatives." Political leaders and the public in both countries need to heed this golden advice.

[26] "Aso Calls for Japan, China to Unite," *AFP*, April 3, 2009.

CHAPTER NINE

THE CLASH OF SOFT POWERS BETWEEN CHINA AND JAPAN: SYNERGY AND DILEMMAS AT THE SIX-PARTY TALKS

LEE GUEN

Introduction

The purpose of this article[1] is to investigate the dynamics of two different types of soft power revealed during the Six-Party Talks, particularly those of China and Japan. The talks are the product of multilateral efforts by the United States, China, Japan, Russia, and the two Koreas to resolve the problem of North Korea's nuclear weapons program. In the course of the talks, the involved countries applied various tactics that aimed at both communal goals and national domestic and foreign-policy goals. The Six-Party process is based upon the premise that the nuclear question on the Korean Peninsula must be answered with peaceful measures. Thus the talks have been an arena for soft tactics rather than hard tactics. This does not mean that coercive "hard power" has been entirely absent during the process, but rather that the strategies and tactics applied to the processes have relied more on "ideational" resources than on material resources, namely, military options or economic sanctions. To be more specific, the Six-Party process has been mostly about venue-making, agenda-setting, facilitating and mediating, idea-seeking, and

[1] The editors gratefully thank the editors and the publisher of *Asian Perspective* for permission to reproduce this article, first published in *Asian Perspective* 34, no. 2 (2010): 113–139. A draft version of this chapter was also presented at the University of Hong Kong, at the Koreas between China and Japan Conference, 2009.

word-finding followed by (supposedly) material incentives or disincentives, at different venues and policy spaces.

As discussed later, soft power in this article is generally defined as "ideational" power that is, in large part, geared toward changing or creating perceptions and images of a particular country or a country's diplomacy. This definition is a somewhat expanded conception of Joseph Nye's concept of soft power because, unlike Nye's definition, soft power in this article includes not only "cooptive power" but also "constructive" power that uses ideational and symbolic resources. During the Six-Party Talks, both China and Japan resorted to very unique and different categories of soft power, and the two different types of soft power clashed directly and indirectly at the talks. This resulted in China's overwhelming diplomatic victory over Japan.

This article seeks to accomplish two goals. First, to develop a conceptual framework that includes both domestic and international levels of soft power so that a complex political context within which a policy maker devises soft-power policies and strategies can be seen. Such a framework is important because a decision maker has to know whether or not he or she is willing to risk domestic or international losses by pursuing a certain soft-power policy or if he or she can chase two rabbits at the same time. Second, to present an empirical case study of soft power to reveal two dynamics of soft power, namely "soft-power synergy" and "soft-power dilemma." For this purpose, China and Japan at the Six-Party Talks are used as a case study because the talks have been the arena for diplomatic manipulation and creativity of ideas, symbols, image-making, and solution formulation rather than coercive diplomacy. Also, China and Japan both had opportunities and incentives to project their soft power at the talks, because China, as a rising power, needed to create a peaceful and responsible image of itself, while Japan, as a declining power, needed to show its ability to reverse such trends without employing hard power. These intersecting incentives make this particular selection of specimens more intriguing.

It is important to note that China and Japan were selected for heuristic reasons and not for the purpose of comparative country analysis. This article does not aim to compare the different policy responses of China and Japan to North Korea's nuclear problem, but rather to highlight their two different dynamics of soft power—the research question, therefore, is not why China and Japan pursued different policies to the same problem, but why the soft-power policy of China ended up with soft-power synergy while that of Japan resulted in a soft-power dilemma. In the context of the Six-Party Talks, China and Japan both vividly display two different dynamics of soft power. The article is organized as follows. First, I introduce the concepts of "soft-power synergy" and "soft-power dilemma" in order to build a conceptual and diagnostic framework, which will be the basis of the evaluation of the diplomatic performances of both China and Japan at the Six-Party Talks. These two concepts assume that soft power frequently works both at the domestic and the international levels (as Robert Putnam's two-level game logic brilliantly illustrates) and that depending upon the different aims and applications of soft power strategies of a country, the result is either a synergy or a dilemma between the two levels. Following this, I analyze the Chinese and Japanese diplomatic strategies at the Six-Party Talks to reveal that China successfully constructed its image as a global power by creating soft-power synergy while Japan gradually slid to the back seat because it fell into the trap of soft-power dilemma.

A Conceptual Framework

Previous Studies

I define soft power as power to construct the preferences and images of self and others, through ideational or symbolic resources, that leads to the behavioral changes of others. This definition of soft power focuses more on the nature of power resources rather than on the nature of power that is being exerted (as Nye previously suggested). In other words, when soft or non-material resources are employed to change the behaviors or preferences of others, this is regarded as soft power. On the other hand, when hard, material resources are employed, this is regarded as hard power.[2] This is a revision and an expansion of Nye's definition for two reasons: it includes not only identification of preferences between the initiators and the receivers of soft power, but also the construction of certain images of countries by employing ideational (soft) resources so as to coerce as well as co-opt others.[3]

---

[2] For details of this new conceptualization of soft power, see G. Lee, "A Theory of Soft Power and Korea's Soft Power Strategy," *Korean Journal of Defense Analysis* 21, no. 2 (2009): 205–218.

[3] Joseph Nye's concept of soft power is based upon a new insight about power. He suggests a cognitive concept of power rather than the previously popular behavioral concept of power. While the behavioral concept of power refers to making others do what they would otherwise not do, Nye's cognitive concept of power refers to getting others to want what you want. In other words, identification of preferences between the initiators and the receivers of soft power is the essential

Previous conceptual studies and empirical research on soft power have focused mostly on subjects such as the "attractive" nature of a country's power and what, and how many, attractive resources a country has in stock.[4] Although such studies are very worthwhile in that they shed light on the neglected nature and sources of a country's influence in international relations, they are not without limitations. One such shortcoming is the assumptions that were mechanically derived from a strictly US-centered perspective in global affairs. The United States, or any other global leader, needs attractiveness to make others willingly follow it or to make others take global leadership for granted. In fact, attractive power is an essential element of a global leader because it has many followers that it needs to lead without always coercing them. But the same cannot be said for lesser powers, because most of the time they are not leaders and they do not have many followers to lead. Therefore, the lesser powers first need to ask themselves why they need to be attractive and what kind of influence they want to exert, and for which foreign-policy goals. For Nye, a policy-oriented American scholar, it was natural to assume the hegemonic position and policy interests of the United States

---

aim of soft power. See J. Nye, *Bound to Lead: The Changing Nature of American Power* (New York: Basic Books, 1990), 188; and J. Nye, *Soft Power: The Means to Succeed in World Politics* (New York: Public Affairs, 2004).

[4] In addition to Nye's works above, notable examples of such works are W. Yasushi and D. L. McConnell, eds., *Soft Power Superpowers: Cultural and National Assets of Japan and the United States* (New York: M. E. Sharpe, 2008); Y. Cho and J. H. Jeong, "China's Soft Power: Discussion, Resources, and Prospects," *Asian Survey* 48, no. 3 (2008): 453–472; D. Leheny, "A Narrow Place to Cross Swords: Soft Power and the Politics of Japanese Popular Culture in East Asia," in *Beyond Japan: The Dynamics of East Asian Regionalism*, edited by P. Katzenstein and T. Shiraishi (Ithaca, NY: Cornell University Press, 2006); A. Chong, "Singaporean Foreign Policy and the Asian Value Debate, 1992–2000: Reflections on an Experiment in Soft Power," *Pacific Review* 17, no. 1 (2004): 95–133; R. Cooper, "The Goals of Diplomacy, Hard Power, and Soft Power," in *American Power in the 21st Century*, edited by D. Held and M. Koenig-Archibugi (Cambridge: Polity Press, 2004).

[5] For that particular reason, Nye's works on soft power tend to focus quite exclusively on leadership studies. See J. Nye, "Transformational Leadership and US Grand Strategy," *Foreign Affairs* 85, no. 4 (2006): 139–148; and J. Nye, *The Power to Lead* (New York: Oxford University Press, 2008).

[6] See J. Kurlantzick, *Charm Offensive: How China's Soft Power is Transforming the World* (New Haven, CT: Yale University Press, 2007); J. A. Garrison, "China's Prudent Cultivation of 'Soft' Power and Implications for US Policy in East Asia," *Asian Affairs* 32, no. 1 (2005): 25–30; Yasushi and McConnell, *Soft Power Superpowers*; and Leheny, "A Narrow Place to Cross Swords."

while he designed the concept of soft power. Without taking account of such a context, however, studies by scholars in other parts of the world tended to mechanically apply those assumptions to non-hegemonic contexts and focus only on the attractive nature of a country's policies.

Furthermore, since Nye did not offer any theoretical framework of his own other than a new dichotomist conceptualization of power, many of the soft-power studies that followed stopped at mere descriptions of a country's attractive resources. But obviously, just being attractive does not automatically lead to influence and power unless that attractiveness is strategically or naturally utilized to achieve certain goals. Nonetheless, soft-power studies, up to now, have not shown any notable interest in the mechanisms and dynamics that are involved in applying attractive resources for both hegemonic and non-hegemonic goals.[5]

As for empirical research on soft power with a particular focus on case studies, previous studies have been immersed in figuring out what kind of "attractive" policies certain countries have pursued, and what "attractive" resources they had in mind when pursuing such policies. Discussion of the policy values of "being attractive" is rarely found. Specifically, when it comes to soft power and the soft-power policies of China and Japan, extensive studies have been conducted to describe China's recent interest in soft power and soft resources, and the history of Japan's policy interests in grooming its image as being attractive and "cool."[6] In addition, with the exception of a few diagnostic policy papers that revealed the sources of American failure in its global war on terrorism and in creating persuasive leadership in coalition-making, most of the empirical research, or even policy papers, on soft power have not shown why non-hegemonic countries like China and Japan, or even lesser powers like South Korea, need soft power at all, or with what kinds of soft-power strategies they can achieve their non-hegemonic political and diplomatic goals. In sum, discussion of the soft power of non-hegemonic states has not earnestly confronted the issue of applicability of Nye's concept to non-American contexts.

Finally, soft-power analysis needs to consider both domestic and international dimensions. A country's power projection, be it soft or hard, cannot be consistently maintained without solid domestic support, and the

---

[5] For a recent attempt at theorizing soft power, see Lee, "A Theory of Soft Power and Korea's Soft Power Strategy"; Kondo Seiichi, "Wielding Soft Power: The Key Stages of Transmission and Reception," in Yasushi and McConnell, *Soft Power Superpowers*.

[6] See Cho and Jeong, "China's Soft Power"; Kurlantzick, *Charm Offensive*; Garrison, "China's Prudent Cultivation of 'Soft' Power"; and Leheny, "A Narrow Place to Cross Swords."

success or failure of the power projection has serious and frequently direct domestic political repercussions. Therefore, when decision makers are contemplating soft-power strategies, they ought to, and in fact do, take into consideration both domestic and international policy goals and implications. For instance, America's recovery of global leadership will create a favorable environment for re-election of incumbent politicians, while at the same time, corruption scandals and the moral hazard of Wall Street will destroy US credibility and its capability to restore global-economic leadership. Therefore, as Robert Putnam brilliantly illustrated, foreign-policy analysis must pay attention to both domestic and international levels. Soft-power analysis cannot be an exception.[7] Nevertheless, no analytical works systematically and seriously examine both the domestic and international dynamics of soft power.

A Conceptual Framework: Soft-Power Synergy and Soft-Power Dilemma

Before offering my conceptual framework to analyze two different dynamics of soft power revealed by the policies of China and Japan at the Six-Party Talks, five different categories of soft-power goals must be introduced, because every power projection within each category has a very specific goal. In other words, one has to know, for example, why a country wants to be attractive, and why a country wants to use certain soft resources. Otherwise, empirical research on soft power will not further develop beyond description of soft resources and soft-power policies, sans knowledge of the implications and outcomes of the policies.

Though this is not an exhaustive list, soft power and application of soft resources can be roughly divided into five different categories in accordance with the policy goals to be achieved by "attractiveness." The five categories of policy goals are construed by empirically and inductively adding up the security and political goals of a government(s) that can be achieved by pulling others favorably towards itself, rather than pushing others away. The main trait of attractiveness is pulling, not pushing. The five categories are located on a scale of passive to active attractiveness. It can be said, with some risk of oversimplification, that some political and security goals can be achieved mainly by passively creating one's own attractive images and perception, while other political

[7] R. Putnam, "Diplomacy and Domestic Politics: The Logic of Two-Level Games," *International Organization* 42, no. 3 (1988): 427–460.

and security goals can be achieved mainly by actively projecting one's attractiveness towards others.

Located on the passive side of attractiveness are soft power to improve the external security environment by conveying peaceful and attractive images of a country, and soft power to maintain unity of a community or community of countries by creating attractiveness of the unit such as the nation-state or a regional community. On the active side is soft power to mobilize other countries' support for one's foreign and security policies by making the policies look attractive and legitimate; soft power to increase the approval ratings of a leader or domestic support of a government by projecting the attractiveness of a country to a domestic audience; and soft power to manipulate other countries' ways of thinking and preferences by projecting attractive ideas, values, and norms.

Figure 1 illustrates the scale of passivity and activity of attractiveness matched by their specific goals. Succinctly, the five goals are *threat reduction*, *unit cohesion*, *support mobilization both at domestic and international levels*, and *idea and preference manipulation*, respectively.[8]

---

[8] Examples of the first category of soft power are China's recent emphasis on "peaceful rising" (or "peaceful development") and "harmonious world," and Japan's post-war efforts to project a peaceful image of herself through her peace constitution, three non-nuclear principles, self-restraint of the Self-Defense Forces, and a limit of 1 percent of GDP on defense spending. The second category of soft power is necessary for effective leadership in mobilizing collective action among countries. Unless an action by a leading country is justified by reasonable rationales or causes, the leading country cannot form an effective coalition of countries for collective action. Recent criticisms of the lack of US soft power in its global war on terrorism or war in Iraq all pertain to this category of soft power. The third category of soft power aims at the more direct consequence of changing preferences and behaviors of others by using ideational resources. Examples of the third category are spreading theories, concepts, or discourses to other countries so that they adopt specific ways of thinking. "Washington Consensus," "neoliberalism," and "globalization" discourses are examples of the theories and discourses developed and spread by the Anglo-American powers. Maintaining large political-economic entities such as an empire, a nation, or a community demands soft power at the center of the entities, because coercive, violent suppression of defectors is too costly and too short-term. Natural identification or loyalty by the members of such entities pertains to this area of soft power. Finally, examples of the fifth category are creating national heroes, invoking patriotism by international sports competition, or showing a leader's outstanding performance in international summits or conferences so as to increase the domestic popularity of a leader or a government. For details, see Lee, "A Theory of Soft Power and Korea's Soft Power Strategy."

Figure 1: Soft Power and Policy Goals

Passive attractiveness ←			→ Active attractiveness
Threat reduction	Unit cohesion	Support mobilization	Idea manipulation

From the perspective of the two levels of domestic and international politics, some categories of soft power are often mutually synergistic, whereas some end up with policy dilemmas between domestic and international goals. For instance, a country's success in improving its security environment by applying soft resources, such as a peaceful image or another attractive resource, reverberates in domestic politics as people will welcome and support such success. In this case, successful soft power abroad leads to a successful soft-power projection inwards as the government hits both domestic and international targets at the same time. A simple synergistic relationship exists between category one and category four above. When a soft-power policy produces a synergistic linkage between international goals and domestic goals (enhancing domestic popularity or national cohesion), I call this phenomenon "soft-power synergy."

On the other hand, there are cases when the success of a certain soft-power strategy negatively affects other soft-power goals. A typical example is the relationship between category four and category one. When a government resorts to an appeal to nationalism to enhance its domestic approval ratings, this can often lead to an antagonistic foreign-policy posture towards its neighboring countries. For example, while Korea's nationalism may be appealing to its people, it is very disturbing to the governments of Japan and China. Sensitive reactions from China and Japan will temporarily, or gradually, result in deterioration of Korea's immediate security environment. On the other hand, even if a government succeeds in mobilizing another country's support for its imperialistic projects, this may invite criticisms from a liberal but powerful electorate at a critical moment, for instance, the election season. From the perspective of two-level games, the success of an outward (or inward) soft-power projection can result in the failure of an inward (or outward) soft-power projection. I call this phenomenon the "soft-power dilemma."

Of course, there is no inherent and fundamental reason or logic that makes certain combinations of categories always synergistic or contradictory. Strategies are similar to the arts in the sense that the creativity of policy makers and strategists can make a difference. In addition, domestic and international audiences are not so unified as to obtain the same response from all segments of society. That means depending on the genius of policies, since a society's responses can fluctuate greatly. Thus, the value of conceptualization of "soft-power synergy" and "soft-power dilemma" resides not in their predictive power but in their heuristic power, and in their utility in revealing some of the unnoticed dynamics of soft power.

In the following sections, I analyze the clash of or competition between China and Japan's soft power at the Six-Party Talks by applying the conceptual tool of "soft-power synergy" and "soft-power dilemma." In the process, I refer to actual policies that were adopted by the two countries.

Clash of Soft Powers between China and Japan at the Six-Party Talks

During the Six-Party Talks, the six parties involved employed many of the above categories of soft power to achieve their common and individual goals. For example, the United States tried to mobilize the support of its allies by depicting North Korea as an "axis of evil" or "outpost of tyranny." The United States also tried to shape the ideas and preferences of others by introducing ideas like CVID (Complete, Verifiable, and Irreversible Dismantlement of North Korea's Nuclear Program) and disablement. South Korea also tried very hard to change the preferences of North Korea by suggesting the idea of providing two million kilowatts of electricity and holding a summit meeting between the two Koreas. Russia's idea of connecting trans-Korean railways to the trans-Siberian railways and building natural gas pipelines that pass through the two Koreas was also an attractive idea aiming at changing the policy preferences of North Korea.

In the case of China and Japan, they also resorted to one or a combination of a few categories of soft powers listed above. China's approach to the Six-Party Talks evolved from being reluctant about multilateral diplomacy in Northeast Asia to becoming an active and positive player and a "responsible stakeholder" in global affairs. These new roles were part of China's soft-power strategy after Zheng Bijian introduced the idea of "peaceful rise" in November 2003 at the Boao Forum.[9] China coaxed and coerced North Korea to come to the Six-Party negotiation table, facilitated bilateral talks between North Korea and the

[9] See Cho and Jeong, "China's Soft Power"; Zheng was the former vice-president of the Chinese Communist Party's Central Party School, as well as the former chairman of the China Reform Forum, a representative semi-governmental organization for China's diplomacy. He also served as Hu Jintao's senior foreign policy adviser.

United States, and became a regular host of the multilateral negotiations. China was frequently criticized for doing less than enough to persuade and coerce North Korea to be more serious about the negotiations. Still, China succeeded in upgrading itself into a responsible superpower able to work together with the United States on the global stage.

On the other hand, Japan's resort to a rather inward-oriented soft power lowered Japan's standing in the Six-Party Talks. Japan was rarely visible at the later stages of the talks. Japan's initial approach to the talks, as well as to North Korea policy during Prime Minister Koizumi Junichiro's bold efforts to normalize relations with North Korea, was quite conspicuous considering the passive and reactive nature of Japanese diplomacy, particularly when it came to US–Japan relations. However, as North Korea's "confession diplomacy" failed to bring a smooth ending to the abduction issue, Japan changed gears, turning inwards to take advantage of the fifth category of soft power, namely, domestic popularity–enhancing soft power. Japan tried to transform the Six-Party Talks' agenda from denuclearization of North Korea to one that more specifically focused on issues surrounding the abduction of Japanese citizens by North Korea. This was the result of the strategy of the conservative Liberal Democratic Party (LDP), and more specifically that of the Abe Shinzo government, to maintain its popularity by taking advantage of the juxtaposed negative images of North Korea and the tough image of the LDP and Prime Minister Abe towards North Korea. While that strategy might have helped the LDP in ushering in the arrival of the Abe government and also in maintaining its edge over the Democratic Party of Japan (DPJ) for a period of time, the same strategy rendered Japan an invisible stranger at the Six-Party Talks.

The Second Nuclear Crisis on the Korean Peninsula and the Introduction of the Six-Party Talks

In October 2002, US Assistant Secretary of State for Asia–Pacific Affairs James Kelly visited North Korea and is reported to have displayed evidence of North Korea's highly enriched uranium (HEU) program to develop nuclear weapons. North Korean officials reportedly acknowledged the evidence but said they were "entitled to have nuclear programs."[10] It is not yet certain whether or not North Korea indeed has developed nuclear weapons through an HEU program. But it became evident that North

[10] See M. B. Nikitin, *North Korea's Nuclear Weapons*, Congressional Research Service (CRS), 7-5700, RL34256, February 12, 2009, 7.

Korea had violated the 1994 Geneva Agreed Framework, the 1992 agreement with South Korea on the denuclearization of the Korean Peninsula, and the International Atomic Energy Agency (IAEA) safeguard agreement under the Nonproliferation Treaty (NPT).

The 9/11 terrorist attacks drastically changed the security landscape of Northeast Asia. Besides the ABC (Anything But Clinton) policy of the George W. Bush administration, the prevention and eradication of terrorist threats to the United States became the cornerstone of US foreign policy. Against this backdrop, North Korea's nuclear program unsurprisingly became a main target of US hardliners, since transfer of nuclear materials from North Korea to the hands of terrorists would be a huge threat to the United States. Publication of the US defense department's 2001 Nuclear Posture Review (NPR) designating North Korea as a possible nuclear target, and President Bush's mention of North Korea as a member of the "axis of evil" in his 2002 State of the Union address, were part of a broad US strategic roadmap in dealing with new security threats in Northeast Asia.

The essence of the changed security landscape of Northeast Asia is the confrontation between the United States and North Korea. The initial North Korean official response after the meeting with James Kelly carried a quite defensive tone. On October 25, 2002, North Korea's foreign ministry proposed a non-aggression pact with the United States.[11] The US response was icy. The United States repeated its position of "no dialogue without the dismantlement of North Korea's nuclear program." In November, under strong US pressure, the Korean Peninsula Energy Development Organization (KEDO) decided to halt delivery of heavy fuel to North Korea, accusing North Korea of violating the Agreed Framework.

Then came the escalation stage between the two countries. On December 9, a North Korean vessel carrying missile exports to Yemen was interdicted by the Spanish navy (having received the information from US intelligence) and shortly afterward released. North Korea became furious, calling this a violation of international law by Spain and the United States. Three days after the interdiction, North Korea declared its intention to reactivate the frozen nuclear facilities to "supplement the electricity shortage" caused by KEDO's decision to stop delivering heavy fuel oil. A week later, North Korea removed the seals from its stock of spent fuel and removed IAEA surveillance cameras at the five-megawatt reactor in Yongbyon. Then, on Christmas Eve, North Korea completed its

[11] M. E. Manyin, E. Chanlett-Avery, and H. Marchart, "North Korea: A Chronology of Events, October 2002–December 2004," CRS Report for Congress, January 24, 2005.

removal of all the seals and surveillance cameras at the radiochemical laboratory in Yongbyon. The IAEA inspectors in North Korea were then expelled.

2003 marked the beginning of a rerun of the events that took place in 1993. North Korea turned into a copycat of its own brinkmanship strategy. On January 10, North Korea again declared its withdrawal from the Nuclear Nonproliferation Treaty. In late February, the United States confirmed the reactivation of North Korea's five-megawatt reactor. North Korea also test-fired three short-range cruise missiles between February 24 and April 1. In mid April, the North Korean foreign ministry announced that North Korea was moving successfully to the last stages of reprocessing eight thousand spent fuel rods, and publicly claimed in late April that the reprocessing was to deter US aggression.

These actions and reactions between the United States and North Korea did not escalate the tension to the point of eruption. In fact, they were interrupted by several attempts to bring the two parties to dialogue. The first attempt was a tripartite talk between the United States, North Korea, and China that was held in Beijing in late April 2003. This tripartite talk was an important turning point because it led both the United States and North Korea to retreat somewhat from their earlier stances. The United States retreated from its previous position of "no dialogue without dismantlement of North Korea's nuclear program," and North Korea retreated from its position of having bilateral talks only with the United States. It was also noteworthy that through the tripartite talk, China made its debut as a critical mediator in resolving the nuclear crisis and arranging venues for further dialogues.

The tripartite talk ended without any immediate concrete result. The United States and North Korea simply reconfirmed their positions, and North Korea's strategy to create a bilateral framework between the United States and North Korea contrasted sharply with the US strategy to make it multilateral. However, as was seen later, this tripartite talk would serve as a springboard to produce genuine multilateral talks later in 2003.

From May onwards, North Korea increasingly showed its willingness to accept the multilateral format in order to cut a deal with the United States. And through arduous efforts by China, North Korea finally agreed to participate in six-party talks that were to be held in Beijing in August 2003. The other parties—South Korea, the United States, Japan, Russia, and China—also accepted the proposal, and the first Six-Party Talks were held from August 27 to 29. Again, the talks ended without a concrete result. However, all the parties concurred on the utility of the talks, and reaffirmed the principle of peaceful resolution of the crisis.

The Six-Party Talks continued turbulently until the fifth round that ended in February 2007, producing agreement on February 13. This document sought to implement the September 19, 2005 Joint Statement that was produced at the fourth round of talks. During the incipient phases of the Six-Party Talks, North Korea tried to escalate the nuclear crisis to draw the attention of the United States so that Pyongyang could have direct bilateral negotiations with Washington, even within the Six-Party Talks framework. Initially, the United States wanted to engage in negotiations with North Korea only after the North had abandoned all of its nuclear programs. On the other hand, North Korea wanted the simultaneous exchange of each and every dismantlement process of its nuclear programs with specific parallel rewards. But as the Bush administration jealously guarded its initial position, North Korea declared possession of nuclear weapons on February 10, 2005, and again in May of the same year announced removal of eight-thousand spent fuel rods from the five-megawatt nuclear reactor at Yongbyon.[12]

Afterwards, North Korea and the United States began to have bilateral talks within the Six-Party Talks. Finally, at the second stage of the fourth round of the talks in September 2005, the six parties were able to reach an agreement to adopt a joint statement which stated North Korea's commitment to abandon all of its nuclear weapons and programs. South Korea reaffirmed its proposal of July 12, 2005 to provide two million kilowatts of electric power to North Korea. The six parties also agreed to take coordinated steps to implement the consensus in a phased manner in line with the principle of "commitment for commitment, action for action," reflecting North Korea's concern. After Assistant Secretary of State Christopher Hill became the US chief negotiator, the United States accelerated its bilateral contacts with North Korea. What's more, Hill showed great interest and will to resolve the nuclear problem.

The first stage of the fifth round of the Six-Party Talks began in November 2005, but North Korea–US relations turned sour again due to the so-called Banco Delta Asia (BDA) incident. The United States accused North Korea of laundering money through the BDA, and imposed "financial sanctions" to sever the financial pipelines of BDA that reached North Korea.[13] Seeing that the sanctions were imposed immediately after the September 19 joint statement, North Korea became frustrated again,

---

[12] S. Squassoni, "North Korea's Nuclear Weapons: Recent Developments," CRS Report for Congress, Order Code RS21391, updated October 18, 2006.

[13] "Treasury Designates Banco Delta Asia as Primary Money Laundering Concern under USA Patriot Act," September 15, 2005, US Department of the Treasury: http://www.ustreas.gov/press/releases/js2720.htm.

and resorted to test-firing long-range missiles. When this did not result in alleviating sanctions, North Korea carried out a nuclear test on September 9, 2006. From that point on, the United States became quite serious in negotiating with North Korea and the six parties were able to produce the February 13 agreement at the third stage of the fifth round of the talks. The United States eventually lifted the financial sanctions.

The February 13 agreement specified "disablement" of North Korea's nuclear programs in exchange for energy, economic, and humanitarian aid. On October 3, the six parties again adopted an agreement involving the second stage of implementing the September 19 joint statement, including the reporting and declaration of North Korea's nuclear facilities and inspection protocols.

The implementation process, however, was stalled again as the United States and North Korea had different interpretations of the inspection protocols. Since then, the Six-Party Talks have yet to resume.

China's Application of Soft Power to the Six-Party Talks

Since the 1990s, China has been heavily engaged in studying and strategically increasing its soft power.[14] One area of China's concerns regarding its soft power is the "peaceful rise and peaceful development" of China. China's major foreign-policy concern at the time was to find an effective response to the "China threat" thesis that was gaining global popularity and to show the world that China is on its way to becoming a responsible, peaceful power without posing threats to the interests of other countries. For that purpose, it was extremely important for China to create a responsible and peaceful image of itself.

For China, the Six-Party Talks gradually became a major venue for it to create such an image. Eventually, China succeeded in producing a worldwide perception that China had become a "responsible stakeholder," able to work cooperatively with the United States. One can observe this Chinese strategy during the Six-Party Talks. They are well documented by Funabashi Yoichi in his book *The Peninsula Question*.[15]

---

[14] On the early works of Chinese scholars on soft power, see Cho and Jeong, "China's Soft Power," nn. 7–19.

[15] Y. Funabashi, *The Peninsula Question: A Chronicle of the Second Korean Nuclear Crisis* (Washington, DC: Brookings Institution Press, 2007). This book is the most detailed chronology and documentary of both China's and Japan's positions, behavior, and strategies at the Six-Party Talks. This article relies very heavily on Funabashi's book about details of both Chinese and Japanese actions and reactions at the talks.

Since the summit meeting between Jiang Zemin and George W. Bush at Bush's ranch in Texas in 2002, improving relations with the United States has become the main pillar of China's foreign policy. China's diplomacy at the Six-Party Talks can be seen as an extension of this new thinking in China's foreign policy. Even though China initially regarded the North Korean nuclear problem as a problem primarily between the United States and North Korea, China eventually accepted to host the talks for the specific objective of improving and stabilizing its own bilateral relationship with the United States. It was key Chinese diplomats who contributed to the expansion of tripartite talks into six-party talks at the strong request of the United States. This was not an easy task. Many of China's diplomats were not keen on creating six-party negotiations. But Deputy Minister of Foreign Affairs Dai Bingguo played a particularly important role in setting up the talks by visiting both North Korea and the United States.[16]

The United States has frequently complained that China did not do enough to dissuade North Korea from proceeding with the development of nuclear weapons. Still, China's efforts regarding the Six-Party Talks were highly regarded by the United States. For instance, in June 2004, James Kelly praised China, saying that China had become a credible partner for increasing regional stability. In doing this, he specifically referred to China's antiterrorism efforts and the Six-Party Talks. He even went on to say that China had promised to take on global responsibilities together with the United States.[17] In another instance, Deputy Secretary of State Robert Zoellick had often demanded that China become a responsible stakeholder in international society, saying so publically in August 2005 at the first high-level strategic dialogue with China, where he met with Dai Bingguo, and again in September 2005 in a speech delivered before the National Committee on US–China relations.[18] Both China and Zoellick found the Six-Party Talks to be a valuable asset for China to prove its willingness to play such a role.

China's adroit handling of multilateral diplomacy was another way of projecting its image as a global player. The Chinese foreign ministry's department of policy planning strongly argued for utilizing the Six-Party Talks as a means to promote China's multilateral diplomacy.[19] According to a Chinese official of that department, who had participated in multilateral

---

[16] Funabashi, *The Peninsula Question*, 278–285.
[17] Funabashi, *The Peninsula Question*, 313.
[18] Funabashi, *The Peninsula Question*, 446.
[19] Funabashi, *The Peninsula Question*, 319.

diplomacy initiatives, the idea began to emerge around the summer of 2002.

China's role as a mediator and facilitator was also quite conspicuous during the Six-Party Talks. When North Korea declared it would boycott the talks after the first round, China's Wu Bangguo, chairman of the standing committee of the National People's Congress, visited North Korea in October 2003 and promised to provide $25 million to help build a glass factory in North Korea. The aid was said to be an incentive for North Korea to stay in the talks.[20] In 2005, Wang Jiarui, head of the international department of the Chinese Communist Party, visited North Korea again after it sent a negative signal on the talks, and played the energy assistance card. In December 2005, President Hu Jintao visited North Korea and was reported to have promised $2 billion worth of economic assistance to North Korea.[21] China also facilitated bilateral meetings between North Korea and the United States while the Six-Party Talks were in session by being creative—deliberately arranging seats so that the representatives of both countries were sitting close to each other or by leaving the North Korean and American representatives alone together in the negotiating room.[22]

China used not only carrots, but also sticks. During the spring of 2003, China stopped supplying heavy oil to North Korea for three consecutive days. Though the official Chinese explanation was that the stoppage was for repair purposes, experts widely interpreted the development as China twisting North Korea's arm, demanding its participation in tripartite talks.[23]

Such evolution did not go unnoticed by the United States. One American participant in the fourth round of the talks commented that China had evolved from a facilitator into chairman. Hill also praised China as a good host.[24] He said that the United States and China shared common interests on the issue of the North Korean nuclear problem and thanks to the Six-Party Talks, US–China relations were improving.

With regard to Sino–Japanese relations, there were not many conspicuous direct clashes or disputes during the talks, but some Chinese concerns were expressed towards Japan indirectly. For instance, Chinese concern about Japanese intentions was frequently observed. One Chinese diplomat said that the denuclearization of North Korea was in China's

---

[20] Funabashi, *The Peninsula Question*, 320–321.
[21] Funabashi, *The Peninsula Question*, 321.
[22] Funabashi, *The Peninsula Question*, 337.
[23] Funabashi, *The Peninsula Question*, 323–324.
[24] Funabashi, *The Peninsula Question*, 381, 384.

interests because a nuclear North Korea might give Japan the pretext to increase its military spending, if not to go nuclear. Another Chinese diplomat at the talks mentioned a rumor that Japan purposely raised the abduction issue at the talks so as not to resolve the nuclear problem and thereby give Japan a rationale for developing its own nuclear weapons.[25]

In sum, China's application of the first category of soft power to the Six-Party Talks has been very successful in terms of creating an international perception of China as a responsible stakeholder in global affairs, and also as a promoter of multilateral diplomacy. By improving cooperation with the United States, China also succeeded in improving its security environment and was able to transform itself from a "threat" to a global partner with the United States. To a certain extent, China is seen as "peacefully developing" in the international society. Yet, China is still criticized for its insufficient efforts to persuade North Korea to give up its nuclear program. China is seen by many as being more interested in maintaining stability in Northeast Asia than pursuing regional nonproliferation of nuclear weapons. Yet, on balance, China has emerged as a responsible global stakeholder.

Japan's Application of Soft Power to the Six-Party Talks

The overall evaluation of Japan's role in the Six-Party Talks by diplomats and scholars is quite negative. One Russian diplomat said Japan's role in the talks was next to nothing, and a Korean diplomat commented that Japan was invisible, particularly during the later rounds.[26] During the talks, Japan was in fact isolated from other participants.[27] The head of Korea's delegation to the fourth round of the talks, Song Min-soon, openly criticized Japanese chief negotiator Sasae Kenichiro's speech, saying that Japan needed to focus on the nuclear issue rather than raising the abduction and missile issues at the talks.[28]

Initially, Japan's approaches to North Korea and the Six-Party Talks were, in fact, not as invisible or as narrow as they became in its later approaches. Prime Minister Koizumi's effort to normalize relations with North Korea was quite bold, since it took place even while North Korea and the United States were in dispute over the issue of the North's HEU

---

[25] Funabashi, *The Peninsula Question*, 301–302.

[26] Personal conversations with a Russian diplomat and a Korean diplomat who participated in the Six-Party Talks and who must remain anonymous.

[27] K. Choi and M. Choe, "Current Status, Prospects, and Countermeasures of the North Korean Nuclear Issue," *IFANS Review* 16, no. 2 (2009): 41.

[28] Funabashi, *The Peninsula Question*, 426.

program. Under the intensive and persuasive advice of Tanaka Hitoshi, the then deputy minister of foreign affairs, Japan had a comprehensive idea about how to resolve the nuclear problem together with other closely connected issues. However, a critical turning point in Japan's North Korea policy came with the partial success of Koizumi's North Korea diplomacy, namely, the partial success at resolving the abduction issue.

North Korea's so-called "confession diplomacy" was first aimed at resolving the abduction issue so that North Korea could move on to strike a comprehensive deal with Japan, which would include large-scale economic aid from Japan. North Korea sent back five abductees and their families to Japan after the summit meeting between Koizumi and Kim Jong-il on September 17, 2002. At the summit meeting, Kim admitted to abducting the Japanese citizens and apologized for the unfortunate wrongdoings that North Korea committed during the Cold War years. North Korea's confession and Koizumi's partial success in bringing back the abductees were meant to become a springboard for the next round of negotiations for North Korea–Japan normalization. But things did not turn out that way. The fact that only five among thirteen abductees survived angered the Japanese public; when it was found via DNA testing that the remains of one of the deceased abductees, Yokoda Megumi, that were turned over, were fake, the public became infuriated.

The confession diplomacy caused Koizumi's North Korea policy, initially led by doves such as Fukuda Yasuo, Tanaka Hitoshi, and Hiramatsu Kenji, to backfire. Japan's North Korea policy soon turned hawkish, reflecting an increasingly "conservative" domestic political environment.[29] The abduction issue became a big political asset for the conservative politicians within the LDP, and Abe Shinzo, the strongest prime ministerial candidate at the time, took the reins over the issue and spurred Japan's North Korea policy in a very hawkish direction.

Such change was not without context. Japan's conservative turn in its domestic politics had started with the demise of the 1955 regime. This was caused by the collapse of the socialist forces in Japanese domestic politics, and the vocal protests by traditional Japanese nationalists against the post-war state of Japan's foreign and security policies.[30] Against this backdrop, conservative politicians within the LDP took advantage of the abduction issue and tenaciously raised it at the Six-Party Talks. Tough stances

[29] H. S. Yun, "Reciprocity and Koizumi Government's North Korea Policy" (in Korean), *Segye Jiyeok Yongu Nonchong* 25, no. 3 (2007): 191.

[30] Y. Soeya, "Japanese Domestic Politics and Security Cooperation in Northeast Asia," Council on Foreign Relations, December 2009, 2: http://www.cfr.org/project/1352/regional_impulses_in_northeast_asia.html.

towards North Korea and adroit manipulation of the abduction issue immensely contributed to the arrival of the Abe administration in September 2006. Despite his weak political base within the LDP, Abe was able to become prime minister owing, mainly, to the abduction issue.[31] The anti-North Korean ambiance in Japan that formed after Kim Jong-il's confession and particularly after North Korea's 2006 missile launches led to a very narrowly focused Japanese policy at the Six-Party Talks.

Within this context, Japan's approach, particularly during the later rounds when Koizumi retreated from Japan's formerly flexible North Korea policy, was the application of the fifth category of soft power, namely domestic-popularity-enhancing soft power by utilizing international events. Japan's Six-Party Talks' policy was based upon two very simple ideas: close cooperation with US hardliners, and maintenance of a tough stance on the abduction issue. These two ideas appealed highly to the Japanese public, and until dovish Christopher Hill took over the US negotiating team, Japanese cooperation with the United States seemed quite effective. However, as all the parties at the Six-Party Talks, including the United States, increasingly took on more conciliatory positions toward North Korea, Japan suddenly slipped into isolation, and became stuck with the abduction issue. Japan was unable to suggest any new ideas or solutions to the main agenda of the talks—the North Korean nuclear problem.

Evaluations and Conclusion

Japan's soft-power strategy at the Six-Party Talks resulted in what I call a "soft-power dilemma." As discussed, a soft-power dilemma refers to a situation in which soft power that appeals and exerts attractiveness to the domestic audience creates a threatening or negative image abroad, thereby causing external security environments to deteriorate. Japan's recent conservative turn may have appealed to the Japanese public by bringing the issue of Japan's history textbooks to the surface, having politicians visit the Yasukuni Shrine, taking a tougher stance towards China, having close cooperation with the United States, and expanding the international roles of Japan's Self-Defense Forces. But such a conservative turn created unstable relations with its neighbors, particularly Korea and China. In other words, excessive or careless application of the fifth category of soft power results in the reduction of the first category of soft power.

---

[31] Y. H. Jo, "Arrival of Abe Administration in Japan and the Prospect for Korea–Japan Relations," (in Korean), *IFANS Policy Brief*, September 29, 2006, 13.

This dynamic of soft-power dilemma was quite vividly illustrated during the Six-Party Talks as discussed above, and the Japanese government ended up isolating itself in the talks. If the Japanese government, at the time, had only its domestic agenda in mind, such isolation might not have been a serious problem. Nonetheless, the result was that Japan revealed its diplomatic weaknesses to the other parties, and lowered its diplomatic standing in the eyes of a very significant group of international powers, including the United States, China, and Russia. At the same time, Japan was not greatly successful in improving its security environment, as was proven by the continued missile launches by North Korea, and the sensitive responses by its neighboring countries to the conservative moves of Japan.

On the other hand, China's soft-power strategy culminated in what I call "soft-power synergy." China's improved status on the international stage, and the gradual recognition of China as a responsible stakeholder by the international society—particularly by the United States—not only improved its security environment, but also certainly amplified the pride of the Chinese people (though an objective opinion survey on that relationship does not yet exist). The China threat thesis was gradually replaced by China's peaceful development, and China became an essential player at the Six-Party Talks. Now it is unimaginable to think of resolving the North Korean nuclear crisis without the presence and participation of China. The success of the first category of soft power resulted in the success of the fifth category of soft power, and to a certain extent in the success of the second category of soft power in terms of enhancing China's leadership.

At the time of this writing, it is uncertain which direction the new DPJ government will take Japan if the Six-Party Talks resume. However, it is recommended that Japan broaden its agenda to escape from the abduction-issue trap, solve the abduction issue within a broader framework of dismantling the last Cold War structure in Northeast Asia, and, thereby, reform North Korea from within and without. As for China, there appears no reason to change its productive soft-power synergy strategy.

CHAPTER TEN

OVERCOMING OBSTACLES FOR CHINA–JAPAN COOPERATION OVER THE KOREAN PROBLEM

ALEXANDER ZHEBIN

Introduction: A Dualistic Relationship

The legacy of numerous Sino–Japanese conflicts on the Korean Peninsula, starting from Toyotomi Hideyoshi's invasion at the end of the sixteenth century (repelled with China's assistance), to World War II, remains the main obstacle for the development of Sino–Japanese cooperation over the Korean problem.[1] This legacy also affects and shapes the interaction of China and Japan on the international scene, as well as on the regional level in Northeast Asia. Today, the transformation of the Northeast Asian region into a zone of peace and prosperity for all appears especially urgent in view of the present situation surrounding the nuclear and missile programs of the Democratic People's Republic of Korea (DPRK). China and Japan must work together to come up with coordinated measures to facilitate this transformation. Both Beijing and Tokyo realize that when the current threat of global nuclear conflict has receded, other global challenges will take center stage: international terrorism; the proliferation of weapons of mass destruction (WMD); drug- and human-trafficking; organized crime; illegal weapons trading; migration, financial, economic, and other crimes; and threats to the environment and health.

At the same time, while Japan continues to consider the US–Japanese alliance as a cornerstone of its security, China is ever more inclined to take a broader approach and, in such cases as the nuclear issue on the Korean Peninsula, believes that a multilateral search for solutions to the problems facing the world community is more feasible. This will require, of course,

[1] A. C. Nahm, *Korea: Traditions and Transformation: A History of the Korean People* (Seoul: Hollym, 1991), 124, 176.

serious efforts to harmonize interests and work out a common strategy for dealing with international problems. The new world order should be based on the broadest kind of multilateral cooperation. The long-term objectives of countering global threats and new challenges objectively outweigh the unilateral approaches, based frequently on *ad hoc* tactical interests and the "Cold War" era mentality and alliances.

Regretfully, Japan's Korea policy still remains in the "Cold War" trenches and is held hostage to the electoral self-interest of certain domestic political groups. Such issues as the Dokdo Islands, the Yasukuni Shrine visits, "comfort women," and the subject of history textbooks, have proved over and over again that Japan still cannot rid herself of the blight of her militaristic past.[2]

By establishing diplomatic relations with the Republic of Korea (ROK) in August 1992, China basically completed the process of reforming its policy toward Korea. The new course takes into account changes both in China's economic development, and her world standing and geopolitical realities in the international arena. China's new foreign policy, including her policy towards the Korean Peninsula, is characterized by a drastic reduction of ideological factors and by an appreciable increase of pragmatism in defining approaches to current global and regional problems.

China's Korea policy currently includes the following major approaches:

1. China is firmly in favor of the denuclearization of the Korean Peninsula. It is difficult to achieve a relaxation of tensions on the Peninsula without ensuring non-proliferation, especially in the Northeast Asian region, and in particular on the Korean Peninsula. After the North Korean missile launch and nuclear test in April and May of 2009, respectively, Beijing did not miss any chance to reaffirm its position that "China would continue to play a constructive role in realizing the denuclearization of the Korean Peninsula."[3]

2. The reconciliation and cooperation between North and South Korea should be developed on the principles agreed upon by the North and the South and their leaders themselves, without outside interference.

---

[2] See D. Hyun, *The Historical Perception of Korea and Japan* (Seoul: Nanam, 2008).

[3] "China urges early resumption of six-party talks," *Xinhuanet*, January 6, 2011: http://news.xinhuanet.com/english2010/china/2011-01/06/c_13679226.htm.

3. All problems on the Peninsula should be solved only by peaceful and diplomatic means.

4. China welcomes the establishment of a peaceful united Korean state, friendly to China and other neighboring countries.

The Korean Crisis: Behind the Scenes

The Six-Party process in Beijing confirmed, once again, that along with the United States, China's position is of key importance in the settlement of this issue. During the crisis, Beijing repeatedly spoke in favor of the denuclearization of the Korean Peninsula. A nuclear North Korea could push Japan, South Korea, and—probably the most dreadful thing for Beijing—Taiwan, along the same path.[4]

At the same time for China, because of her strategic, political, and prestige considerations, liquidation of the DPRK is absolutely unacceptable. Such an outcome would result in US control over the whole Korean Peninsula and the stationing of American armed forces directly on China's borders.

The United States seems to have far-reaching and, for the time being, covert plans concerning the Korean Peninsula. These plans call for securing a stronghold on the Chinese border in view of the ever-growing US–China rivalry and the US "hedging" strategy towards China.

After the disappearance of the USSR and the collapse of socialism in Eastern European countries, Washington expected an early collapse of the North Korean regime. Absorption of the North by the South under the military/political aegis of the United States would allow the Americans to establish control over unique strategic vantage points in Asia, located on the borders of Russia and China, the very powers which could still potentially challenge US global dominance.

Liquidation of the DPRK would conclude the process of revision of the results of World War II in Northeast Asia, but would also mean a revision of the results of the Korean War of 1950–53. The deployment of US armed forces, with their precision weaponry, along the almost 1,400 km-long overland border with China and the 17 km-long border with Russia, would result in cardinal changes in the military–political situation in this region and in the Asia-Pacific region as a whole.[5]

---

[4] *Nezavisimaya gazeta*, April, 28, 2003.

[5] A. Zhebin, "Some Aspects of Korea's Nuclear Crisis," in *Russia and Korea in the Changing World Order*, edited by V. Tkachenko (Moscow, 2003), 48.

Some Russian observers are inclined to consider the US attack on Iraq, as well as the Washington-sponsored "anti-terrorist operation" in Afghanistan, as pretexts used by the United States to obtain military bases in Central Asia. Such a view make sense if contextualized in the larger framework of a struggle between the United States and China for dominance in the Asia-Pacific region. Russian General Shebarshin believes that bases in this region are necessary for the United States, "not for fighting terrorism, but for control over the northwest part of China." Moreover, in his opinion, the Americans would be able to "encircle" not only China but also Russia with military bases.[6]

In view of such plans, Washington's appeals to Beijing to take part in certain multilateral efforts, which are covertly directed at regime changes and liquidating the DPRK, appear somewhat arrogant. The Chinese are actually being called upon to help, with their own hands, bring American soldiers to China's borders.

China cannot afford to lose North Korea. Beijing suspects that such a development would lead to the whole Peninsula being turned into a US forward-deployment base to threaten China, in the case that bilateral relations deteriorate. Loss of the DPRK would seriously undermine China's prestige and international standing in Asia and all over the world. China's plans to reclaim Taiwan would be also in jeopardy.

There is only one sound explanation for the actions of the US administrations, starting with Clinton administration's demonstration of cautiousness in resolving the North Korean nuclear issue to the present day "accommodation" of the DPRK: China shares a common border with North Korea, and during the Korean War she demonstrated her resolve to keep the northern half of the Peninsula as a buffer zone between herself and the United States. The United States is certainly unwilling and, as the recent financial crisis has shown, incapable of risking a major conflict with China over North Korea.

Chinese Premier Wen Jiabao's visit to the DPRK in October 2009, and his act of placing flowers on the grave of Mao's son, killed when fighting against US-led troops during the Korean War, was a signal that even amateurs in the world of Asian political symbols could read. Wen's gesture was, undoubtedly, a symbolic one, in that particular case. At the same time, it was also clear that China was not going to forget the sacrifices of the Korean War, and not going to "cede" North Korea to the "imperialists."

Therefore, it seems apparent that the United States is trying to entice

---

[6] *Nezavisimaya Gazeta*, March 24, 2003.

the Chinese with promises that after the demise of the DPRK, US forces will not be deployed in the North, and will return the south of the 38th parallel—or, alternatively, that American strikes will be limited only to the North Korean nuclear facilities. Simultaneously, the Americans are in every way possible trying to sow alienation and mistrust between China and North Korea, particularly by the use of compliments, including those made at the top-level, concerning a "constructive role" allegedly demonstrated by Beijing during the crisis.[7]

In view of the specified interests on the Korean Peninsula, Beijing will try, no doubt, to mobilize all political and diplomatic methods available, as well as necessary economic resources, to ensure the DPRK's survival. At the same time, China will induce North Korea in every possible way to exercise restraint in foreign policy and to continue with economic reforms that will lessen China's political and economic burdens.

China's leadership is vitally interested in the creation of favorable external conditions for the country's further development. Therefore, Beijing has already shown that, more than ever before, it is ready to influence Pyongyang. The Chinese representative to the International Atomic Energy Agency on February 12, 2003 voted for the resolution to refer the North Korean nuclear problem to the UN Security Council (UNSC). During the same month, according to some reports, China blocked the only oil pipeline between the two countries for several days "for technical reasons," thus signaling to Pyongyang its displeasure with the latter's behavior on the nuclear question. China supported both UNSC resolutions condemning North Korean nuclear tests in 2006 and 2009 and the UNSC president's statement condemning North Korea's missile launch in April 2009.

North Korea's seemingly arrogant challenge to the superpower can be explained partly by Pyongyang's understanding that China's national security interest, in the long run, will compel it to support the DPRK. Having taken advantage of this "stalemate" between the United States and China, and feeling incapable of defending herself with her obsolete conventional armaments, North Korea resorted to the development of missile and nuclear weapons to deter a possible US attack. The US invasion of Iraq probably gave the final push for the North Korean leadership's "strategic decision" to go ahead with practical implementation of its previously mostly experimental program. Since then, North Korea has repeatedly claimed that the country "was compelled to go nuclear in

---

[7] "Bush urges leaders to unite against North Korea," *USA Today*, May 7, 2006: http://usatoday30.usatoday.com/news/washington/2006-07-04-us-north-korea_x.htm.

the face of the US hostile policy and its nuclear threats."[8]

The Nuclear Problem in Korea: A View from Beijing and Tokyo

The explosive situation on the Korean Peninsula has been the subject of grave attention on the part of China. The Peninsula has an almost 1,400 km-long land border with China. In the interests of China, as well as other states, the preservation of the denuclearized status of the Peninsula and the development of peaceful cooperation in Northeast Asia is of paramount importance.

The current nuclear crisis in Korea has brought about discussion in China on how Beijing should handle the situation. From the very outbreak of the crisis there has been a tendency to approach the situation as a mainly bilateral dispute between the United States and the DPRK. At the same time, a number of observers have argued that China's position on the matter should be determined by Beijing's new standing as a "responsible stakeholder" and as a nuclear power vitally interested in strengthening the nuclear non-proliferation regime.

Some experts have even expressed opinions in favor of creating a united front with the United States and its allies to demonstrate "collective rigidity" towards the DPRK, to put an end to its nuclear ambitions. Opponents of such an approach have pointed out China's traditional, centuries-long security interests on the Peninsula, which have compelled China to repeatedly send in its troops to ensure peace and stability there.

China's position is that the nuclear problem needs to be resolved by taking all aspects of the situation into consideration. On the one hand, it is important to secure the DPRK's return to the Non-Proliferation Treaty (NPT) and, generally, to ensure the nuclear-free status of the Korean Peninsula. But on the other hand, it is necessary to provide the DPRK with security guarantees and to remove obstacles for those players from the international community who are willing to help North Korea to cope with its complex economic problems.

As for the various problems raised by participants of the Six-Party Talks, China believes that it would be desirable, during the course of the negotiations, to concentrate on the most important issue: how to handle the nuclear problem and how to create conditions whereby the issue would be

---

[8] "DPRK Foreign Ministry Declares Strong Counter-Measures against UNSC's 'Resolution 1874'." *Korea Central News Agency of the Democratic People's Republic of Korea*, June 13, 2009.

resolved once and for all. As for the remaining problems, including the abduction issue in Japan–DPRK relations, these could also be discussed, but it would be necessary to hold additional meetings and negotiations. However, these other issues should not hinder the steady progress being made towards the main aim—denuclearization of the Peninsula.

It is worth noting that China did not hesitate to express her displeasure with the DPRK's decision to withdraw from the NPT in 2003, and with Pyongyang's missile launches and nuclear tests in 2006 and 2009. However, China's UN envoy reiterated Beijing's position that the reaction from the Security Council "has to be cautious and proportionate."[9]

Finally, China's unequivocal siding with the DPRK's position after the Cheonan and Yongphendo incidents in 2010 caused a deep disappointment in Tokyo. Some experts, analyzing Tokyo's behavior during the Six-Party Talks on the nuclear problem in Korea, noted that Japan on some questions failed to support the United States. They said that Japan could take a position in Northeast Asia similar to a position taken by Turkey during the Iraq war.[10]

At the same time, visible differences between China and Japan's approaches to the solution of the North Korean nuclear and missile problem testify that both sides have a great deal of work to do to ensure stable and fully fledged cooperation on the issue. Another conclusion made from the case is that outstanding issues in bilateral relations between Beijing and Tokyo are serious enough to hinder Sino–Japanese cooperation on a number of international issues of great importance to both countries and to the rest of the world.

The Unification of Korea

Beijing's position concerning the inter-Korean rapprochement and its possible results is determined by China's national interests, which will certainly benefit from liquidation of the "hot spot" right next to her eastern border, and, in the long-term, from founding a unified Korea capable of maintaining good relations of friendship and cooperation with China.

At the same time, as Chinese Foreign Ministry spokesman Ma Zhaoxu made clear, Beijing's priority remains the maintenance of peace and

---

[9] "Chinese envoy: Security Council response to DPRK launch should be cautious, proportionate," *Sina English*, April 14, 2009: http://english.sina.com/china/p/2009/0413/233565.html.

[10] *Information and Analytical Agency MiK*, January 13, 2005.

stability on the Peninsula.[11] It is also important for China to ensure the outcome of the most predictable results of the reunification process. Considering the high degree of uncertainty concerning the foreign policy of a united Korea, as well as her possible participation in the military-political alliances with other states and the orientations of such alliances, China is being compelled, while welcoming an inter-Korean détente, to take a more cautious stance on the reunification issue.

China is seemingly unwilling to face the US troops on the Korean–Chinese border in the context of the unresolved Taiwan problem and the developing Sino–American political and economic rivalry, while other major interested parties also harbor their respective concerns about a united Korea's foreign policy.

The United States feels uneasy concerning the prospect of being compelled to put an end to the American military presence in South Korea, and the Japanese are reluctant to see the emergence of a strong adversary full of desire to exact revenge for the historical humiliations of a past colonial age.

Both Beijing and Moscow can hardly welcome as a new neighbor a state with a population of 70 million under the prevailing influence of the United States with troops stationed in its territory. In Russia's case, it would be equivalent to the emergence on her eastern borders of an Asian clone of NATO. Some prominent Russian experts believe that the stationing of US troops in South Korea is an anachronism of the "Cold War" period.[12]

Generally, however, for China the real task is not to obtain a position on the Peninsula, especially in view of her present capabilities, but to prevent a situation whereby Korea would be placed under the influence of another state, especially one unfriendly to China.

Since, under the present balance of power in Northeast Asia, one cannot exclude such a development occurring, the existence of the DPRK as a friendly sovereign state, carrying out the role of a buffer against the geopolitical ambitions of the United States in this region, is favorable to Beijing (and to Moscow as well).

In view of the factors specified above, and from the point of view of China's security interests, the DPRK's unification formula, which calls for the creation of a neutral, non-aligned state on the Peninsula, looks more

---

[11] "China calls for maintaining peace and stability on the Korean Peninsula," *Xinhuanet*, October 10, 2012: http://news.xinhuanet.com/english/video/2012-10/10/c_131897621.htm.

[12] V. I. Denisov, "Inter-Korean Settlement and Russia's Interests," *International Affairs* 51, no. 3 (2005): 125–136.

attractive than the South Korean commitment to US military presence, even after the reunification of Korea.

Normalization of relations between the DPRK and the ROK, and the eventual reunification of both parts of the Peninsula, are expected to provide more favorable opportunities for the development of trade and economic cooperation between China and both parts of a unified Korea.

Some experts believe that a unified Korea would be a good political and economic counterbalance to Japan, especially in view of the latter's obvious inability to play a more independent role in international affairs.

Obstacles for Sino–Japanese Partnership in Korea

There are quite a number of factors that drastically limit opportunities for China–Japan cooperation on the Korean Peninsula. These factors are caused by delicate issues in bilateral Sino–Japanese relations and their respective policies both on the Korean Peninsula and in Northeast Asia. Among them it is possible to name the following major factors:

1. Japan's position concerning the Taiwanese issue.

2. Unresolved territorial disputes over the Senkaku/Diaoyu Islands.

3. Strengthening the US–Japanese military-political alliance and attempts to use it as a cornerstone for encircling China by linking Australia and other US allies to the alliance.[13]

4. Deployment of theater missile defense (TMD) systems in Northeast Asia by the United States with Japan's participation. There are fears that TMD will result in a sharp change of strategic balance in the region, thus giving a push to a new arms race and leading to the emergence of new lines of division and discord in Northeast Asia.

5. Incessant attempts to conduct a revision of Japan's constitution with the purpose of allowing *de jure* use of armed forces outside the country (this has already been implemented *de facto* in Iraq).[14]

[13] Defense White Paper, Seoul, Republic of Korea: The Ministry of National Defense, 2008, 15.
[14] *Nezavisimaya Gazeta*, November 1, 2005.

6. Fears concerning the transformation of Japan's nuclear policy. They are caused by both Japan's technical capabilities and its stocks of plutonium, as well as statements by some Japanese politicians. North Korea's first nuclear test in 2006 opened the gates for a public discussion on nuclear weapons. It is possible that under a certain combination of domestic and international factors, Japan might reconsider the existing nuclear policy.

7. Contrary to Japan, which so far has failed to establish diplomatic relations with the DPRK, China maintains diplomatic relations with both Korean states. Besides, China and the DPRK have a long history of friendship and cooperation in various spheres. While China–DPRK relations during recent years have demonstrated a clear tendency to strengthen both political and economic spheres, Japan's ties with North Korea have proved to be moving in the opposite direction. The DPRK is the only country with which China still has a military-political treaty, signed in 1961, on friendship, cooperation, and mutual assistance.

8. China has none of the fears concerning North Korea's missiles and nuclear weapons which exist in Japan. It is highly unlikely that the DPRK will ever use its nuclear weapons against China; however, most experts agree that they could be used against the US bases in Japan in case of an attack on the DPRK.

9. China sympathizes with Japan's efforts to find a solution to the issue of abducted Japanese citizens. At the same time, Beijing believes that the search for a resolution to the problem should not hinder the achievement of the main objective of the Six-Party Talks—to ensure a non-nuclear status for the Korean Peninsula. It seems that the unwavering priority given by Tokyo to the abduction issue has deprived Japan's foreign policy of the flexibility which the present complicated circumstances necessitate.

10. Beijing and Tokyo have different approaches to the solution of the nuclear problem on the Korean Peninsula. These disagreements include responsibility for the current situation, the scope of the DPRK's nuclear program, which part of it should be eliminated (only that meant for military use, or all of it, including that intended for peaceful use), the scale and depth of forthcoming inspections, the conditions and character of security guarantees, and the degree

of economic assistance to be given to the DPRK. Beijing believes that the solution to the problem is to be found not merely through those methods which Japan recently has been pursuing, e.g., Japan's policy of unilaterally applying sanctions even before the UNSC makes a decision on the matter.

11. Beijing and Tokyo have differing visions of the future of a united Korea in the regional and global systems of international relations. Tokyo sees unification within the framework of a tripartite alliance with Washington and Seoul.[15] Such an approach can hardly satisfy Beijing and Moscow. Both of them are likely to perceive such an alliance as a mechanism of containment, or even deterrence, against China and Russia. This is also the perception of these two continental powers concerning the continued presence of foreign troops on the Korean Peninsula, even after reunification the country. This difference is of such importance that, in the author's opinion, it deserves a detailed explanation.

In Search of a New Security Order in Northeast Asia

Our experience of the negotiations on the Korean Peninsula for the resolution of the nuclear issue leads us to conclude that without a solution to certain fundamental problems directly related to the region's future security structure, we will not be capable of tackling the nuclear crisis.

The fundamental key issue to be resolved is how to find a place for a future unified Korea within the regional security system, which is acceptable to all the "big countries." Many politicians and experts in the United States, Japan, and the ROK have already listed the reunified Korea as a member of the tripartite alliance of the US–Japan–ROK, to which Australia has been linked since March 2007.[16]

However, such an approach is unlikely to satisfy Beijing and her strategic partner, Moscow. Both countries are likely to perceive such a union as a deterrent against Russia and China. For Russia, such an alliance would be tantamount to the emergence on its eastern borders of a body similar to NATO, under the umbrella of the TMD system which is actively deployed by the United States and its allies in the region.

---

[15] H. Yamaji, *Policy Recommendations for Japan: Unification of the Korean Peninsula* (New York: The Brookings Institution, 2004), 6.

[16] *The Japan Times*, June 15, 2008.

At the same time, the DPRK stands for the establishment of a neutral, non-aligned state on the Korean Peninsula. This approach appears, in terms of ensuring the security of China and Russia, more attractive than some experts' insistence on the need to maintain the US military presence on the Peninsula even after Korea's unification.

The claim that the division of Korea is one of the worst legacies of the "Cold War" has become almost commonplace in all discussions on the situation in the region. However, analysts and policymakers tend to link the resolution of this legacy to the need to achieve change in the foreign and domestic policies of the DPRK that would be desirable for the United States and its allies, or, even better, to realize a regime-change scenario in North Korea.

But are not the US military alliances with Japan and the ROK the same legacy of the "Cold War"? It has been almost two decades since the West announced its victory in the "Cold War," but these alliances have far from been dissolved; on the contrary, one can see incessant attempts to have them strengthened and enlarged.

Some American experts are demanding that the issue of the US military presence on the Korean Peninsula, and in East Asia in general, should not be discussed at any multilateral forum that debates the establishment of regional institutions.[17] They believe that any peace regimes and mechanisms in Northeast Asia should not "put at risk" the existing American military-political alliances with Japan and South Korea, which are expected to remain the foundation of the United States' strong position in Northeast Asia.[18]

Thus, any future mechanism for peace and security in Northeast Asia is actually viewed by many American politicians and experts as a kind of "appendix" to bilateral military-political alliances the United States has had with some countries in the region since the "Cold War" era. This type of mechanism will be assigned two main objectives: consolidating and legitimizing US military and political domination in the region, and exercising control over the policies of those countries with no bilateral alliance with the United States—such as China.

Calculations to the effect that a future united Korea will be a *de facto* forward base of maritime powers (the United States and Japan) against continental powers (China and Russia), can hamper, and is already hindering, both the establishment of a reliable and sustainable peace

---

[17] PacNet Newsletter, no. 35, 2007.
[18] PacNet Newsletter, no. 35, 2007.

system in Northeast Asia, the solution of the nuclear problem, and the reunification of Korea.

The history of the Six-Party Talks shows that this multilateral mechanism for security and cooperation in Northeast Asia could become a credible forum only if it provides for finding and implementing mutually acceptable compromises, and does not become a tool for imposing the interests of one country, or a group of countries, onto other participants of such an organization.

Possible Solutions

Traditional political and economic instruments employed for achieving a Korean settlement so far have not brought any tangible results. Certainly, there was a period of visible progress in political, economic, and humanitarian spheres of exchange between North and South Korea after the first inter-Korean summit of 2000. However, since 2008, inter-Korean relations have been deteriorating rather rapidly. Notwithstanding all positive results brought by the Six-Party process, North Korea is now a *de facto* nuclear power.

Any search for a diplomatic solution to the North Korean problem would be doomed to failure should the blame for these developments fall on the DPRK only. The policy of the United States and Japan towards North Korea during the last two decades has provided Pyongyang's leadership with enough solid ground to suspect that the non-proliferation agenda is employed merely as a tool to achieve their more important foreign or domestic policy goals, that stipulate as a precondition the realization of a regime-change scenario in North Korea.

The United States and its allies should address the North Korean ruling elite's legitimate security concerns and worries. Unless the DPRK's *kanbu* can be provided with clear guarantees of their personal safety, adequate social status, and a certain level of well-being after reunification, the North Korean ruling elite will stay united and remain very reluctant to abandon its nuclear weapons.

This is especially true in view of the unfortunate fates of the ruling elites in Eastern Europe, Yugoslavia, Iraq, and, quite recently, in Libya, which were watched and studied very closely by Pyongyang. The more we wish North Korea to open up and cooperate in various spheres, the more urgent and unavoidable will be the discussion of the future of the North Korean ruling elite in a reunified Korea.

The process of economic integration and globalization in Northeast Asia seems to provide us with new instruments for resolving the problem.

It is highly likely that the more active the involvement of the DPRK in globalization and cooperation processes in Northeast Asia, the more likely it may bring about positive changes in Pyongyang's international behavior. Experience in dealing with the DPRK testifies that excessive pressure and coercion have led, in the majority of cases, to greater suspicion and hostility, while engagement and respect for certain positions shaped by history's legacies have brought about cooperation and compromise.

It appears that the United States is finally starting to realize that it needs to be more specific in its so far rather vague promises to North Korea. A comprehensive package has never been proposed to North Korea, in comparison to what was offered by the EU to Iran. China, and especially Japan, can contribute greatly to such a package designed to solve the Korean Peninsula nuclear problem.

Inviting North Korea to honest participation in the realization of multilateral economic projects, such as the construction of gas and electricity lines from Russia to the Republic of Korea, via North Korean territory, or connecting Korean railways with the Trans-Siberian railway, may convince Pyongyang that the international community has taken a road leading to the DPRK's gradual and peaceful integration into the existing international political and economic order, rather than forcing a regime-change scenario onto the country. Both China and Japan can open a new unexplored field for cooperation on that road.

This is why Russia disagrees with those advocating postponing practical implementation of multilateral economic cooperation projects until the nuclear problem in Korea is resolved. The assumption does not look convincing, considering the fact of ever-growing trade and economic cooperation between China, Russia, and both Korean states.

The current situation on the Korean Peninsula can be resolved satisfactorily only if the legitimate security concerns and economic needs of all states located in the region, including those of the DPRK, are taken into account.

Opportunities for China–Japan Cooperation on the Korean Peninsula

In spite of the above-mentioned differences it is possibly to identify the following similar—perhaps even identical—goals for China and Japan in Korea:

1. Preventing a major military conflict on the Peninsula, since such a conflict inevitably would threaten the security of China and Japan.

2. Ensuring the non-nuclear status of the Korean Peninsula, the non-proliferation of WMD, and preventing the means of their delivery.

3. Encouraging the establishment, on the Korean Peninsula, of a unified state that would not take an unfriendly position towards China or Japan, or provide any third party with the opportunity to endanger China or Japan's security from the Peninsula.

4. Maintaining relations with both Korean states at such a level that would allow China and Japan to have effective leverage to ensure that both Korean states, while pursuing their respective foreign policy goals, would pay due consideration to China and Japan's interests in the spheres of security, politics, economy, and other areas.

5. Ensuring participation of the two Korean states, or a unified Korea, in future implementations of international economic projects which suit the interests of China, Japan, and other Northeast Asian countries.

It is necessary to note that Tokyo is well aware of China's influence on the Peninsula and recognizes China as an important player in the region. However, the Japanese side, as a rule, has preferred to forget about China's own legitimate security interests on the Peninsula, and has attempted to utilize China's influence almost exclusively for exerting additional pressure onto Pyongyang.[19]

Support by China of then Prime Minister Koizumi's visits to Pyongyang in 2002–04, with the aim of normalizing relations with the DPRK, became clear proof of the fact that China considers Japan an important partner in the efforts towards normalization of the situation in the region.

Beijing has hoped that reconciliation between Tokyo and Pyongyang would bring about a relaxation of tension in Northeast Asia and help to put the negotiation process regarding Korea back on track.

One can hope that the recently established trilateral China–Japan–ROK economic cooperation mechanism, with its joint Secretariat and other channels of communication, especially trilateral summits among participants, will contribute to a better understanding of mutual concerns,

---

[19] V. A. Grinyuk, "The Problem of Abduction of Japanese Citizens by the DPRK's Special Services, in *Korea: A View from Russia*, edited by A. Z. Zhebin and K. V. Asmolov (Moscow, 2007): IFES RAS, 89, 91.

curing old grievances and preventing the emergence of new obstacles to genuine reconciliation and friendly relations.

Certainly, opportunities for Sino–Japanese cooperation aimed at the maintenance of peace and stability in Northeast Asia and on the Korean Peninsula are far from exhausted. There are still new fields to explore.

Conclusion

The incumbent Chinese leaders have demonstrated a proactive policy towards the nuclear problem on the Korean Peninsula and on other aspects of the Korean settlement. "The Korean theme" has become one of the main topics of China's top-level contacts, not only with the United States and Russia, but also with Japan.

However, any cooperation between China and Japan on the Korean problem will be more limited compared to a similar scenario with other neighboring countries, unless Japan takes a more independent and constructive approach to the situation.

The experience of the Korean settlement since the first nuclear crisis on the Peninsula in 1993/94 is not a good one. The process has been unproductive, and has experienced abrupt policy changes and political declarations, unilateral sanctions, and excessive pressure. The suspension of the Six-Party Talks, along with long interruptions in Japan–DPRK normalization talks, has vividly demonstrated the kind of results such an approach could bring about. It is especially important to take these circumstances into consideration in East Asia where "a face-saving" solution of a dispute is generally considered a much more important and acceptable outcome than one side's victory.

CHAPTER ELEVEN

JAPAN–CHINA COOPERATION IN FUTURE SCENARIOS FOR THE KOREAN PENINSULA: SOFT-LANDING, COLLAPSE, AND MUDDLING-THROUGH CASES

HIROYASU AKUTSU

Introduction: How can Japan and China cooperate in future Korean Peninsula scenarios?

Kim Jong-il died in December 2011 after nearly three years of rapid-paced power succession to his third son, Kim Jong-un. In August three years earlier, Kim Jong-il had reportedly suffered from a stroke, causing the twelfth Supreme People's Assembly election slated for September to be postponed. It was not until November that reports surfaced on Kim Jong-il's activities and visits to military facilities, with photos showing him in a state of good health. Regardless of this incident, an election was eventually held in March and the first session of the twelfth Supreme People's Assembly was held on April 9, 2009, when Kim Jong-il was re-elected as Chairman of the National Military Commission. Simultaneously, the membership of the Commission was also refreshed to solidify leadership under Kim Jong-il. A long-range rocket/missile had been launched from *Musudanri* on April 5, and the launch was used to surround the new leadership with fanfare and raise the dignity of the regime. Furthermore, North Korea conducted its second nuclear test on May 5, and since then has continued to conduct missile tests in defiance of United Nations Security Council (UNSC) Resolution 1874.

As of February 2012, the Six-Party Talks, that were addressing North Korea's nuclear problem and aiming to comprehensively solve other political and security issues concerning the Korean Peninsula, have been stuck in deadlock. International efforts are ongoing to bring North Korea back into dialogue and to implement UNSC Resolution 1874 to sanction North Korea for launching a *Taepodong-2* missile on April 5, for conducting a second nuclear test on May 25, and for launching an advanced long-range missile on July 8. With hindsight we can see that these events, and the Cheonan and Yonpyong incidents in 2010, were closely related to the power-succession process. One could interpret these offensive attacks as Kim Jong-un's "military achievements" to legitimize Kim Jong-un as Supreme Commander of the North Korean People's Army. As of April 2012, the new North Korean regime, under Kim Jong-un, seemed likely to complete the power-succession process in a relatively smooth way.

However, the ongoing stability of the political process in and around North Korea cannot be guaranteed. As suggested by several intelligence and academic assessments,[1] in the long term the North Korean regime can still be seen as highly fragile. Before any contingencies occur, it is important to study potential critical scenarios for the Korean Peninsula to manage and minimize the impact of uncontrollable possible situations, so that countries in the surrounding region can reduce uncertainties pertaining to their own security and maintain regional stability. This kind of study can also provide some useful hints, or serve as a guide for policy experts, regarding a response to any type of contingency on the Korean Peninsula.[2]

Generally speaking, analyzing scenarios for international contingencies or future courses of events helps illuminate the possible cooperative and confrontational elements amongst the different parties. In the case of the Korean Peninsula, undertaking scenario analysis could help both Japan and China make better choices on future policies geared towards stability and peace-building in the region. Given that Japan and China have already been developing their "strategic relationship based on mutual benefits" (戦略的互恵関係), it would be useful for both countries to clarify their position in the case of various contingencies on the Korean Peninsula, and also regarding the unification of the two Koreas.

---

[1] See, for example, A. A. Dynkin, *Strategic Global Outlook 2030* (Moscow: Institute of World Economic and International Relations, Russian Academy of Sciences, 2011), 43.

[2] One of the most recent and well-known studies is P. B. Stares, J. W. Vessey, and J. S. Wit, *Preparing for Sudden Change in North Korea* (New York and Washington: Council on Foreign Relations Press, 2009), Council Special Report No. 42.

Setting a "realistic" assumption: More restrained behavior by neighboring countries

Numerous war games and simulations regarding contingencies and other less critical situations on the Korean Peninsula have been carried out for the past decade in Japan and, most likely, in other Northeast Asian countries as well. Both governmental and non-governmental policy experts have tried analyzing a number of dire scenarios involving the two sides of the Korean Peninsula, the United States, China, Russia, Japan, and the international community.

As long as tension on the Korean Peninsula continues to fluctuate according to the changing situation, these efforts will not cease. At the same time, the Peninsula has managed to avoid any scenarios that could lead to the sudden collapse of the regime in North Korea in one way or another. Consequently, the ruling regime has survived to this day. North Korea's regime survival has been reinforced by economic, humanitarian, and political aid from China, South Korea, Russia, the United States, Japan, and the international community. The Agreed Framework of 1994 and the Korean Peninsula Energy Development Organization (KEDO), founded in 1995 to implement the Agreed Framework, with a ten-year target time frame, was the most comprehensive institutional arrangement in this category. The Agreed Framework and the KEDO were terminated under the George Bush administration, but the current Six-Party Talks have functioned as a less institutionalized, but the only *de facto*, regional arrangement to replace the Agreed Framework and the KEDO. The talks still hold some potential to become a more institutionalized arrangement.

The Six-Party Talks have come to a standstill due to North Korea's second nuclear test and her launching of ballistic missiles in 2009. The possibility of North Korea returning to the talks is still very slight and it is difficult to anticipate the full achievement of the expected results of the Six-Party Talks in the future.

Regardless, it is likely that the five remaining countries in the talks will continue acting to avoid any confrontational scenarios that involve direct US military strikes against North Korea and/or complicate their strategic calculations. At the same time, the five countries may shift their focus to consultation and coordination among themselves, through what is called the "Five-Party Talks." What is of interest is the tendency, on the part of the United States, to avoid any preemptive military strikes against North Korea, even though in reality North Korea has a limited advantage in conventional weaponry over the South Korean and US forces, located between Seoul and the demilitarized zone. Specifically, North Korea has approximately twelve thousand artillery guns deployed underground in the north of the demilitarized zone, most of which were believed to be targeting both the US Army Second Infantry Division and a major part of Seoul.[3] In the event of an escalation, the United States may well successfully bomb the suspected nuclear sites, but North Korea could still execute a massive artillery strike against Seoul and US forces.[4] US military planners and administration officials have expressed their concerns, especially after 9/11, about the possibility that North Korea's artillery guns could carry biological and chemical warheads. The potential consequences of these kinds of strikes had worked to restrain the Clinton administration from actually bombing North Korea's recognized nuclear facilities in Nyongbyon/Yongbyon and Taechon in 1994. Although threats of such strikes could be shown, in one way or another, to warn North Korea against provocation, US military strikes on North Korea are unlikely for the time being. Therefore, any kind of engagement policy by the United States, South Korea, China, Russia, and Japan, and economic and other humanitarian aid from the international community, would only continue to help sustain the longevity of the regime.

In retrospect, in the past fifteen years we have witnessed a relatively stable Korean Peninsula in the sense that no large-scale war has actually broken out between North Korea and the US–South Korea alliance, and the neighboring countries are exercising restraint towards North Korea's provocations. Even when North Korea conducted a nuclear explosion test in October 2006, the five countries did not respond aggressively, and showed their preference for stability over the uncertain development of military conflict.

For Russia, the linkage of its Trans-Siberian railway to the potential North–South Korean railway would be critical to its economic development. From a traditional strategic point of view, although Russia's *de facto* relationship with North Korea is less than that of purely military allies, the continuation of the DPRK to serve as a buffer state against the US–South Korea alliance would not harm its interest in the least. Thus, Russia would wish to opt for stability over military conflict on the Peninsula. In fact, Russia has been opposed to any military confrontation on the Peninsula since the 1993/94 nuclear crises.

China would also act to avoid the negative ramifications of chaos or the collapse of the regime in North Korea, especially around the China–

---

[3] Gary Luck and William Perry, "Testimony at the US Senate," US Department of State transcript, January 15, 1995; see also D. Oberdorfer, *The Two Koreas: A Contemporary History* (Massachusetts: Addison-Wesley, 1997), 313–314.

[4] Oberdorfer, *The Two Koreas*, 313–314.

North Korea border area. However, the possibility of incursion into North Korean territory by the People's Liberation Army to rescue civilians, or to prevent critical sites from allowing dangerous materials to be taken outside of North Korea, cannot be precluded. According to a report released by the Center for Strategic and International Studies in Washington DC in January 2008, some researchers in the People's Liberation Army would consider taking control of such dangerous material in such a situation.[5] Geo-strategically speaking, too, China would wish to maintain North Korea as a buffer state against the US–South Korea alliance. China would also choose to maintain the status quo of the divided Korean Peninsula until North Korea's economy becomes more controllable, in favor of the Chinese economy.

What about Japan? Japan would also wish to avoid any military conflict on the Peninsula. In the case of direct military confrontation between North Korea and the US–South Korea alliance, Japan would play only the minor role of providing logistic support for the United States, its only ally. Even if South Korea were attacked by the North Korean artillery and a major part of Seoul turned into a "sea of fire," Japan would have to depend on the United States or South Korea to rescue Japanese residents there. Only when South Koreans have overcome their negative sentiments towards the Japanese would Japan be able to send in her own Self-Defense Force for rescue missions. In addition, it has become clear that there are more Japanese civilians who were abducted by North Korea, which Kim Jong-il himself confessed to during his meeting with Prime Minister Junichiro Koizumi in 2003. Even though Kim had promised the return of several abductees to Japan, the fate of those remaining in North Korea is still a major subject of concern in Japan, and would remain so if the situation in North Korea deteriorates.

North Korea's missile and nuclear tests in 2006, and missile/rocket launch in 2009, have raised concerns about the fate of missile, nuclear, and other military sites in North Korea during, or after, a possible regime collapse or leadership change in Pyongyang. Apart from those located underground, US intelligence satellites may have already identified these sites. Even though the United States, Russia, and China may have their own separate intelligence on those sites, through their contact with North Korean former officials who had defected to a third country, there will always be ambiguities with regards to this intelligence. North Korea has

---

[5] B. Glaser, S. Snyder, and J. S. Park, *Keeping an Eye on an Unruly Neighbor: Chinese Views on Economic Reform and Stability in North Korea*, United States Institute of Peace Working Paper, January 3, 2008, 4–5 and 19–20.

been opportunistic enough to take advantage of such ambiguities and the neighboring countries have tended to act in a restrained manner.

Will the above observation in favor of cautious and restrained behavior by the Korean Peninsula's neighbors be likely to hold in the future? Now that the Six-Party Talks are in place, the tendency of the northeastern countries to share information and to cooperate may have been reinforced. I argue that under conditions of greater uncertainty—for example, when faced with the impending collapse of the regime in North Korea—then information-sharing would be less forthcoming. Below, I will outline a very brief scenario analysis concerning three divergent cases.

Three divergent scenarios: Soft-landing, collapse, and muddling-through cases

Scenario One: The Soft-landing

The soft-landing scenario envisaged here is that the Six-Party Talks, which have actually been the only formal part of the diplomatic and multilateral framework, would lead to a successful soft landing for the North Korean regime, and the eventual reunification of the two Koreas.

As of mid-2009, the Six-Party Talks stalled during the middle of the second phase of the denuclearization of North Korea, or the "Korean Peninsula": namely, the disablement of the Nyongbyon/Yongbyon nuclear facility. The disablement work will not be restarting anytime soon due to the current political and diplomatic deadlock between North Korea and the other member countries of the Six-Party Talks. It seems that more cooling-off time will be needed before the talks can resume.

However, if we assume that the Six-Party Talks will continue as planned in the Joint Statements of September 19, 2005 and February 13, 2007, the second phase of the denuclearization of North Korea will end when the disablement of the Nyongbyon/Yongbyon nuclear facility is completed. If the second phase is completed, then the third phase would proceed with progress on the other four areas of cooperation within the Six-Party Talks program. Since 2006, there have been five working groups within the Six-Party Talks based on the five areas of cooperation stipulated in the Joint Statement of September 19, 2005. They are: (1) disablement/dismantlement of North Korea's nuclear programs/weapon(s), (2) economic and energy assistance to North Korea, (3) normalization of bilateral relations between the United States and North Korea, and Japan and North Korea, (4) construction of a peace regime on the Korean

Peninsula, and (5) the establishment of a peace and security mechanism beyond the Korean Peninsula and in Northeast Asia.

In this scenario, it is easy to see the role of China and Japan in the disablement/dismantlement of North Korea's nuclear programs/weapon(s). For the disablement and dismantlement work, both countries can provide technical personnel in cooperation with the other three member countries and the International Atomic Energy Agency (IAEA) or the broader non-proliferation community.

In terms of energy and economic assistance (item 2), both countries can make great contributions. If North Korea were to be provided with light-water nuclear reactors (the country was supposed to receive two light-water nuclear reactors through the KEDO), Japan and China could provide financial, technical, and personnel assistance to North Korea in cooperation with other Six-Party Talks member countries.

Regarding the normalization of bilateral relations between the United States and North Korea, and between Japan and North Korea (item 3), although they are bilateral issues, China would be able to strengthen her support for the improvement of relations between Japan and North Korea.

As for the construction of a peace regime on the Korean Peninsula (item 4), China is directly involved in this discussion because she was on North Korea's side against the South Korea–US side during the Korean War. Japan is not a direct party to this discussion, but given that Japan was on the side of the United States and South Korea, Japan would be willing and able to provide some support in the course of this discussion.

The establishment of a peace and security mechanism beyond the Korean Peninsula in Northeast Asia (item 5) is supposed to materialize only after the successful denuclearization of North Korea. Under the current situation, this seems to be the most challenging task for the member countries of the Six-Party Talks. However, under Russia's chairmanship, the working group for this task has been held several times and several experts have already put forward their own designs for such a multilateral security mechanism.[6]

---

[6] One of the most recent and detailed proposals of a Northeast Asian security mechanism would be that suggested by Charles L. Prichard, President of the Korean Economic Institute, former US ambassador and special envoy for negotiations with North Korea, and representative to the KEDO. See C. L. Prichard, *Failed Diplomacy: The Tragic Story of How North Korea Got the Bomb* (Washington, DC: The Brookings Institution, 2007), 176–184.

Scenario Two: The collapse of the North Korean regime

As mentioned earlier, there are a large number of contingency and scenario studies regarding the Korean Peninsula. Instead of reviewing all of the existing studies, I briefly discuss two major potential consequences of the collapse of the North Korean regime, or the loss of state control in North Korea.[7] The definition of "collapse" is controversial and the task of defining the term poses an intellectual challenge in itself. For the sake of analytical utility, this chapter makes no assumption on the nature of the collapse and focuses instead on the aftermath of such an event, concerning itself with a chaotic situation involving an exodus of refugees, and dangerous materials, related to weapons of mass destruction (WMD), falling into the wrong hands, such as those of terrorists and radicals.[8]

Refugee flow

Refugee flow is a common subject of discussion among the countries of the region. It has been recognized as one of the consequences of regime collapse or other similar situations. China has the longest land border with North Korea and should therefore have the largest concern about incoming refugees. China has already had to deal with refugees during normal and/or less critical times. Russia, which has a shorter borderline with North Korea, has also been concerned about such refugees. South Korea has been the main "final" destination for refugees from China and Russia in the past, and the refugee issue has become a major social concern in South Korea. In the event of a North Korean collapse, this chapter argues that South Korea would take some measures to address this scenario, regardless of whether America's help might be forthcoming.

From Japan's standpoint, the most pressing problem would be a refugee exodus from North Korea into Japan. The Japanese government has already analyzed a number of scenarios that deal with such an eventuality.[9] The Japanese government has forecast a rise in the number of refugees to around 100–150,000 and Japan's principal concern, from the point of view of Japan's national security, is the flow of North Korean

---

[7] This chapter will not define "collapse" in detail, but one can categorize collapse into regime collapse, systemic collapse, and state collapse.

[8] It should be noted that refugee and WMD material flows out of North Korea could also occur during the process of a regime collapse or some kind of chaos rather than as a consequence of such a situation.

[9] Kim Yun-gi, "150,000 North Korean Refugees reach Japan in Korean Peninsula Contingencies," *Jungan Ilbo*, January 6, 2007.

agents, disguised as refugees, into Japan.[10] The actual number of potential North Korean refugees into Japan is controversial and could be found to be much lower than current estimates if more detailed analyses were conducted regarding physical conditions in North Korea, but the possibility of such a contingency happening cannot be precluded.

Chaos over the nuclear and other WMD-related sites

Another major common concern among the neighboring countries would be the fate of North Korea's nuclear and other WMD-related sites, and the experts in those technologies. If these weaponry, materials, and experts could be quickly subsumed under the control of the new leadership in North Korea, then the five powers—the United States, the PRC, the ROK, Japan, and Russia—could be given some kind of assurance by the new leadership, thereby alleviating their fears. However, if this should not be the case, the situation might deteriorate as these weapons, materials, and experts fall into the hands of terrorists outside the country. The possible reactions of Japan, China, Russia, and the United States are listed in Table 1.

Table 1: Initial responses of neighboring countries under limited information sharing in case of contingencies

Country	Refugee exodus	Chaos in WMD-related sites
United States	Containment	Non-intervention or more limited intervention
China	Containment	Non-intervention or more limited intervention
Russia	Containment	Containment or more limited intervention
Japan	Limited acceptance	Non-intervention

Containment

The United States and South Korea might strengthen the security of the borderline with North Korea, including the demilitarized zone and the Northern Limit Line, to prevent North Korean refugees from entering South Korea. South Korea, China, and Russia would also tighten security controls over their border with North Korea. Yet, regardless of the added

[10] Yun-gi, "150,000 North Korean Refugees."

security, these borderlines remain porous, and it is entirely possible that many desperate North Korean refugees would still be able to successfully enter China or Russia. While China and Russia might be able to "round up" these refugees, they might be forced to exercise restraint in their treatment of them, in the presence of human rights NGOs that would most likely be present in the border areas. Japan is more fortunate in the sense that it has a natural maritime barrier, i.e., the Sea of Japan. Nonetheless, Japan would strengthen its maritime security against the North Korean "boatpeople," especially when some of these refugees may be North Korean special agents. However, if they are found to be "clean," then Japan might have to accept them for some period of time. While some experts estimate that there would be only a small number of such refugees entering Japanese waters, in the case of a regime collapse in Pyongyang, others estimate that between 100,000 and 150,000 North Korean refugees would come from Wonsan and Chongjin towards Kyushu and Shikoku.[11]

Intervention

The United States, or the US–South Korea alliance, might directly advance into North Korea to take control of its nuclear or other critical sites. However, they might be faced with a lack of intelligence reports on the whereabouts of these facilities, and on how to reach the core part of the existing regime leadership.

The United States has done much work on the various cost–benefit profiles of strikes on North Korean capabilities. For example, the US Clinton administration had seriously considered surgical/limited bombing strikes on North Korea's recognized nuclear facilities and concluded that doing so would bring about major military, economic, political, and social repercussions on and around the Korean Peninsula.[12] The problem was the possibility that artillery guns, located in the Northern part of the demilitarized zone, might cause major damage to Seoul and the US Second Infantry Division, located between the demilitarized zone and Seoul.[13]

Another military option the United States might consider would be a large-scale military attack on North Korea. However, again, the possibility of Seoul and the US Army Second Infantry Division being attacked in retaliation cannot be precluded. In addition, the United States has learned

[11] Yun-gi, "150,000 North Korean Refugees."

[12] Luck and Perry, "Testimony at the US Senate"; see also Oberdorfer, *The Two Koreas*.

[13] Oberdorfer, *The Two Koreas*.

many lessons from the War on Terror in Iraq, and as a consequence this option holds limited appeal.

In either case, the possibility of the collapse of the North Korean regime under US military strikes seems too costly for the United States and its consequences too risky for the neighboring countries to take.

Limited information-sharing and the difficulty of coordination

It is difficult for the involved parties to coordinate their policies and measures in advance given that information-sharing among them is, in reality, very limited. Moreover, because of the "political incorrectness" of multilateral coordination (except for cooperative "engagement" with North Korea) and the sensitivity of intelligence-sharing, it would be even more difficult for them to take coordinated actions as a group, even though the United States, South Korea, and Japan could more easily cooperate with one another within the US–South Korea alliance and the US–Japan alliance frameworks. China and Russia could act, both individually and within the Six-Party Talks. However, conventional wisdom tells us that nation-states would not easily share sensitive information.

Scenario Three: A muddling-through and "nuclearized" North Korea

This muddling-through scenario assumes that North Korea manages to survive and eventually become a nuclear weapons' state with a fragile economy. This is one of the most appalling situations, for both the region and the world. In such a scenario, Northeast Asian neighbors are forced to coexist with a hostile nuclear North Korea, and South Korea, in particular, would be faced with the danger of being absorbed into the North by force. As North Korea's security autonomy from China and Russia increases, the relative influence of the two allies on North Korea would decline. Consequently, Japan would feel even more threatened by North Korea's mid-range ballistic nuclear-tipped missiles, and the United States would have to strengthen its capabilities to defend its military bases, facilities, and citizens in the region. In particular, the United States might either voluntarily enter, or become pressured into, a position where it has to strengthen its alliance ties with South Korea and Japan. Thus, this muddling-through and a "nuclearized" North Korea would eventually reinforce the continuation of the status quo, the divided Korean Peninsula.

Japan–China cooperation in the Korean Peninsula unification process

The case of the "successful" scenario of future cooperation between Japan and China assumes a better-informed situation where Japan and China would share more information with an eye towards some kind of soft-landing result.

On the other hand, the hard-landing scenario invariably involves the assumption that such a scenario would entail much less information for the parties involved, uncertainties could become even more enlarged, and the parties' mutual suspicions could be reinforced. This provides an opportunity and a need for international cooperation, and Japan and China would be compelled to coordinate their actions under this dire scenario. Victor Cha, former Director for East Asian Affairs in the US National Security Council, has called for preparations to be made for contingencies in the wake of a possible collapse of the North Korean regime.[14] Under Cha's proposal, the United States should discuss countermeasures with South Korea and would involve Japan in a three-way discussion on refugee-related measures and additional logistical assistance. The United States would consult with China as well.[15]

In addition, there are reportedly researchers within the People's Liberation Army who support entering into formal discussions with the United States to ensure the common objective of securing the safety of nuclear weapons and materials.[16] There is no reason to exclude the possibility of Japan–China cooperation under such a scenario. Especially from the standpoint of crisis management, this paper proposes that Japan and China should start discussing how to share information, provide joint humanitarian assistance and rescue operations, coordinate measures dealing with refugees, and prevent nuclear, biological, and chemical material flows. In the situation of anarchy in North Korea, Japan and China might have to discuss how to provide provisional governance for stabilization in the country.

Finally, under the scenario of a muddling-through and a "nuclearized" North Korea, Japan–China cooperation would revolve around the following two possibilities: joint roll-back/elimination measures, and joint accommodation/cooperative threat-reduction (CTR) measures. For roll-back/elimination of North Korea's nuclear weapons, Japan and China

---

[14] Victor Cha, "We Have No Plan," *Chosun Ilbo*, June 9, 2008.

[15] Cha, "We Have No Plan."

[16] Glaser, Snyder, and Park, *Keeping an Eye on an Unruly Neighbor*.

would have to resort to a more offensive approach towards North Korea. Such an approach would involve what is called counter-proliferation, which may be accompanied by increased military pressure, or threat of use of military force.

Table 2: Japan–China cooperation in the unification process and after

Scenario	Japan–China cooperation
Soft-landing through the Six-Party Process	*Multilateral cooperation* –Technical assistance to disablement and dismantlement towards full denuclearization –Economic and energy assistance –Improving bilateral relations towards normalization –Supporting a peace regime on the Korean Peninsula –Promoting the discussion of security issues in Northeast Asia *Bilateral cooperation* –Promoting the above efforts through Japan–China joint activities –Encouraging general confidence-building measures
Collapse and chaos	–Sharing information –Joint humanitarian assistance including joint rescue operations and coordinated measures for refugees –Joint measures for the prevention of nuclear, biological, and chemical material flows –Helping to provide a provisional governance for stabilization
Muddling-through and acquiring a limited nuclear deterrent	–Joint roll-back/elimination measures –Joint accommodation/joint cooperative threat-reduction measures –coexistence with a "nuclearized" North Korea

Regarding joint accommodation, Japan and China could provide some incentives to North Korea in exchange for North Korea making significant progress in nuclear disarmament. For example, cooperative threat reduction (CTR) would be a promising strategy. CTR is similar to what can be done between Japan and China within the framework of the soft-landing process discussed earlier in this chapter. If Japan and China could jointly establish a project to denuclearize North Korea, and encourage North Korea to become a more open and freer political entity and economy by providing political and economic incentives, then this would be another favorable course of events for Japan, China, and the rest of the region and the world.

Alternatively, if North Korea would not agree to denuclearization and Japan and China had to accommodate the country and treat it as a *de facto* nuclear weapons state, both Japan and China would have to learn to coexist with the regime. This scenario would be the worst possible scenario for both Japan and China.

Conclusion

The three representative scenarios examined in this chapter reaffirm the necessity of cooperation between Japan and China with regards to issues on the Korean Peninsula. The hard-landing and muddle-through scenarios all entail negative consequences, indicating that China and Japan must work closely together to overcome these challenges. This chapter is not arguing for "cooperation for the sake of cooperation" between China and Japan over future events on the Korean Peninsula. However, if Japan and China are to make *strategic* choices over the Korean Peninsula in the future, and if both countries want to materialize their *strategic* relations based on mutual benefit (戦略的互恵関係), then Japan and China need to have specific discussions on what contingencies could occur and how both countries can work together in the various phases of those contingencies. It is never too late to begin discussing. If this is difficult on the Track 1, or governmental, level, it could be done on the Track 1.5 or Track 2 levels.

As mentioned at the beginning of this chapter, the future of the Kim Jong-un regime in North Korea is uncertain and the possibility of dire scenarios cannot be precluded. Hopefully, this chapter will serve to make a meaningful addition to the existing contingency studies over the Korean Peninsula and help provide some basis for future cooperation between Japan and China over the Korean Peninsula.

CHAPTER TWELVE

THE DEMOCRATIC PEOPLE'S REPUBLIC OF KOREA (DPRK) IN JAPAN'S NORMALIZATION AND CHINA'S PEACEFUL RISE: PROSPECTS AND CHALLENGES

VICTOR TEO

Over the last two decades, the profiles of the two Koreas—North and South—in global affairs[1] have never been higher. Both countries make the international headlines regularly, though for radically different reasons, and both seem to exercise an influence in international diplomacy that is disproportionate relative to their size. The Republic of Korea (South Korea) has clearly emerged as the most prominent of the four Newly Industrialized Economies (NIES) in Asia in the post–Cold War world. The renaissance of South Korea after the 1997 Asian Financial Crisis has been remarkable, and today her innovative economy has emerged to be one of the strongest in East Asia. Thanks to the ROK–United States Alliance, Korea has one of the most modern and well-equipped conventional forces[2]

[1] The article draws in part on the conceptual work done in a project funded by the Hong Kong Research Council (Project Number HKU 753310H) on Japan's normalization and the implications for her foreign policy. The author gratefully acknowledges the support of the Hong Kong Research Council for their generous assistance with this research theme.

[2] The Republic of Korea (ROK) has an active combined force of 655,000 personnel with 4.5 million troops in reserve and 3 million in the paramilitary forces. In 2010, ROK military expenditure was 29.1 trillion US dollars. The Democratic People's Republic of Korea (DPRK) has the fourth-largest standing Army in the world with an active combined force of 1.19 million, with another 6

in East Asia, with well over 2,400 main battle tanks as the backbone of her mechanized forces, as well as a fleet of advanced fighters with ten squadrons of F-16C/D Fighting Falcons and three Squadrons of F-15K Eagles.[3] South Korea is also at the forefront of regionalization[4] efforts in their bid to wrest some degree of control from ASEAN, which arguably has been in the driver's seat for the last two decades. Ban Ki-moon, a former foreign minister, assumed the office of the Secretary-General of the United Nations in 2007,[5] while in April 2008 Yi So-yeon became the first Korean national[6] and the second Asian female astronaut in space. South Korea's impeccable handling of high-profile international sporting events such as the 1988 Olympics and 2008 World Cup with Japan has shown the world that South Korea consistently punches above its weight in international affairs. The Hallyu[7] (Korean Wave) has struck Southeast Asia and the world, bringing to Korea an unprecedented degree of cultural influence and softpower. Like the J-pop wave during the 1970s and 1980s, more people across Asia—Japan included—are learning the Korean language, watching Korean dramas, indulging in Korean cuisine, and

---

million in reserve. Most remarkably, North Korea has a Special Forces Command with 88,000 troops. See "The Military Balance 2012," published by the International Institute for Strategic Studies, http://www.tandfonline.com/doi/pdf/10.1080/04597222.2012.663215: 255–262.

[3] The Military Balance 2012, 259.

[4] The China–Japan–South Korea Trilateral was first raised by South Korea in 2004, ostensibly to wrestle some form of control of regionalization from ASEAN-led efforts. The first meeting was held in 2008, and in 2013 the sixth meeting between the leaders of China, Japan, and Korea took place. The scope and depth of the cooperation, however, is still relatively limited. There are institutionalized meetings of the heads of governments and foreign ministers, and talks are limited to economic and financial cooperation and disaster relief and recovery.

[5] Ban Ki-moon's candidacy was supported by the majority of the fifteen UN Security Council members as evidenced by the informal polls leading up to the nomination. Japan was apparently horrified by the prospects that a Korean national would become the Secretary-General but, later on, changed her position to abstention when it became evident that the majority of the Council members had supported Ban, and that all the other members had at least an objection from the Permanent Members.

[6] "Woman to be first South Korean in Space," *New York Times*, 10 March, 2008: http://www.nytimes.com/2008/03/10/world/asia/10ihtastro.1.10867611.html?_r=0.

[7] "K-Drama leads Hallyu," http://www.koreatimes.co.kr/www/news/culture/2012/12/201_117894.html; see also D. Shim, "Hybridity and the Rise of Korean Popular Culture in Asia," *Media Culture and Society* 28, no. 1 (2006): 25–44.

visiting South Korean destinations.[8] South Korean companies, such as Samsung and Hyundai, have influenced the lives of people the world over with their cheap and reliable goods, to the extent that many Japanese and American companies are losing their market share to the Korean Chaebols. Most recently there has been significant press coverage of the global legal battle between Apple Inc. and Samsung Corporation over their intellectual property rights[9] and smartphone designs.[10]

The People's Democratic of Korea (DPRK), on the other hand, has been making headlines for very different and usually negative reasons. The DPRK is portrayed as ruled by cognac-sipping despots[11] who live a life of debauchery[12] while maintaining an iron grip over the failing economy, where people are starving to death[13] under the ideology of *juche*

---

[8] At the time of going to press, Korean pop sensation Psy holds the world record for largest number of YouTube hits (1.33 billion), for his song "Gangnam Style."

[9] "Apple versus Samsung: The Clash of the Smartphones," August 13, 2012: http://kwhs.wharton.upenn.edu/2012/08/apple-vs-samsung-the-clash-of-the-smartphones/.

[10] CNN Wire Staff, "Samsung to Fight Court Ruling in Apple court dispute," *CNN*, August 27, 2012, http://edition.cnn.com/2012/08/25/tech/mobile/apple-samsung-case.

[11] See comments by Wolf Blitzer, "North Korean Leader Loves Hennessy, Bond Movies," January 8, 2013, http://articles.cnn.com/2003-01-08/us/wbr.kim.jong.il_1_north-korean-leader-house-arrest-hennessey?_s=PM:US; see also NBC report, " Cigars, Cognac and Mass Starvation: 10 Facts that Divide North Korea from the World" *NBC News*, December 19, 2011, http://www.msnbc.msn.com/id/45725040/ns/world_news-asia_pacific/t/cigars-cognac-mass-starvation-facts-divide-north-korea-world/#.UPozEKVC9hI; "Kim Jong-il, the Tyrant with a Passion for Wine, Women and the Bomb," *The Independent*, October 21, 2006: http://www.independent.co.uk/news/world/asia/kim-jong-il-the-tyrant-with-a-passion-for-wine-women-and-the-bomb-421016.html.

[12] The DPRK leadership is known to maintain "pleasure squads" (known as Kippumjo) which are estimated to be made up of 2,000 young girls to service the sexual, physical, and entertainment needs of the ruling class. Little is known about these groups but there is emerging testimony from defectors who have escaped from North Korea. See "'Pleasure Squad' Defector Sheds Light on Life of Kim Jong Il," *The National*, January 8, 2010, http://www.thenational.ae/news/world/asia-pacific/pleasure-squad-defector-sheds-light-on-life-of-kim-jong-il#page1; also see "The Commander's Special Pleasure, the 'Pleasure Group'," *Daily North Korea*, September 25, 2005:
http://www.dailynk.com/english/read.php?cataId=nk02300 &num=289.

[13] There are unsubstantiated but widespread reports in the media suggesting that starving North Koreans have resorted to cannibalism; see B. Demick, *Nothing to*

(self-reliance). With the largest standing army in the world, the Kim regime maintains power through thorough control of all aspects of the lives of the North Koreans, to a degree unseen even in the Soviet Union. The DPRK is characterized as inherently evil, as using the instruments of the state to print counterfeit US dollars and stamps, as manufacturing amphetamines,[14] and as involved in all manner of transnational crime:[15] money laundering, gunrunning, and/or exporting missile parts[16] and nuclear materials to other "pariah" regimes such as Iran, Syria, and Sudan.[17] There is, of course, the familiar pattern of the DPRK breaking off nuclear talks by attaching a string of demands—ranging from food aid to a formal end to the Korean War—as preconditions to returning to the negotiating table. Beyond that, the DPRK has admitted to the kidnapping of Japanese and South Korean nationals, military incursions[18] into South Korea, and increased aggressiveness, as evidenced by the sinking of the

---

Envy: Ordinary Lives in North Korea (New York: Spiel & Grau, 2010); also "North Korean Cannibalism Fears Amid Claims Starving People Forced to Desperate Measures," *The Independent*, January 28, 2013: http://www.independent.co.uk/news/world/asia/north-korean-cannibalism-fears-amid-claims-starving-people-forced-to-desperate-measures-8468781.html; also "The Cannibals of North Korea," *Washington Post*, February 5, 2013: http://www.washingtonpost.com/blogs/worldviews/wp/2013/02/05/the-cannibals-of-north-korea/.

[14] Raphael F. Perl, *Drug Trafficking and North Korea: Issues for US Policy*, CRS Report for Congress, Washington DC, Library of Congress, January 2007; also see Balbina Y. Hwang, "Curtailing North Korea's Illicit Activities," *Backgrounder*, no. 1679, Washington, DC Heritage Foundation, August 25, 2003.

[15] See S. Chestnut, "Illicit Activity and Proliferation: North Korea Smuggling Networks," *International Security* 32, no. 1 (2007): 80–111.

[16] J. Joby Warrick, "On North Korean Freighter, a Hidden Missile Factory," *Washington Post*, August 14, 2003 and "North Korea Shops Stealthily for Nuclear Arms Gear," *Washington Post*, August 15, 2003.

[17] Chaim Braun and Christopher F. Chyba, "Proliferation Rings: New Challenges to the Nuclear Nonproliferation Regime," *International Security* 29, no. 2 (Fall 2004): 5–49.

[18] For example, in 1968, North Korean Commandos (Unit 124, Korean People's Army) infiltrated South Korea in an attempt to attack the Blue House and assassinate President Park Chung Hee. In 1996, North Korean commandos infiltrated South Korea with a naval submarine, which launched one of the largest manhunts for them spanning over forty-six days. According to a Korean *Herald* report January 5, 2011, North Korea has violated the armistice 221 times and conducted actual military attacks over 26 times; "NK Commits 221 Provocations Since 1953," *Korea Herald*, January 5, 2011: http://nwww.koreaherald.com/view.php?ud=20110105000563.

South Korean Warship Cheonan[19] on March 26, 2010 and the shelling of Yeonpyeong Island on November 23, 2010.

Even though North and South Korea are technically still at war, these sworn enemies do, however, share a few commonalities beyond kinship and shared history. First, North and South Korea[20] spend a disproportionate amount of effort and resources[21] on the standoff with each other, each claiming to be the legitimate government of Korea—but, paradoxically, neither appears to be in a hurry to move towards reunification. From the ROK standpoint, the only viable option for reunification would lie in the collapse of the North Korean regime; and from the DPRK's perspective, reunification would probably only happen through all-out war. Second, the division of the Korean Peninsula from 1953 onwards presented Korea's immediate neighbors with two Korean political entities—complete with their own versions of modernity, sovereignty, and geostrategic orientation. Third, both North and South Korea tend to exhibit similar nationalistic tendencies in their foreign policy outlooks, and both Koreas have tended to side with each other (or at least not dispute each other's narratives) in their quarrels involving either China or Japan when it comes to territory or

[19] The evidence presented by the international fact-finding board has not met with widespread acceptance, even in South Korea herself. Bloomberg reports that 24% of South Koreans do not trust the government's evidence in a poll by a Korean newspaper *Hanbook Ilbo*, "South Korea Faces Skeptics at Home Over Evidence Linking North to Torpedo," *Bloomberg*, May 29, 2011: http://www.bloomberg.com/news/2010-05-29/south-korea-faces-skeptics-at-home-over-evidence-tying-north-to-torpedo.html.

[20] Even though North Korea's weaponry is stronger in numerical terms, it is generally acknowledged by military experts that the combined US and South Korean forces are superior in quality and technological terms. In fact, some of the experts are of the view that South Korea alone would not have any problem in defending themselves from the North Koreans should a war start. See Michael E. O'Hanlon, "Stopping a North Korean Invasion: Why Defending South Korea Is Easier Than the Pentagon Thinks," *International Security* 22, no. 4 (1998): 153–156.

[21] Moon Chung-in and Sangkuen Lee estimate that the defense budgets of South and North Korea in 2009 were 28,980.3 billion won and 482,600 billion won respectively. The authors note, ironically, that as a result an asymmetric pattern of defense spending has emerged since the mid-1970s in which the North has been reducing its spending on the defense sector whilst the South as been accelerating its military spending. Moon Chung-in and Sangkuen Lee, "Military Spending and the Arms Race on the Korean Peninsula, Japan Focus." http://japanfocus.org/-Chung_in-Moon/3333.

history.[22] Fourth, despite their disparities, both North and South Korea exercise an influence disproportionate to their relative size in East Asian international relations. This is especially striking given that the United States—the sole superpower—is deeply entrenched in this environment, and that China and Japan, the second and third largest economies, are located on either side of the Korean Peninsula. Considering the political clout, strategic weight, and economic prowess of these countries, the Koreas have done remarkably well in maintaining a balance between them—something, perhaps, that the Koreans have grown adept at over the centuries. Yet even if this is the case, the viability of either of the Koreas surviving, if not thriving, as an independent state cannot be taken for granted. Like China, Korea for part of her history (at least until the Goguryeo dynasty in 37 BC) was never a unified single state.

Born out of the Korea War, both the ROK and DPRK governments have professed from day one that they are the sole legitimate government of Korea. The creation of the two Koreas meant that there is a certain bifurcation in the United States, Russia, China, and Japan's foreign policies towards the two Koreas. As the Cold War progressed and the superpowers reached a détente, it became clear to the PRC and the USSR that they could not ignore the Republic of Korea, just as the United States and Japan had to factor the DPRK into their strategic calculus. In the same vein, however, the end of the Cold War does not mean that traditional sentimentality has no place in Northeast Asia politics. On the contrary, China's and Russia's policy towards the DPRK, in the post–Cold War period, appears to be based on both a healthy dosage of ideological nostalgia and political solidarity, beyond their usual hard-core interest calculations—albeit constrained by the limits both countries faced. Even though the DPRK might feel that both the PRC and Russia could have been more forthcoming in their assistance, the fact remains that both China and Russia are still the largest supporters of the DPRK regime. This is the case even though South Korea has substantially improved her relations with both China and Russia since the mid-1980s. Mikhail Gorbachev's *Perestroika* and *Glasnost* campaigns and Deng's economic reforms meant that South Korea has, in many ways, become a more

[22] Both Koreas are immensely unhappy with what they perceive as Chinese hegemony over the Koguryo controversy, in which China (and Chinese historians) claim that the ancient Kingdom of Koguryo (27 BC–AD 668) was a Chinese vassal state. See Peter Hays Gries, "The Koguryo Controversy, National Identity and Sino–Korean Relations Today," *East Asia* 22, no. 5 (Winter 2005): 3–17.

natural economic partner for Russia and China than North Korea is. Yet this is not enough to erode either China's or Russia's support for the DPRK completely. If South Korea's international image today is enjoying some sort of renaissance, then the DPRK is certainly the posterboy for all things negative in international affairs: a rogue state, a nation of brain-washed peasants, a member of the Axis of Evil bent on acquiring nuclear capabilities, and, ultimately, a destabilizing influence in a region of prosperity. Outside of South Korea, nowhere is this image more pronounced than in Japan. Japanese domestic opinion took a sharp dive in the late 1990s after the DPRK conducted a missile test that saw two missiles landing in the Sea of Japan. This was soon overwhelmed by a diplomatic standoff between the DPRK and Japan over the kidnapping of Japanese nationals during the Cold War. Underneath Japan's insistent public narratives and diplomatic focus on the abductee issue lie both an exasperation and an impotence in her management of relations with the DPRK, in the context of a difficult strategic environment. This image of the DRPK, however, is not universally acknowledged or adopted. As far as the DPRK is concerned, China is often caught in the middle between her desire to maintain loyalty to her ally, and her long-professed principle of non-interference in the affairs of others—as well as the expectation that she live up to the image of the responsible power that she is so eager to fulfill. This dilemma is compounded by the fact that the destabilizing role of the DPRK might draw the PRC into a conflict she doesn't want or need with the United States and Japan. Beijing is frustrated with Pyongyang's apparent neglect of her advice, and is astounded at Pyongyang's arrogant and hardline posture of the last few years.

This chapter focuses on the role North Korea plays in Japan's and China's post–Cold War thinking, and argues that—contrary to what is commonly assumed—the DPRK's behavior is actually important for China's and Japan's foreign policy posture and grand strategy development. Understanding this helps lend an insight into how North Korean issues are evaluated, interpreted, and manipulated in both capitals. Unless and until one can understand how the Chinese and Japanese view DPRK-related issues, one cannot be reasonably clear on how Chinese and Japanese interests are juxtaposed against those of the United States, the dominant actor in East Asian politics. This has important implications: Japan is often discounted as an international actor in DPRK-related issues because of the Yoshida Doctrine, the cardinal pillar in Japan's foreign policy since the end of the Pacific War that mandates Japan to follow the United States in foreign and strategic affairs. China is often discounted as the patron and ally of the DPRK, suggesting that China can hardly act independently and judiciously insofar as North Korean issues are concerned. These general assumptions are carried surreptitiously in many narratives that dominate media reports and editorials. Yet many of these analyses are hardly fair portrayals of reality. This chapter first highlights the important role of domestic politics in Japan in enhancing our understanding of North Korean issues, and argues that Japan's normalization agenda could be construed as the principal driver in her approach towards the DPRK issue, rather than vice versa. In other words, the DPRK issue is dressed up as a policy issue to drum up public opinion and electoral support, predominantly to justify the normalization agenda by right-of-center Japanese politicians. The way the DPRK issue is being approached reveals cracks in Japan's long-professed stance in following the United States. At worst, it might point to the beginning of an era where a strategic maturing Japan is moving towards eventual independence from the United States' strategic orbit. Second, the chapter notes that discussions of China's role often assume her to be a reluctant actor, heavily constrained as regards any action she might undertake towards North Korea. This perspective, however, overestimates China's influence in North Korea, downplaying real bilateral issues that dog the Sino–DPRK relationship. This chapter argues that a better understanding of how the DPRK is debated and perceived among Chinese strategists reveals a schism in China's ability to operationalize its doctrine of Peaceful Rise and its image of a responsible power amid the geo-strategic realities she faces. Third, this chapter suggests that even though the DPRK represents an important opportunity for China and Japan to cooperate (and improve Sino–Japanese relations in the process), domestic circumstances and strategic realities have made it difficult for both Beijing and Tokyo to seize this opportunity. The DPRK actually represents an important opportunity for China and Japan to cooperate on a critical issue that would adversely affect their national security—something rarely seen in contemporary Sino–Japanese relations. Unfortunately, because of the domestic constraints and inertia of their previous policy stances, these two powers have yet to capitalize on the opportunity provided by the improvement in the strategic environment, and work hand in hand to help ameliorate the situation on the Korean Peninsula.

Bonafide Threat or Strawman: The DPRK in Japan's Normalization Discourse

The collapse of the Soviet Union and the subsequent end of the Cold War removed ideology as the overriding consideration in the region's geopolitics. This also brought about a certain incentive on the part of the traditional allies of the United States to move beyond their traditional "diplomatic" comfort zone to engage their former adversaries. The United States's principal ally in East Asia, Japan, was mired in intense domestic debate over the strategic future and direction of the country and the region. The loss of the ideological anchor, coupled with the possibility that the United States no longer required Japan's assistance in the containment of the USSR and her allies, prompted a severe introspective examination of Japan's own foreign and strategic policy and outlook.

The angst that the Japanese faced in their foreign policy was intricately linked to the prevailing international climate, as well as to domestic considerations. The diplomatic context by which this period was characterized was one of intense debate in Tokyo. First, the collapse of the Soviet Union meant that the entire Cold War structure that had informed and governed the Japanese foreign policy worldview during the previous era had ceased to exist. The criticism Japan received after the Gulf War for her checkbook diplomacy, and her failure to "contribute" to the liberation of Kuwait, left Japan both dumbfounded and dismayed. Second, this not only jarred with the self-image as a responsible member of the international community that Japan had construed for herself since the end of the Pacific War, but also raised questions about the viability of the US–Japan partnership in general and the continued viability of the Yoshida Doctrine in particular for Japan in the post–Cold War era. Third, the domestic debate on Japan's future strategic posture and orientation was compounded by concerns about the prospects of US withdrawal from the Western Pacific and what this meant for Japan. This all took place within the context of the rise of China and the debate over what this meant for Japanese normalization, given the diametrically opposed trajectories of the Chinese and Japanese economies in the previous decade.

One of Japan's priorities in this environment was therefore to improve her relations with countries in the former Soviet bloc, especially those that bordered Japan. Beyond China and Russia, Tokyo considered it important to improve relations with the DPRK. By September 1990, Japan had issued a Three-Party joint declaration (with the ROK) that paved the way for Track One normalization talks from 1991 until the end of 1992. The utter failure of these talks reflected not only the intractable nature of the various issues[23] involved, but more importantly the over-estimation of

[23] The issues include Pyongyang's demand for compensation from Japan for suffering and losses incurred during the colonial period up to World War II. Japan conversely demanded Pyongyang resolve the difficulties concerning nuclear

Tokyo and Pyongyang regarding the efficacy of diplomatic talks in the resolution of these issues. The impetus for Tokyo to improve her relations was also constrained by Japan–ROK relations, given the ROK's reluctance for Japan–DPRK relations to develop along an independent track from ROK–DPRK negotiations.

Japan was forced by international circumstances to adopt a tougher stance towards the DPRK from the mid-1990s onwards because of the first nuclear crisis in 1993/94. As Pyongyang engaged in a standoff with the United States and the International Atomic Energy Agency over her alleged nuclear weapons program, Tokyo faced a dilemma with which she would become increasingly familiar in the post–Cold War period. Tokyo found herself torn between the pressure to follow the United States' posture and her own desire to improve relations with Pyongyang. The North Korea issue, therefore, represented one of the first challenges to Tokyo's steadfast alliance with the United States in the post–Cold War era, and, ironically, Tokyo's reluctance to join with the United States' hardened stance towards the DPRK marks the first of many difficult moments in post–Cold War Japanese foreign policy. Japan was spared the angst of her decision thanks to the agreement on DPRK–US negotiations and the implementation of the KEDO framework (i.e., a shift in US policy), as well as the Japanese preference for engagement rather than containment of the DPRK's nuclear ambitions. Ironically, even as the international climate changed for the better—with DPRK–US relations improving with the implementation of the KEDO framework, and the institution of the Sunshine policy by President Kim Dae-jung of South Korea—Japan–DPRK relations showed no corresponding sign of improvement.

Three developments accounted for this. First, North Korea increasingly provided both the impetus as well as the justification for the Liberal Democratic Party's (LDP) normalization agenda in Japanese domestic politics. With the rise of right-of-center prime ministers such as Ryutaro Hashimoto, Keizo Obuchi, Junichiro Koizumi, Shinzo Abe, Yasuo Fukuda,

---

inspections, provide information about 1,828 Japanese citizens who had migrated to the DPRK (1959–63 Zainichi Koreans repatriation campaign) with their Korean spouses, and address the question of Japanese soldiers taken by the Soviets in World War II and sent to the DPRK. See Yong Mok Kim, "The Dilemma of North Korea's Japanese Wives," *JPRI Critique* 4, no. 10 (November 1997); Kang Cheol Hwan, *Ethnic Koreans in Japan Victimized by the North Korean Regime's Fraud*, Korean Unification Research Institute of Chosun Ilbo, http://www. dailynk.com/english/keys/2003/12/05.php.

and Taro Aso (until the Democratic Party of Japan ascended to power), mainstream Japanese politics continued to exhibit strong undercurrents of Japanese nationalism. Second, changing political and economic circumstances within the DPRK drove the country to harden its foreign policy position. Third, the evolution of the US–Japan Security Alliance, alongside the increased tensions in East Asia, provided for a re-evaluation of Japan's strategic policy and considerations. Certain quarters within Japan started to use the DPRK as an important argument for greater strategic autonomy—either within the framework of the US–Japan alliance, or even outside it—as well as for the strengthening of Japan's alliance with the United States.

The Rise of the Neo-Conservatives in Japan and the US–Japan Security Alliance

The rightwards shift in Japanese mainstream politics and public opinion did not occur immediately after the Cold War. With the demise of the USSR and the growing popularity of the "China Threat" thesis from the early 1990s, Tokyo has been in a constant state of debate as to her strategic mission and outlook. From 1993 to the end of 1995, the two non-LDP prime ministers Mirihiro Hosakawa (August 1993–April 1994) and Tomiichi Murayama (June 1994–January 1996) broke the LDP stranglehold on Japanese domestic politics. These two prime ministers took a very different political and diplomatic approach to that of their LDP predecessors. During a visit to Beijing in 1994, Prime Minister Hosakawa sought Beijing's assistance to rein in DPRK's nuclear ambitions, noting that China had the "deepest" relations with the DPRK.[24] He also said he believed that China's military secrecy was of "no threat" to Japan, albeit that greater openness would give rise to greater confidence. Hosakawa also sidestepped whether Japan would move to curb the millions of dollars flowing from Japan to North Korea.[25] Prime Minister Tomiichi Maruyama, who inherited the coalition government from Hosakawa's interim successor (Tsutomu Hata), took a very similar approach to that of Hosakawa with respect to his policy agenda. Maruyama built on what Hosakawa had achieved, extending the most direct apology to Japan's Asian neighbors

---

[24] *Associated Press*, March 20, 1994.

[25] E. David Sanger, "Hosokawa's Report, à la Clinton," *New York Times*, February 12, 1994: http://www.nytimes.com/1994/02/12/world/hosokawa-s-report-a-la-clinton.html.

when he finally acknowledged Japanese misconduct during World War II.[26] While there is no evidence that Hosakawa and Maruyama's actions had any direct bearing on Japan's foreign policy, their actions did strike a reconciliatory tone with China, Japan, and countries in Southeast Asia. Of course, these developments also meant that both prime ministers came under attack from their political opponents in the Liberal Democratic Party, as well as certain right-wing political elements and organizations. These concerns were also compounded by Washington's worries over what these gestures might mean for the US–Japan alliance and the United States' position in Asia.

Consequently, when the LDP was restored to power in early 1996, there was a significant change in Tokyo's prevailing mood. The ascension of Ryutaro Hashimoto meant that Japan was once again led by the Liberal Democratic Party, and opinion in both Tokyo and Washington began to move towards the consensus that post-War Japan still saw the US–Japan security alliance as the central pillar of Japan foreign policy, as well as of US grand strategy in the Asia-Pacific. In February 1996, within three months of coming into the post, Hashimoto visited the United States, and President Clinton returned his visit in April 1996, whereupon Japan and the United States announced the "Japan–US Joint Declaration on Security Alliance for the 21st Century," endorsing a plan to reduce the scope and intrusiveness of US forces in Okinawa and signing several accords to strengthen the US–Japan security alliance (April 16–18, 1996).[27] In September 1997, the new US Defense guidelines were announced,[28] imparting renewed vigor to Japan in promoting the US–Japan alliance as the fundamental basis for her foreign and strategic policy outlook. The DPRK's ballistic and nuclear program formally replaced the Soviet Red Army as the fundamental threat in Japan's strategic narratives and

---

[26] Statement by Prime Minister Tomiichi Murayama "On the Occasion of the 50th Anniversary of the War's End," August 15, 1995: http://www.mofa.go.jp/announce/press/pm/murayama/9508.html.

[27] "Chronology of US–Japan Relations," September 30, 2013: http://aboutusa.japan.usembassy.gov/e/jusa-usj-chronology.html.

[28] The first defense guidelines were signed in 1978 and revised in 1997. The 1997 revision introduced the concept of "situations in areas surrounding Japan" to expand roles and missions for the Self-Defense Forces in case of a regional contingency, in addition to the defense of Japan's national security. See Sugio Takahashi, "Upgrading the Japan–US Defense Guidelines: Towards a New Phase of Operational Coordination," http://project2049.net/documents/japan_us_defense_guidelines_takahashi.pdf.

provided a strong justification for the LDP's political agenda, as it provided the overriding framework for the reaffirmation of the US–Japan Security Alliance. Yet there are, of course, wider considerations regarding the reaffirmation of the US–Japan alliance. Hashimoto's political agenda and platform in many ways mirrored the traditional conservativism that had dominated Japan since the end of World War II. The reaffirmation of the US–Japan Security Alliance was one of the fundamental directions in which the LDP saw Japan heading, but more importantly it was a means to implement the overall political goal of the normalization of Japan. Admittedly, there was no constant vision what this normalization entailed—and among the many Japanese specialists who discuss normalization, there are different versions and narratives of what Japan should and could do to achieve it.[29] One of the primary drivers behind this re-evaluation was the rise of China—and by the mid-1990s, both the United States and Japan were concerned with her growing power,[30] even though both parties at that point vehemently denied that that was the main reason for sustaining their alliance.[31]

Concurrently, the diplomatic climate surrounding the DPRK was not much better. The nuclear crisis of 1993/94 effectively froze any attempt to resume normalization talks, but in December 1994 the Hosakawa administration agreed to help part-finance the KEDO project. In 1995 Maruyama attempted to normalize relations with North Korea through Watanabe Michio's LDP-SDPJ-Sakigake delegation to the DPRK. This was followed by governmental assistance comprising half a million tons of rice from June to October 1995. The following year, Hashimoto's administration agreed to help North Korea after famine struck once again. In 1997, again during Hashimoto's administration, there was another mission

---

[29] Yoshihide Soeya, David A. Welch, and M. Takokoro, eds., *Japan as a "Normal Country"?: A Nation in Search of its Place in the World* (Toronto: University of Toronto Press, 2011).

[30] When Seiroku Kajiyama announced that the revised guidelines would compel Japan to assist the United States in the event of a conflict in the Korean Peninsula or the Taiwan Straits, it provoked much anger in China, thereby confirming Japanese perceptions with regard to the Chinese threat. This is one significant difference between post-war conservatives and the neo-conservatives in Japan today.

[31] This has been somewhat inconsistent, but since 2005 Japan has explicitly identified China, through the annual Defence White Paper, as a threat to her national security.

led by Mori Yoshiro.[32] Unfortunately, the negotiations and the attempt to normalize were largely stalled over the DPRK and Japan's disagreement over the return of Japanese wives of North Koreans (*Nihonjin tsuma*), as well as the abduction issue—this having dampened domestic consensus on resuming normalization talks with the DPRK from 1995 onwards. As the Hashimoto administration moved to solidify Japan's alliance with the United States, Japan's domestic opinion concerning the DPRK took a nose dive. It was therefore ironic that as the international environment began to improve in a way that might have permitted better relations with the DPRK, Japan's leaders began to articulate a very different approach towards North Korea (and implicitly towards China). In retrospect, the real motivator for the consolidation of Japan's hardened position over North Korea came when the DPRK allegedly test-fired a missile which flew over Japan in August 1998 (although the DPRK maintained that it was a satellite launch). That missile test foreshadowed many more to come, as recorded in Table 1. The thorough sensationalism of this incident caused public opinion in Japan to further harden against North Korea, boosting the popularity of right-wingers within the LDP. Under Prime Minister Obuchi's leadership, Japan emphasized the need for a "comprehensive" approach towards the DPRK, namely to ask the DPRK to abandon its missile and nuclear programs in return for expanded economic aid.[33] This episode, in turn, provided the needed justification for the United States and Japan to rally domestic and international opinion behind the reaffirmation of the US–Japan alliance—although analysts suspected that the real intention of the alliance was to constrain China, rather than the DPRK. At least in the mid-1990s, both Japan and China were careful not to make this explicit, and the DPRK became a strawman in their official narratives. This proved to be the beginning of a political and diplomatic strategy that Japan would follow for the next fifteen years. However, by 2005 Japan had identified both the DPRK and the PRC as explicit threats. The abduction issue today remains unresolved, and the mutual demonization between the DPRK and Japan continues even in the post–Kim Jong-il era. The DPRK continues to be a powerful symbol in the neo-conservatives'

---

[32] See Christopher W. Hughes' very insightful paper on "The Political Economy of Japanese Sanctions towards North Korea: Domestic Coalitions and International Systemic Pressures," *Pacific Affairs* 79, no. 3 (2006): 455–481; paper also available at University of Warwick Institutional Depository, http://wrap.warwick.ac.uk/1016/1/WRAP_Hughes_9871481-080709-political_economy_of_sanctions_towards_north_korea_wrap.pdf.

[33] "Obuchi, Perry go over Pyongyang Policy," *Japan Times*, May 24, 1999.

narrative, and serves as propaganda in their bid to reframe and reform Japan's strategic thinking and policy.

Table 1: Selected Missile Tests of the DPRK

Date	Locality	Type of Missile	Range of Missile	Rationale / Remarks
May 29/ 30, 1993	Wonsan to Sea of Japan	Nodong-1	Short-range; landed in Sea of Japan	Testing model for export order (300 missiles) to Iran in exchange for oil
August 31, 1998	Tonghae Launching Site (Musudan-ri) in North Hamgyong Province	Taepodong rocket	Flew over Japan and landed in Pacific Ocean	Launch of Kwangmyongsong-1 satellite. Japan insists this was a missile that flew over the sea of Japan; the DPRK insists it was a satellite launch. China was involved in the development of this satellite.
July 5, 2006	Tonghae launching site (Musudan-ri) in North Hamgyong Province	Taepodong-2 missiles & 6 Scud (Rodong) missiles	1 x long-range; 6 x short-range landed 600km north of Hokkaido; 100 km south of Vladivostok	Follows the agreement of the United States and Japan to produce Anti-Ballistic Missile technology and the conduct of large-scale war games in the Western Pacific in June 2006 by the United States.
April 5, 2009	Tonghae launching site (Musudan-ri) in North Hamgyong Province	Unha 2 rocket (allegedly replicate of China's Dongfeng 2) rockets	Estimated about 3,850 kilometers from the launch site	Launch of Kwangmyongsong 2 satellite (Bright Lode Star)

May 27/ 28, 2009	6 short-range missiles were fired, including one ground-to-ship and one surface-to-air missile from Wonsan	Rodong / Scud-C Missiles	Fired away from South Korea in northeast direction; range of 1,000–1,500 km	DPRK hosted missile launch after conducting a nuclear test on miniaturized warheads on May 25, 2009. Leadership transition and possible legacy quest for Kim Jong-il. Violated UN Resolutions 1695, 1718, 1874
July 2, July 4, 2009	Launched 2 missiles into the Sea of Korea Launched 7 short range missiles into the Sea of Korea on the 4th	Scud / Rodong	Rodong, short-range, 1,000 to1,500 km	Aimed at improving missiles' accuracy; In violation of UN Resolution 1874. Timed for US Independence Day.
May 18–19, 2013	Launched 4 short range missiles northeasterly direction away from ROK	Musudan	Short range, 4,000km	This launch can be construed as part of the Korean Peninsula crisis; aimed at bolstering Kim Jung-un's popularity at home and showing defiance in face of greater cooperation between the ROK and the US.

The DPRK's Regime Transition and Survival Diplomacy

Viewed from the prism of the DPRK, the joint maneuvers by Japan, the United States, and South Korea concern not only foreign affairs, but also the continued existence of the regime and the DPRK. As such, the hardened position of the DPRK from the early 1990s onwards must be seen in the context of the general development of the DPRK in the same period. By all measures, the failure of the central economic planning system of the DPRK had become so pervasive that with the dissipation of the aid from the former USSR and the PRC, economic conditions had become extremely severe. In particular, from 1994 until 1998, the DPRK also suffered unprecedented flooding that destroyed not only precious arable grain and crops, but also depleted the strategic grain reserves. This period also coincided with the leadership transition, the death of Kim Il-sung compounding the difficulties faced by the regime. For the first time since its founding, the DPRK found herself facing the most serious challenge to regime survival and sovereign integrity. The reaffirmation of the US–Japan Security Alliance created security anxieties within the DPRK, and it certainly did provide the external "threat" necessary for the DPRK regime to rally the nation behind the new regime of Kim Jong-il. The singling-out of the threat from the United States and Japan provided a good excuse for the new regime to boost the Songun (선군정치)[34] policy and to push ahead with the missile and nuclear programs. The US–Japan Security Alliance is promoted within the DPRK to serve the ruling elite's agenda just as the North Korean threat is promoted within Japan for the LDP's. Relations between the DPRK and Japan could be described as "frosty" at best, and at worst outright hostile. Yet, in reality, Tokyo and Pyongyang show a certain symbiosis in their interactions due to their public display of hostility.

By and large, even as Kim Jong-il had managed to fend off the challenges created by the twin difficulties of famine and the succession, the DPRK he inherited was extremely poor, weak, and on the verge of collapse. Having spent much of his life waiting in the wings for the succession to his father's position, his tenure as the leader of the DPRK was relatively short. The Communist fraternity had always frowned upon dynastic succession. Even within the DPRK, there was a groundswell of discontent regarding this succession. To maintain regime legitimacy, he had to promote the military-first policy, and correspondingly increase spending on these domestic constituents in order to maintain his patronage. The diversion of resources to this end, as well as to the maintenance of the personality cult, meant relegating important economic reforms to the background. This is a self-reinforcing problem that has plagued the DPRK till this day. The biggest problem confronting Kim Jong-il was, however, the systemic problem that he had encountered himself—the question of the succession. When news broke that his eldest son and anointed successor Kim Jong-nam had been arrested in Japan after

[34] For a "traditional" DPRK interpretation of "Songun," see Ri Jong-chol, *Songun Politics in Korea, Pyongyang* (Democratic People's Republic of North Korea: Foreign Languages Publishing House, 2012). The author considers this to be a "revolutionary mode of socialist leadership and socialist mode of politics that gives priority to military affairs, and defends the country, the revolution … ." The dominant view of Songun outside the DPRK, however, is drastically different—many scholars consider Songun a version of pork-barrel politics whereby the ruling elites use this policy to justify privileging the Korean class.

traveling on a fake passport ostensibly to visit Tokyo Disneyland,[35] a new layer of difficulties arose for Kim Jong-il. With his health failing, he had to reconfigure his plans in order have a more "legitimate" successor—this was Kim Jong-eun, his third son after the removal of Kim Jong-nam as a viable heir.

Notwithstanding, Kim Jong-il did manage to improve DPRK relations with the South, keeping intra-Korea ties warm for a decade. Kim Dae-jung's Sunshine policy was instituted from 1998 onwards, and until 2008 and the election of South Korea President Lee Myung-bak, the DPRK and the ROK remained cordial, for lack of a better word. Ironically, the mutual demonization between the DPRK, on one hand, and Japan and the United States, on the other, did not stop. The success of Kim Dae-jung's Sunshine policy did move North–South Korean relations forward, and for a brief period it did appear that there was a respite in intra-Korean tensions. Without any doubt the most successful event of this diplomacy was the Summit, at which a number of cooperative projects were kickstarted. The most well known of these was the Mount Kumgang Tourist Region project, which lasted until 2008 when there was a shooting accident involving a tourist.[36] The momentum of the North–South summit was sustained through the Roh Moon-hyun administration. With President Lee Myung-bak's ascendance, the Korean government instituted policies that unraveled the achievements of the Sunshine policy, and the resumption of the arms race and confrontation between North and South undid most of the confidence and goodwill that the Sunshine policy had accomplished. The events of September 11 and the total reorientation of the United States towards the War on Terror in Afghanistan and the Middle East, coupled with the election of Prime Minister Junichiro Koizumi, brought new challenges for the DPRK. With Sino–Japanese relations spiraling downwards, a glimmer of hope appeared on the horizon when Japan assiduously courted the DPRK to hold the Japan–DPRK summit between Koizumi and Kim Jong-il. By 2002, the situation in North Korea had largely stabilized and the DPRK leadership was extremely keen to reconcile with Japan. The DPRK regime, of course, hoped that normalization would bring compensation and economic aid, assistance which the DPRK badly required. In the meantime, Prime Minister Koizumi was beleaguered by troubles in Sino–Japanese relations and was

[35] "Japan Expels North Korean Leader's Son," May 4, 2001: http://news.bbc.co.uk /2/hi/asia-pacific/1310374.stm.

[36] "South Korean Tourist Shot Dead by North Soldier," *Reuters*, July 11, 2008.

looking for a foreign policy victory to improve his image at home. A summit with North Korea would boost his foreign policy credentials at home and shore up his popularity for the next election. Indeed, Koizumi[37] got more than he bargained for.

In a startling admission, Kim Jong-il admitted that North Korea had been involved in kidnapping Japanese nationals from 1977 to 1983, the total number eventually being ascertained by Japan as seventeen.[38] Beyond that, Japan also obtained an apology from the DPRK for this incident as well as concessions for the return of some of the kidnapped people. Yet although this trip was hailed as a success, it raised more questions than it answered, sending Japan into a media frenzy over the DPRK and the kidnapping issue. Under intense public scrutiny and public pressure, Prime Minister Koizumi attempted another diplomatic visit to the DPRK eighteen months later. While his trip cannot be considered a failure, it is clear that the results did not meet the expectations of the Japanese public. There was significant blowback in terms of public opinion towards the North Korean issue, and the perceived failure of the Koizumi mission killed any hope of future normalization between Japan and the DPRK. Beyond that, Japan began to differ from the United States on how to handle the crisis. The United States was adamant that complete nuclear disarmament could proceed, whilst the Koizumi administration believed that through engagement they could perhaps then work on the issues that were important to them. Nonetheless, the expectations and the media attention did not help. Japan's insistence on the resolution of the kidnapping issue, which was required by the exigencies of domestic politics, increased the strain on the US–Japan Security Alliance and affected the Four-Party Talks. There is little doubt that Shinzo Abe, Chief Cabinet Secretary under Prime Minster Koizumi, had completely co-opted this issue. Despite this, throughout the administrations of Shinzo Abe, Taro Aso, and Yasuo Fukuda, until the LDP's defeat by the Democratic Party of Japan, DPRK–Japan relations have remained relatively stable. Even though there is evidence that the DPRK tried to reach out to the Democratic Party of Japan, the short tenure of Prime Minister Hatoyama, and the difficulties that his successor faced in combating the fallout of

---

[37] Prime Minister Shinzo Abe was Prime Minister Junichiro Koizumi's chief cabinet secretary and took the lead in the DPRK policy.

[38] See "National Association for the Rescue of Japanese Kidnapped by North Korea," http://www.sukuukai.jp/narkn/.

Fukushima, meant that Japan–DPRK relations have largely remained in a political and diplomatic lull.

Viewed from Washington,[39] Japan's obsession with the abduction issue was impeding the diplomatic efforts at bringing the DPRK back to the negotiating table in the quest to dissuade them from going nuclear. In Japan, for all intents and purposes, the issue took on a life of its own, creating a domestic consensus so powerful that no politician could afford to ignore it. The insistence on the abduction issue created a schism between the United States and Japan, the former being worried about the nuclear issue above all else, including the fate of the abducted Japanese. With the launch of more test missiles, the narratives about the DPRK in Japan have become more and more radical.

Yet, amidst the façade of this hostility, Japan still maintains ties to North Korea through the existence of a large community of ethnic North Koreans in Japan.[40] The *Zanichi* is not only an important source of information on how the DPRK is perceived in Japan, but more importantly provides extremely important functions as regards public relations and the supply of hard currency to the DPRK.[41] The latter is estimated at various levels, but Eberstadt puts the figure at around 650–880 million in 1994 International Dollars, and this amount probably omits the amount carried by the *Chosen Soeren* in suitcases when they visit the DPRK.[42] These linkages are well-known to the Japanese. More importantly, the DPRK community in Japan has intricate links to LDP politicians as well.[43] The DPRK is also known to have intricate ties to the DPJ, to whom they reached out after Hatoyama's rise to power.[44] Since the confrontation, the

[39] The United States is somewhat ambivalent about Japan's position. On the one hand, there is much appreciation for Japan's staunch support for the US–Japan alliance, but on the other, they are dismayed at Japan's insistence that the hostage issue be placed above all other goals, including denuclearization, which Washington considers to be of paramount importance.

[40] Matsubara Hiroshi and Tokita Mayuko, "Japan's Korean Residents Caught in the Japan–North Korea Crossfire" (originally published by Asahi Shimbun and the *International Herald Tribune*, Jan 2–6, 2007), accessed January 20, 2007: http://www.japanfocus.org/-M-Tokita/2327.

[41] N. Eberstadt, "Financial Transfers from Japan to North Korea estimating the Unreported Flows," *Asian Survey* 36, no. 5 (1996): 523–542.

[42] Eberstadt, "Financial Transfers."

[43] M. E. Manyin, *Japan–North Korea Relations: Selected Issues*, CRS Report for Congress, 14.

[44] K. Chung, "Japanese–North Korean Relations Today," *Asian Survey* 4, no. 4 (1964): 788–803. Interestingly, it was the father of former Prime Minister

Zanichi has come under heavy scrutiny, as, unlike the Koreans from South Korea, the North Koreans show very little sign of assimilation into the Japanese community.

The DPRK and China's Peaceful Rise

The DPRK–PRC relationship remains one of the most enigmatic and opaque in the world. Their interactions are a foreign policy "black box," with most of the world, including the United States and Japan, knowing very little about what is going on—akin to the PRC–USSR relations during the 1950s. After the Chinese People's Volunteers (CPV) crossed over the Yalu River to defeat the UN troops, the DPRK and the PRC began a partnership that lasted more than four decades. Pyongyang was less than thrilled when in 1992 China normalized relations with South Korea. This meant that of all the significant powers, only China had access to both the South Korean and North Korean leadership, something which the United States, Japan, and even Russia cannot claim to have. This diplomatic advantage is not something that the Chinese have cultivated assiduously, nor flaunted without much forethought.

China's motivation to establish ties with South Korea is one borne out of economics—and even though the relationship began that way, the tone and direction have rendered China's traditional ally very uncomfortable with this.[45] There are, of course, added benefits. A closer relationship with Seoul would certainly mean having a better handle on affairs on the Korean Peninsula, and directly diluting the influence of the United States. Beyond that, it places pressure on North Korea to re-evaluate her way of handling difficult issues with China. For the South, the normalization of her relations with her sworn enemy's principal supporter certainly brings direct benefits. Even though the United States is the principal deterrent against potential North Korean aggression, China might represent a real opportunity to perhaps ameliorate North–South tensions and relations. Today, the Beijing–Pyongyang relationship appears to be less resilient than the PRC's relations with South Korea, but, nonetheless, is still

---

Hatoyama who reached out to Japan during the early years of the Cold War. The North Koreas reached out to the DPJ the moment Yukio Hatoyama won the premiership, but unfortunately their efforts were largely in vain.

[45] Kongdan Oh Hassig, "China's Strategic Relations with the Two Koreas, Institute for Defense Analyses," September 1997: http://www.dtic.mil/cgi-bin/GetTRDoc?AD=ADA331317.

enduring the test of time despite their divergent paths and systemic differences. After the implementation of the Chinese economic system, China's foreign policy has always been driven by her need to satisfy the exigencies of her economic reforms. North Korea, therefore, remains somewhat of an anomaly in Chinese foreign policy, in the sense that China has always considered the DPRK to be important and a special neighbor, albeit an economic liability. To that end, the PRC has tried to provide crude oil shipments and military equipment along with frequent exchanges between Chinese and North Korean leaders. By the 1980s, it was clear that Kim Il-sung's *Juche* philosophy had caused economic stagnation, as the DPRK had cut off trade even with her two most important supporters—China and the Soviet Union. The late Kim made it a priority to revive the country's economy, and worked hard to re-cultivate and re-balance the DPRK's relations with the two antagonistic communist giants—the USSR and the PRC. Ironically, even while North Korea was improving on her goals, South Korea was making more headway in reaching out to the Soviets and Chinese. President Roh Tae-woo assiduously courted both Mikhail Gorbachev and Secretary General Zhao Ziyang after the 1988 Seoul Olympics, taking advantage of the ROK's economic utility for the modernizing Soviet and Chinese economies. By the early 1990s, however, it was clear that Russia did not have economic clout or geopolitical influence in the affairs of both Koreas, and China emerged as the clear winner insofar as North Korean affairs were concerned.

From the viewpoint of Beijing in the 1990s, China–North Korea relations presented a clear dilemma. On the one hand, Beijing cherished the warm embrace of a staunch political ally in the aftermath of the June 4 Tiananmen incident; but on the other, having the DRPK as an ally hardly sat well with the image of a China keen on playing a major role in international affairs. By the mid-1990s it had become exceedingly clear to Beijing that the DPRK was an unvarnished example of a Cold War relic, a strategic liability, and an extremely unpredictable neighbor. Major questions faced the Chinese leadership concerning North Korea. First, would China perpetually be able to provide food aid and financial resources to support the DPRK regime, the North Koreans showing no signs of going beyond lip service in reform of their economy? Second, even if there was political will on the part of the Koreans, were the practicalities of modernizing the North Korean economy something that the Chinese felt they could shoulder alone? The question of reforms and reconstruction of the North Korean economy is a regional, if not international, problem. Third, with the North Koreans perpetually antagonizing the United States, Japan, and South Korea, what would

Beijing do if there were a serious conflict on the borders (with the attendant problems of refugees) associated with regime collapse—or, worse, if she became entangled in a conflict she had no interest in?

Beijing has often reiterated in public that China has neither a privileged access to, nor a special influence over, Pyongyang,[46] and that, like all members of the international community, China is befuddled and frustrated by Pyongyang's intentions and policies. Even though China and North Korea are linked by the same ideological umbilical cord, and christened by the Korean War, there is no reason to expect any sort of Sino–DPRK alliance in today's world. There are, of course, views to the contrary—ranging from China being tolerant of the DPRK's recalcitrance[47] as a deterrent to US and Japanese strategic moves, to downright collusion by the Chinese military in order to establish some sort of "Manchukuo" in North Korea and manipulate the strategic environment in Northeast Asia.[48] This, of course, is consonant with the view that the DPRK is perceived as a strategic buffer to US forces on the Korean Peninsula.[49]

Beijing's rhetoric on the DPRK is shaped by her own interests as much as it is guided by Beijing's goal for the world to perceive China's ascendance as a "Peaceful Rise." This doctrine,[50] first articulated by Zheng

[46] Personal communication with scholars in China from the period 2010 to 2012. Most Chinese scholars are of the view that Western, in particular, American and European, scholars overestimate the kind of clout that the Chinese have in North Korea. This opposing view typically informs the staple diet reflected in op-eds published by organizations such as the Council of Foreign Relations: see, for example, Xu Benia and Bajoria Jayshree, "The China–North Korean Relationship," February 18, 2014: http://www.cfr.org/china/china-north-korea-relationship/p11097#p5.

[47] Bates Gill, for example, argues that Beijing appeared to be relatively tolerant of North Korea's provocative actions. See Bates Gill, *China's North Korea Policy: Assessing Interests and Influences*, United States Institute of Peace Special Report July 2011: http://www.usip.org/files/resources/China's_North_Korea_Policy.pdf.

[48] See Masako Ikegami, "China and North Korea: Renewal of the 'Blood Alliance'," *Asia Pacific Bulletin* 158, no. 5 (April 2012).

[49] Andrew Scobell, "China and North Korea: The Close but Uncomfortable Relationship," *Current History* (September 2002): 279; Liu Ming, "China and the North Korean Crisis: Facing the Test and Transition," *Pacific Affairs* 76, no. 3 (Fall 2003): 350–351.

[50] See Zheng Bijian, "China's Peaceful Rise to Great Power Status," *Foreign Affairs* 84, no. 5 (September/October 2005); also John L. Thornton, *China's Peaceful Rise: Speeches of Zheng Bijian 1997–2004* (Washington, DC: Brookings Institution): http://www.brookings.edu/fp/events/20050616bijianlunch.pdf.

Bijian (then then vice-principal of the Chinese Communist Party School) was formally adopted by President Hu Jintao as the foreign policy "thinking" to be utilized in official discourse, in tandem with the doctrine of "harmonious society" which informs the thinking on China's domestic politics. Essentially, this doctrine states that the international community need not be perturbed by the rise of China, for that rise essentially presents an opportunity rather than a threat for all neighboring countries. In China's official narrative, China would seek to abide by her international obligations and treaties rather than challenge the rules and norms of the current international system. In this context, North Korea becomes one of the important focal points by which the international community, and in particular the countries in the region, measure the sincerity of the Chinese rhetoric over her alleged peaceful rise.

This, in turn, becomes a particular dilemma for Beijing, for several reasons. First, Beijing is extremely reluctant to swap the "peaceful rise" for an interventionist foreign policy, especially one involving her close neighbor. Second, this would mean departing from one of the most cherished principles that has guided China's foreign policy—that of non-intervention in the affairs of others. Third, this would also mean endorsing the expectations that the international community (led by the United States and other chiefly OECD countries) has demanded of China—namely to shoulder responsibilities commensurate with her rising international status. Such open acquiescence would, no doubt, lead to a slippery slope towards further evaluation, criticism, and demands that Beijing could hardly afford. Fourth, from a geopolitical standpoint, analysts have pointed out the utility of having the "North Korean" card in Beijing's diplomatic arsenal. Furthermore, China's security is clearly being served by having the current regime hold the DPRK together. Any scenario involving a regime change in the DPRK is likely to shift the strategic tilt in favor of a US- or South Korea–friendly regime, something which Beijing would not wish. Fifth, there are plenty of issues within the PRC–DPRK relationship that have yet to be resolved, such as history,[51] border demarcation,[52] and

[51] In the Koguryo controversy between China and South Korea, the North Koreans maintain a position that is quietly in congruence with South Korea. The South Koreans are particularly concerned about the Chinese position on Koguryo because of the implications it might have for possible Chinese claims in the event of a North Korea regime collapse, as well as the possible aspersions cast on the loyalty of Chinese Koreans. For an interesting take on the DPRK's position, see http://news.naver.com/main/read.nhn?mode=LPOD&mid=sec&sid1=&oid=078&aid=0000026912 [in Korean]. For an interpretation of the controversy on the

trade and customs disagreements—although these issues are not well known in wider political circles. Rightly or wrongly, the DPRK perceives that the richer Chinese state is not giving them the respect that they deserve.[53] This situation is not very much different from the grievance the PRC harbored about the Soviet Union in the period leading up to the Sino–Soviet rivalry. Sixth, and perhaps most important, the Chinese themselves are not confident that they would be able to have any sort of real influence on the North Koreans. Even at the height of their difficulties, the North Koreans adopted a very hardline stance towards any sort of conditions attached to aide—owning to a combination of pride, paranoia, and fierce adherence to their *Juche* philosophy. Chinese analysts have privately acknowledged that the PRC lacks any sort of real clout in the country, since the DPRK leadership considers issues very independently of Beijing,

---

Chinese side, see Chen Dingding, "Domestic Politics, National Identity, and the International Conflict: The Case of the Koguryo Controversy," *Journal of Contemporary China* 21, no. 74 (2012): 227–241. It is important to note that in 2001, Pyongyang and Beijing filed competing applications to UNESCO for the recognition of ancient tombs dating back to the Koguryo period, recognized as a world heritage site.

[52] The main dispute between the DPRK and the PRC concerns the "White-headed" mountain on the Sino–DPRK border. Known to the Koreans as "Paektu Mountain" and "Baitoushan" in Chinese, this mountain is part of the Changbaishan mountain range and straddles China's Jilin province and Korea's Ryanggang Mountain. For the Koreans, this mountain is central to Korean folklore and nationalism and its importance is not dissimilar to Mount Fuji to the Japanese or Mount Tai in Shandong Province China. According to the DPRK's narrative, Kim Jong-il was supposed to have been born in Paektu Mountain in 1942 (as opposed to Khabarovsk, where Kim Il-sung was a serving officer). The territory in dispute is a tract of land about thirty-three square kilometers around the summit, which the Koreans feel has been appropriated by China. The DPRK and the PRC are also at odds over the demarcation of some of the river estuary islands near the mouth of the Yalu River, i.e., Chouduandao/Pidan and Shindao/Shindo. There is also much unhappiness over China's demand for greater access to the Sea of Japan through the mouth of the Tumen River, and her ambitions to develop a Special Economic Region at the border town of Fangchuan. See Daniel Goma, "The Chinese–Korean Border Issue: An Analysis of a Contested Frontier," *Asian Survey* 46, no. 6 (November/December 2006): 867–880.

[53] You Ji, "China and North Korea: A Fragile Relationship of Strategic Convenience," *Journal of Contemporary China* 10, no. 28 (2001): 387–398. You Ji has a very interesting discussion on the differences between the Chinese leadership and Kim Il-sung's take on the DPRK's leadership succession, and how Kim Jong-il has never quite forgiven the Chinese for not backing his accession.

and at the same time has a complete grip on the country's institutions. Beyond that, there appears to be a lack of concern for their own citizens, rooted in the regime's priorities. Nonetheless, the PRC is still best placed to encourage gradual economic reforms and restrain the DPRK from unnecessary military adventurism in times of uncertainty.

Beijing's position over the Korean issue has therefore been a narrative of caution and balance. China's public position is that the DPRK is a sovereign country and has a right to self-determination and to put in place policies that are in her best interests (signaling non-interference and mutual respect). At the same time, Beijing has always openly articulated that the DPRK should abide by international regimes and UN mandates such as the Missile Technology Control Regime (MTCR) and IAEA inspection requests, and urges the peaceful settlement of any dispute that might arise between the DPRK with Japan, South Korea, or the United States (as in the case of Cheonan). Beijing also desires denuclearization on the Korean Peninsula: but her position appears somewhat ambiguous, as she does not appear to endorse the "complete and verifiable" disarmament that the United States, Japan, and South Korea demand, and seems rather to have a relatively lower threshold. Ideally, Beijing would like to modify Pyongyang's behavior without running the risks associated with a regime change. To that end, China has also worked quietly on the diplomatic front to persuade the North Koreans to reform their economy, negotiate with the United States, and enhance their relations with Seoul and Tokyo. What China will not do, however, is to go all out to threaten the DRPK, since the Chinese realize how insecure the leadership is. China has often remained relatively neutral in most instances of North–South altercations, and has often resisted calls from Washington, Tokyo, or Seoul to put more pressure or take punitive actions on Pyongyang.

Although there is no explicit linkage between the North Korea issue and China's Peaceful Rise, Beijing's handling of the DPRK issue is indicative of what she could do as a responsible member of the international community and aspiring Great Power. Of course there are other indicators, and China does appear keen to live up to the hype on its peaceful rise. During the Financial Crisis of 1997/98, Beijing's refusal to partake in competitive currency devaluation allowed most of the region to export themselves out of the crisis. Beijing's ascent and commitment to live up to her obligations under the World Trade Organization, her acquiescence to cooperate (not without resistance) with the World Health Organization during the SARS crisis, and the economic opportunities accorded to Southeast Asian states as a result of the growth, are often-quoted examples of her peaceful rise. But China surely must realize that her peaceful rise does not stop at China becoming one of the significant powers in the region or, indeed, the world, but rather that most countries view China to be the second most powerful country after the United States. To that extent, China should view the problems that afflict the region and the world beyond the myopic lens of national interest, and rather should adopt the perspective of the global good.

Unlike Japan, China's handling of the North Korean issue has always been subtle and understated. Unfortunately, this is not how Pyongyang perceives Beijing's position. The North Koreans perceive that the Chinese have not fulfilled their obligations, which stem from ideological fraternity and political solidarity built up over the years, and think they have been dragging their feet on economic assistance. The expectations of the United States and her allies (Japan, South Korea) run counter to the direction that North Korea expects China to take—with the former lobbying China to get "tougher" with North Korea as a way of making good her promise to be a responsible member of the international community. This weighs tremendously on China's aspiration to become a responsible member of the international community. As North Korea becomes increasingly bolder and more assertive, despite the PRC's quiet diplomacy, China is becoming faced with an increasingly difficult dilemma: how could and should she steer the DPRK to be less aggressive and provocative and more conciliatory, as China ascends to be one of the world's great powers? Like Japan's normalization, the debate on China's Peaceful Rise and North Korea is fraught with disagreements and ambiguity, to the extent that one might think it to be an abstract academic exercise rather than a concrete question of foreign policy. How, then, do we locate and contextualize North Korea as between China and Japan?

New Thinking on North Korea for Sino–Japanese Relations

If there is anything to be learnt about the DPRK's international behavior over the past two decades, it is that the DPRK is relatively insensitive to international pressure. Threats of sanctions and recriminations almost invariably bring about harsher responses in rhetoric from Pyongyang, rather than concessions of any lasting sort. Unlike most other alleged "rogue" states (e.g., Iran), the DPRK's economy is in an extremely bad shape, and increased sanctions against the DPRK are of only marginal significance to an already suffering regime. In fact, sanctions would only reduce pressure on the ruling regime, as the foreign powers and their sanctions can then be blamed for the miserable state of affairs. Arguably, more than any of her neighbors, North Korea's foreign policy is guided by domestic political considerations, as are her decisions regarding nuclear weapons. North Korea's desire to pursue nuclear weapons stems from a deep-seated insecurity.[54] The strategy to acquire weapons of mass destruction is not built on a fancy or whim on the part of the DPRK leadership from the mid-1990s onwards, but represents a concerted effort since the early 1950s[55] when Kim Il-sung learned of the United States'[56] and USSR's Atoms for Peace program.[57]

Nuclear weapons provide an existential guarantee to the DPRK regime, shore up the Korean Workers Party's domestic political legitimacy, lend it diplomatic leverage, assist in the extraction of continued economic aid, and provide a strategic equalizer in what most analysts would agree is a rough strategic neighborhood.[58] Not only is Pyongyang threatened by the United States, but North Korea probably feels that none of her neighbors—Russia and China included—can be relied on to help ensure her security. Today, the North Koreans have crossed the threshold of simply "experimenting" with nuclear technology. While it is probably true that the North Koreans are using their nuclear weapons program as a bargaining chip, one must acknowledge the utility of their strategy. If the international community cave in to their demands, all that the North Koreans are promising to do is halt (or more likely slow down) their

---

[54] For an extremely useful summary of North Korea's nuclear ambitions and history, see Walter C. Clemens, "North Korean's Quest for Nuclear Weapons: New Historical Evidence," *Journal of East Asian Studies* 10 (2010): 127–154.

[55] The Woodrow Wilson International Center for Scholars has a digital archive which examines the primary historical documents pertaining to DPRK nuclear ambitions dating back to the 1950s. For example, see Soviet Foreign Minister Andrei Gromyko's observation that the North Koreans were eager to start their own nuclear program: A. Gromyko, "From the Journal of Gromyko, Record of a Conversation with Ambassador Ri Sin-Pal of the Democratic People's Republic of Korea," April 30, 1958: http://digitalarchive.wilsoncenter.org/document/116019.

[56] Address by President Dwight D. Eisenhower to the 470th Plenary Meeting of the United Nations General Assembly, December 8, 1953: http://www. world-nuclear-university.org/about.aspx?id=8674&terms=atoms%20for%20peace.

[57] Siegfred S. Hecker, "Lessons Learned from the North Korean Nuclear Crises," *Daedalus* 139, no. 1 (Winter 2010): 44.

[58] The South Koreans, Russians, Chinese, and Japanese would most likely share this perception even though the "threat" is probably differently defined in each neighborhood. The Chinese, for example, would fear North Korea's nuclear capability as less threatening than, say, Japanese strategic independence, or the United States' direct intervention in North Korea as more threatening.

nuclear program; and if they don't, they will go ahead with building better and more powerful warheads and missile systems.

In President Bush's 2002 State of the Union Speech, he explicitly labeled North Korea as a member of the "axis of evil," one of a set of governments he saw as hell-bent on aiding terrorism and developing weapons of mass destruction. With the two-theatre war in Iraq and Afghanistan in full swing, the United States managed the North Korean problem with limited attention and resources. In January 2003, Pyongyang unilaterally withdrew from the Non-Proliferation Treaty (NPT), yet, a few months later, the DPRK proposed that the Six-Party Talks be resumed.[59] This proposal was ignored by the United States. Rather than a complete dismantling of the weapons, the North Koreans were hoping to provide evidence that all nuclear activities had been "frozen," thereby generating support in exchange for some sort of security exchange with the United States. By 2006 the North Koreans had conducted an atomic test,[60] officially giving the Chinese government twenty minutes advance warning.[61] Yet there were speculations over the efficacy of the technology held by the North, and especially as to the capability of Pyongyang's nuclear powers. By February 2007, North Korea had agreed to close its main nuclear reactor in exchange for fuel aid, and in June of the same year it shut down the main reactor at Yongbyon. By the summer of 2008, North Korea had made a declaration of her nuclear assets, and the United States removed North Korea from the list of countries that sponsor terrorism.[62] Yet by January 2009, the "honeymoon" period whereby the DPRK was engaged in international political deals, appeared to have all but dissipated. The DPRK's second nuclear test in May 2009, detonating a second device that was about twenty-times stronger than the previous,

---

[59] The six parties are instituted to help bring about an end to North Korea's nuclear program through negotiations. The talks began in August 2003 and have been disrupted by different political goals and interests and often contrasting diplomatic agendas. For a detailed report, see Benia Xu, "The Six-Party Talks on North Korea's Nuclear Program," February 29, 2012: http://www.cfr.org/proliferation/six-party-talks-north-koreas-nuclear-program/p13593.

[60] For a detailed report, see the Center for Non-Proliferation Studies, Monterey Institute for International Studies, "North Korea Conducts a Nuclear Test," October 10, 2006: http://cns.miis.edu/stories/pdfs/061010_dprktest.pdf.

[61] *Washington Post*, Oct 9, 2006.

[62] "US Declares North Korea off the Terror List," *New York Times*, October 12, 2008.

reaffirmed her nuclear capabilities.[63] In August of the same year, Pyongyang launched a rocket which it said was a communications satellite, demonstrating to the world once again the North Koreans' ability to launch satellites. The DPRK conducted a third nuclear test on February 13, 2011.

Consequently, the portrayal of the DPRK has taken on a life of its own in the United States, China, and Japan. If anything, though, the narratives playing out in the three powers have been quite different. In the United States, the DPRK is cast as a global threat and geopolitical nuisance, a member of the axis of evil bent on the acquisition of nuclear weapons, a sponsor of global terrorism, and an enemy of the free world. In Japan, the dominant perception of the Japanese people is that it is a rogue nation that endangers Japan, as evidenced by the DPRK's frank and startling admissions that Japanese nationals were kidnapped and brought to North Korea. Beyond that, the DPRK's flagrant violation of the UN moratorium on missile technology transfers, and its accelerated military buildup while naming Japan and the United States as principal threats to the nation, are also causes for alarm. The DPRK's 1998 missile tests, which saw the *Taepong-2* missiles fly over Japan, as well as her nuclear tests, deeply violated the non-nuclear principles cherished by the Japanese since the end of World War II. In short, for the Japanese, the DPRK poses an existential threat. Yet to the Chinese, the DPRK is an old friend with an outdated way of economic thinking, and is an extremely threatened ally. Certainly, the DPRK is not the global sponsor of terrorism that the Americans cast it as, nor a nation that threatens the existence of others as Japan would believe. Even with these very different perceptions and thinking, the Chinese, Japanese, and Americans can agree on the lowest denominator: it is imperative that the North Koreans be brought back in to the fold of proper international behavior and that, if at all possible, the Korean Peninsula issues be resolved without the use of force.

These developments should not be perceived in a vacuum. North Korea has been extremely important for the domestic debates by the new conservatives in Tokyo, and to a lesser extent for China's discussions on her Peaceful Rise. The emergence and coincidence of these two narratives both inspires and draws from political conservatism in both countries, thinly veiling the Great Power aspirations in both Tokyo and Beijing today. The "escalation" of the problems on the Korean Peninsula have

[63] "North Korea Conduct a Second Nuclear Test," *BBC News*, May 25, 2009: http://news.bbc.co.uk/2/hi/8066615.stm.

corresponded to a "deterioration" in Sino–Japanese relations over the last decade and a half. Since 1995 we have seen a dramatic downward spiral in relations between China and Japan. As the second and third largest economies in the world, China and Japan appear to be at loggerheads over everything: from history-related issues (e.g., the Yasukuni Shrine visits, arguments over revisionist history, wartime responsibility, and apologies), to intractable material issues that appear to be premised on geopolitical notions of national interest (e.g., East China Sea energy deposits, the territorial dispute over the Senkaku/Diaoyu islands). At the center of their acrimonious relations is an intersection between contested memories and identities and clashing interests. As China seeks to demonstrate that its rise is peaceful and Japan looks to the international community for her "normalization," the intense competition between China and Japan appears to be evolving beyond East Asia. If press reports are to be believed, China and Japan are engaged in a war to win the hearts and minds of their neighbors in Southeast Asia as to the sourcing of mineral resources in Africa and the Middle East. Narratives of competition and conflict are of course a lot sexier than mundane stories of international cooperation and diplomatic goodwill. Academics expound on such things to highlight the importance of their research, policymakers emphasize them to boost their powers and policymaking portfolios, and newspapers report them to increase their sales.

As mentioned, although this competition might appear detached from the events on the Korean Peninsula, in reality there are intricate linkages. One underlying commonality is the rigid sense of state-based nationalism, coupled with increased security concerns and demonization, designed to feed the nationalisms in the Koreas, China, and Japan. This in turn has enabled conservative elements in Japan and China to thrive. They have continued to rise politically, and now dominate the debates in the country with accentuated tensions and insecurities on all sides. Admittedly, the United States also plays an important part in the dynamics of the domestic politics of these countries, but, nonetheless, one cannot deny that in practice, China and probably Japan could do much more to influence the tone and direction of developments on the Korean Peninsula. We often assume it is the United States alone which is able to influence the course of events, and this significantly underestimates the potential for China and Japan to improve the situation with regards North Korea. Additionally, the Korean issue is not given enough consideration with respect to Sino–Japanese relations. While it is true that both China and Japan have played a relatively negative role in the history of the Koreas, through their hegemonic contentions and imperialistic ambitions, one cannot discount the potential for these two great powers to ensure that the Korean Peninsular remains nuclear free and that inter-Korean relations develop on an even keel. This should not be seen as something that is outrageously difficult, nor for that matter something that falls outside the sphere of interests of Japan and China—or, indeed, of South Korea or United States.

From Beijing's handling of trade disputes between China and South Korea (the so-called Garlic War, 1999/2000) and China and Japan (the so-called Mushroom War, 2001), it is clear that Beijing treats Japan with more consideration and sensitivity—even though Beijing has retaliated against Seoul's and Tokyo's protectionism.[64] On issues pertaining to the DPRK, the South Koreans have found themselves being tied to the Americans more than they desire—even if they often find themselves compromising between China and the United States.[65] If South Korea sees China's rise as a China threat, there is no question that this limits South Korea's strategic options.[66] In a strange turn of events, the Japanese too have found themselves disagreeing with the United States. Yet the United States' standoff with the North Koreans is much more than a case of North Korean recalcitrance—the reunification scenarios and the nuclear problem is very much tied to the United States' presence in East Asia. It is the Korean threat that provides the domestic justification to the American taxpayers to foot the bill for the US presence and persuades much of the international community to enable US (and UN) forces to be stationed

[64] In South Korea's case, Beijing employed severe sanctions on industrial goods, i.e., mobile handsets and polyethylene products, whilst in the Japan's case, China imposed softer measures in the form of higher tariffs. It has been suggested that in the Japanese case, both the Chinese and the Japanese were more aware of the "face" factor which might aggravate the situation. In the Korean case, the Chinese were keen to "teach" the South Koreans a lesson for hastily putting in place the harsher sanctions. See Jae Ho Chung, "From a Special Relationship to a Normal Partnership?: Interpreting the 'Garlic Battle'," *Sino–South Korean Relations in Pacific Affairs* 76, no. 4 (Winter, 2003/04): 549–568.

[65] Jae Ho Chung, "South Korea between Eagle and Dragon," *Asian Survey* 41, no. 5 (September 2001): 778–779.

[66] Chung, "South Korea between Eagle and Dragon": 777–788; Chung identifies nine available options for South Korea's policy. They include: (1) preventive war, (2) jumping on a bandwagon, (3) distancing (i.e., downgrading a relationship), (4) neutrality/self-help, (5) binding, (6) engagement, (7) balancing/containment, (8) hedging, and (9) issue-based support. These options are drawn from Randall L. Schwaller, "Managing the Rise of Great Powers: History and Theory," and Alastair Ian Johnston and Robert Ross, "Conclusion," both in *Engaging China*, edited by Johnson and Ross (London: Routledge), 7–17, 273–78.

south of the 38th parallel. This is linked to the continued strategic alliance between South Korea and the United States, and contributes to the strategic environment that necessitates an American forward presence in East Asia. In short, the continued strategic eminence of the United States in the Asia-Pacific relies, in part, on the existence of the current regime. Regime survival in the DPRK might, ironically, be as important to the Kim family and the Korean Worker Party elites as it is to the more conservative forces in Washington DC. What this means is that prospects of a peaceful Korean reunification or even cordial relations might be exceedingly hard to realize, as long as the United States is left to "lead" or manage the relations on the Peninsula.

In the same light, Japan's alliance with the United States is also extracting a heavy price on the latitude of Japan's strategic options in dealing with the North. Japan's normalization agenda certainly, today, appears to be premised upon a staunch reaffirmation of the US–Japan alliance, with a heavy dose of anti-PRC element—such as was never seen before, even in Japan's political conservatism of the 1950s to 1980s. Yet when one considers how the North Korean issue is driving (and is used to drive) Japanese politics and foreign policy from a macro-perspective, it becomes evident that the prospects for achieving the goals of returning the abductees and denuclearization are becoming more distant by the day. The rhetoric of the DPRK as a threat and its relations to domestic politics and foreign affairs is much like what Shakespeare's Porter remarks about alcohol: "it provokes the desire, but it takes away the performance."

Conclusion

To that end, China and Japan should consider North Korean issues not, so to speak, as a standalone "problem," but as a "common" problem. China and Japan should together consider how North Korean issues impinge on their foreign relations and relations with other parties. As noted above, Japan has been extremely resistant to follow the United States' lead on North Korea, with Tokyo insisting strongly on the resolution of the kidnapping issues before all else. Even as the conservative element of the Liberal Democratic Party has successfully brought the DPRK issue to the forefront of Japan's strategic agenda, there are opportunity costs. The DPRK issue is actually creating a schism in the US–Japan Security Alliance while driving the United States and China closer—even if the United States and China disagree as to what extent and with what means to deter North Korea. The United States' position has always been clear: complete and utter abandonment of the DPRK nuclear weapons program, and its opening up to IAEA inspections. China, on the other hand, appears to be ambiguous and more lenient than the United States (or Japan). Yet on a more fundamental level, both analysts in the PRC and in Japan know that the DPRK's posture with the bomb is more for political posture and regime longevity than as an offensive military weapon.[67] As Siegfried Hecker notes, there is "actually no price high enough for Pyongyang to sell. It is not about to give up nuclear weapons first as a condition of denuclearization. Pyongyang may agree to denuclearize in principle, but it will drag out implementation as it did during the six-party process."[68]

If Japan would indeed like to handle the North Korean issue in a manner that is different from the United States, the first point of departure would perhaps be to convince China that it might be in her best interest to persuade the DRPK to adopt a more enlightened policy towards Japan. China, more than the United States, could help persuade the North Koreans to take the Japanese request more seriously. The reason is simple: China and Japan have relatively similar goals on the Korean Peninsula, and, unlike the United States, China's sway over both the DPRK and ROK is substantial. Unfortunately, the same conservatives in Tokyo who are highlighting the North Korean threat are the same group who encourage the military build-up to "balance" China, just as they are the same collective who insist on more "equal" relations with the United States. Unless the conservatives are considering a state of perpetual confrontation with an insecure (nuclear) North Korea and an ascendant rising China—something which would not seem to be a good idea alongside their adjustment of "relations" with the United States—then surely it would be in their interests to quietly ameliorate their political platform and so work with the Chinese in the resolution of the issue. Beyond that, surely the same group must recognize that Japan–ROK relations are not all that rosy, and given the strategic situation of Northeast Asia, working together with the Chinese to rein in North Korea might actually increase the strategic latitude available to them. Even with her current problems with Pyongyang, China's relations with the DRPK are still considerably less toxic than United States' or Japan's relations with North Korea. The value of Chinese acquiescence and facilitation in order to bring North Korea

---

[67] This, however, is contested. The DPRK's nuclear ambition might no longer be a negotiating tactic but, rather, one borne out of a conscious attempt to become a nuclear state.

[68] Hecker, "Lessons Learned from the North Korean Nuclear Crises," 53.

back to negotiations with the United States and Japan cannot be underestimated.

China's leaders might recognize that the PRC's own goals on the Korean Peninsula might be more achievable if the Chinese could help the Japanese people recognize that the DPRK actually is not hell bent on destroying Japan, thus undermining North Korea's role as the strawman in Japanese politics. Of course, analysts might be tempted to consider the adage "my enemy's enemy is my friend," but the utility of such geopolitical thinking only goes so far. If China is able to modify North Korea's behavior towards Japan, not only does this affirm the Peaceful Rise thesis, but, more importantly, undermines the view that China is a bully and a threat in East Asia. Beijing could acknowledge privately that there are concerns about how the North Koreans are interacting with the Japanese. Hardening their position against the Japanese might do well for domestic legitimacy, but at the same time it vindicates the Japan conservatives' call not to "kowtow" to North Korea (and China) as well. It also might enable Japan to reach a more lasting understanding with the Japanese public itself. After all, Prime Minister Koizumi did visit Pyongyang, and during the DPJ years[69] Pyongyang did try to reach out to them.

Beijing and Tokyo surely must understand that if the Pyongyang regime is to be made to understand that giving up its nuclear programs will ensure its survival, while clinging on to them is a sure fire way to invite external intervention, then Pyongyang might be likely to denuclearize. Pyongyang is able to get away with what it is doing today largely because China, the United States, Japan, and Russia all hold very different positions with regards to the DPRK. Given the tensions in Sino–Japanese relations, Pyongyang would never believe that Beijing could assist Japanese goals and vice versa. Unless there is an improvement here, there is no way that the situation will improve on the Korean Peninsula. Beijing has not shown much interest in international sanctions on Pyongyang. The reasons are a complicated mix of geopolitics, concerns about the regional impact on Jilin and Liaoning provinces, and perhaps ideological affinity

[69] Interestingly, it has been argued that the brief interruption to the rule of the Liberal Democratic Party by the Democratic Party of Japan has not unleashed significant policy transformation in Japan, owing to a variety of reasons such as that party positions have been increasingly harmonized, and the presence of inexperienced legislators preventing much-needed reforms. See Phillip Lipscy and Ethan Scheiner, "Japan under the DPJ: The Paradox of Political Change without Policy Change," *Journal of East Asian Studies* 12 (2012): 311–322.

for their comrade-in-arms. Nonetheless, if Beijing decides to act against Pyongyang, then surely helping to enforce the sanctions would increase the pressure on the regime—given that a regime change is the ultimate security goal that the current Korean Workers Party is trying to forestall.

Given the new leadership that has recently been installed in China, Japan, and North Korea, it might actually benefit the region if both China and Japan can come to a consensus to take the lead in striking a "grand bargain" with North Korea.[70] In essence, North Korea could be offered a package that involves development aid, economic engagement, and political assurances, in return for concessions on partaking in state-sponsored terrorism, returning all kidnapped nationals, abiding by international conventions such as the MTCR, and IAEA inspections. Most importantly, China and Japan must persuade the United States from unnecessary diplomatic rhetoric, and encourage the United States to end economic sanctions and engage the DPRK in a dialogue in an effort to get the North Koreans to agree to a No-First-Use of Weapons of Mass Destruction, and if possible sign an agreement to end the Korean War. In short, China and Japan could help bridge the gap between North Korea and the United States' positions on a host of issues, and this would, at root, be to their own benefit.

---

[70] Mike Mochizuki and Michael O'Hanlon have argued persuasively that it would be possible for the United States to strike a grand bargain with the DPRK by persuading all parties to partake in a broad plan to address the issue at the core of the problems in the Korean Peninsula—that of the failure of the North Korean Command economy and the DPRK's economic atrophy through demands that the nuclear issues are not negotiated separately and on a piecemeal basis. M. O'Hanlon and M. Mochizuiki, "Toward a Grand Bargain with North Korea," *Washington Quarterly* 26, no. 4 (Autumn 2003): 7–18.

SELECTED BIBLIOGRAPHY

"Aso Calls for Japan, China to Unite." *Associated Free Press*, April 3, 2009.

Akihiko, T. *Nicchu kankei, 1949–1990* [Japan–China Relations, 1949–1990]. Tokyo: University of Tokyo Press, 1991.

Amako, S. *China in Japanese Eye*. Beijing: Social Sciences Academic Press, 2003.

Bercovitc, J., K. B. Huang, and C. C. Teng. *Conflict Management, Security and Intervention in East Asia: Third-Party Mediation in Regional Conflict*. London and New York: Routledge, 2008.

Betts, R. K. "Wealth, Power, and Instability: East Asia and the United States after the Cold War." *International Security* 18, no. 3 (1994): 34–77.

Butler, M. J. *International Conflict Management: An Introduction*. London and New York: Routledge, 2009.

Buzan, B. and G. Segal. "Rethinking East Asian Security." *Survival* 36, no. 2 (2010): 3–21.

Calder, K. E. "US Foreign Policy in Northeast Asia." In *The International Relations of Northeast Asia*. Edited by S. K. Samuel. Lanham, MD: Rowman & Littlefield, 2004.

Campbell, K. M., N. Patel, and V. J. Singh. *The Power of Balance: America in Asia*. Center for New American Security, 2008. Available at: http://www.cnas.org/files/documents/publications/CampbellPatelSingh_iAsia_June08.pdf.

"Caring for Korea: US Must Be Open to Offering Concessions to Pyongyang." *Financial Times*, March 31, 2009.

Carr, E. H. *What is History?* New York: Alfred A. Knopf, 1961.

Center for Non-Proliferation Studies, Monterey Institute for International Studies. *North Korea Conducts a Nuclear Test*. October 10, 2006.

Cha, H. "Pyongyang, 1,575 years." *Pyongyang Times*, November 16, 2002.

Cha, V. "Abandonment, Entrapment, and Neoclassical Realism in Asia." *International Studies Quarterly* 44, no. 2 (2000): 261–291.

—. "We Have No Plan." *Chosun Ilbo*, June 9, 2008.

Cha, V. D., "What do they want?" *PacNet*, no. 36, May 18, 2009.

Chan, J. "Japan's Alarmist Reaction to North Korean Missile Test." *World Socialist Website*, April 16, 2009.

Chan, Y. Y. "North Korea's Resurgence and China's Rise: Implications for the Future of Northeast Asian Security." *East Asia* 25 (2008): 293–316.

Chestnut, S. "Illicit Activity and Proliferation: North Korea Smuggling Networks." *International Security* 32, no. 1 (2007): 80–111.

Chen, D. "Domestic Politics, National Identity, and International Conflict: The Case of the Koguryo Controversy." *Journal of Contemporary China* 21, no. 74 (2012): 227–241.

Cheng, J. Y. "China and the Korean Situation: The Challenge of Pyongyang's Brinkmanship." *East Asia: An International Quarterly* 20, no. 4 (2003): 52–76.

"China Calls for Maintaining Peace and Stability on Korean Peninsula." *Xinhuat*, October 10, 2012.

"Chinese President Meets DPRK Premier, Urges Resumed Nuclear Talks." *Xinhua*, March 19, 2009.

Cho, Y. and J. H. Jeong. "China's Soft Power: Discussion, Resources, and Prospects." *Asian Survey* 48, no. 3 (2008): 453–472.

Choi, K. and M. Choe. "Current Status, Prospects, and Countermeasures of the North Korean Nuclear Issue." *IFANS Review* 16, no. 2 (2009): 41.

Chong, A. "Singaporean Foreign Policy and the Asian Value Debate, 1992–2000: Reflections on an Experiment in Soft Power." *Pacific Review* 17, no. 1 (2004): 95–133.

Choo, J. "Mirroring North Korea's Growing Economic Dependence on China: Political Ramifications." *Asian Survey* 48, no. 2 (2008): 343–372.

Christensen, T. J. *Useful Adversaries: Grand Strategy, Domestic Mobilization, and Sino–American Conflict, 1947–1958*. Princeton: Princeton University Press, 1998.

—. "China, the US–Japan Alliance, and the Security Dilemma in East Asia." *International Security* 23, no. 4 (1999): 47–98.

—. *Fostering Stability or Creating a Monster?: The Rise of China and US Policy toward East Asia. International Security* 31, no. 1 (2006): 81–126.

Chung, J. H. "South Korea between Eagle and Dragon." *Asian Survey* 41, no. 5 (2001): 777–796.

—. "From a Special Relationship to A Normal Partnership?: Interpreting the 'Garlic Battle' in Sino–South Korea Relations." *Pacific Affairs* 76, no. 4 (2003): 549–568.

Chung, K. "Japanese–North Korean Relations Today." *Asian Survey* 4, no. 4 (1964): 788– 803.

Clemens, W. C. "North Korea's Quest for Nuclear Weapons: New Historical Evidence." *Journal of East Asian Studies* 10, no. 1 (2010): 127–154.

Collingwood, R. G. *The Idea of History*. Oxford: Oxford University Press, 1946.

Committee for the Development though Truth Finding, National Intelligence Agency, ed. *Kwago wa taehwa, mirae ui songchal: chuyo uihok sagon pyon* [Dialogue with the past, reflections for the future: Main mysterious incidents] Seoul: National Intelligence Agency, 2007.

Cooper, R. "The Goals of Diplomacy, Hard Power, and Soft Power." In *American Power in the 21st Century*. Edited by D. Held and M. Koenig-Archibugi. Cambridge: Polity Press, 2004.

Cossa, R. A. "Continuity and Change: US Asia Policy," *PacNet*, no. 18, March 6, 2009.

Cossa, R. A., B. Glosserman, M. A. McDevitt, N. Patel, J. Przystup, and B. Roberts. "The United States and the Asia-Pacific Region: Security Strategy for the Obama Administration." Co-published by IDA, Pacific Forum CSIS, INSS, CNA, and CNAS, 2009.

Croce, B. *History as the Story of Liberty*. London: George Allen & Unwin, 1941.

Dalby, S. "Crossing Disciplinary Boundaries: Political Geography and International Relations after the Cold War." In *Globalization: Theory and Practice*. Edited by E. Kofman and G. Youngs. London: Pinter, 1996.

Demick, B. *Nothing to Envy: Ordinary Lives in North Korea*. New York: Spiel & Grau, 2010.

Denisov, V. I. "Inter-Korean Settlement and Russia's Interests." *International Affairs* 51, no. 3 (2005): 125–136.

Dollar, D. "South Korea–China Trade Relations: Problems and Prospects." *Asian Survey* 29, no. 12 (1989): 1167–1176.

Doi, A. "What Hillary Should Tell Japan." *PacNet*, no.8, February 4, 2009.

Dong X., X. Wang, and Y. Li. *How the Koreans View China*. Beijing: Social Sciences Academic Press, 2012.

Duffield, J. S. "Asia-Pacific Security Institutions in Comparative Perspective." In *International Relations Theory and the Asia Pacific*. Edited by G. J. Ikenberry and M. Mastanduno. New York: Columbia University Press, 2003.

Dynkin, A. A. *Strategic Global Outlook 2030*. Moscow: Institute of World Economic and International Relations, Russian Academy of Sciences, 2011.

Eberstadt, N. "Financial Transfers from Japan to North Korea Estimating the Unreported Flows." *Asian Survey* 36, no. 5 (1996): 523–542.

Embassy in Tokyo to the Minister of Foreign Affairs. "Mi-Il sunoe hoedam ui p'yong'ga pogoso" [Analysis report on US–Japan summit]. Iljong 700-5157, September 12, 1972. In *Tanaka Kakuei Ilbon susang Miguk pangmun* [Japanese Prime Minister Tanaka Kakuei's visit to the United States]. August 31/September 1, 1972. C-0052 (ROK diplomatic archive).

Friedberg, A. L. "Ripe for Rivalry: Prospects for Peace in a Multipolar Asia." *International Security* 18, no. 3 (1994): 5–33.

Funabashi, Y. *The Peninsula Question: A Chronicle of the Second Korean Nuclear Crisis*. Washington, DC: Brookings Institution Press, 2007.

Gaddis, J. L. *Strategic Containment: A Critical Appraisal of American National Security Policy during the Cold War*. Oxford: Oxford University Press, 2005.

Garrett, B. and B. Glaser. "Looking across the Yalu: Chinese Assessments of North Korea." *Asian Survey* 35, no. 6 (1995): 528–545.

Garrison, J. A. "China's Prudent Cultivation of 'Soft' Power and Implications for US Policy in East Asia." *Asian Affairs* 32, no. 1 (2005): 25–30.

Gilpin, R. *War and Change in World Politics* Cambridge: Cambridge University Press, 1981.

Gomà, D. "The Chinese–Korean Border Issue: An Analysis of a Contested Frontier." *Asian Survey* 46, no. 6 (2006): 867–880.

Gries, P. H. "The Koguryo Controversy, National Identity, and Sino–Korean Relations Today." *East Asia* 22, no. 4 (2005): 3–17.

Haggard, S. and M. Noland. "North Korea in 2007: Shuffling in from the Cold." *Asian Survey* 48, no. 1 (2008): 107–115.

Hagström, L. and M. Söderberg. "Taking Japan–North Korea Relations Seriously: Rationale and Background." *Pacific Affairs* 79, no. 3 (2006): 373–385.

He, F. "A Study on 'Imperial Tributary System'." *Journal of Peking University (Humanities and Social Sciences)* no. 6 (1998): 30–45.

Hecker, S. S. "Lessons Learned from the North Korean Nuclear Crises." *Daedalus* 139, no. 1 (2010): 44–56.

Hensley, G. "Asia-Pacific Security: Paradox and Riddle." *New Zealand International Review* 23, no. 1 (1998): 33–37.

Hirotaka, W. "Dealing with Pyongyang." *Japan Echo*, February, 2003.

Hisahiko, O. and N. Yasuhiro. "Negotiate Patiently with North Korea." *Japan Echo*, February, 2003.

Howe, C. "China, Japan, and Economic Interdependence in the Asia-Pacific Region." *China Quarterly* 124 (1990): 662–693.

Hsu, J. W. "MOFA Reiterates Claim over Diaoyutai Isles." *Taipei Times*, February 28, 2009.

Hughes, C. W. *The Political Economy of Japanese Sanctions Towards North Korea: Domestic Coalitions and International Systemic Pressures*. University of Warwick Institutional Repository, 2006. Available at: http://wrap.warwick.ac.uk/1016/1/WRAP_Hughes_9871481-080709-political_economy_of_sanctions_towards_north_korea_wrap.pdf.

—. *"Super-Sizing" the DPRK Threat: Japan's Evolving Military Posture and North Korea*. University of Warwick Institutional Repository, 2009. Available at: http://wrap.warwick.ac.uk/1015/1/WRAP_Hughes_9871481-080709-super-sizing_the_dprk_threat_wrap.pdf.

—. "Japan–North Korea Relations from the North-South Summit to the Koizumi-Kim Summit." *Asia Pacific Review* 9, no. 2 (2010): 61–78.

Hughes, C. W. and A. Fukushima. "US–Japan Security Relations: Toward Bilateralism Plus?" In *Beyond Bilateralism: US–Japan Relations in the New Asia-Pacific*. Edited by E. S. Krauss and T. J. Pempel. Stanford: Stanford University Press, 2004.

Hwang, J. "Lee, Hu Share Concern about North Korea Launch." *Korea Herald*, April 3, 2009.

Hyun, D. *The Historical Perception of Korea and Japan*. Seoul: Nanam, 2008.

Ikegami, M. "China–North Korea: Renewal of the 'Blood Alliance'." *Asia Pacific Bulletin*, no. 158 (2012): 5–7.

"Ilbon ui tae Pukhan kyongje kwan'gye chuyo hyonan munui e taehan hoesin" [Reply to the inquiry into the main issues related to Japan's economic relations with North Korea], from the Korea Central Intelligence Agency to the Minister of Foreign Affairs, Chungjaehaeng 150. In *Ilbon–Pukhan kyongje kwan'gye, 1972* [Japan–North Korea economic relations, 1972]. 725.6JA, 1972, D-0012 (ROK diplomatic archive).

"Ilbon ui tae Pukhan plant suchul mit suchurip unhaeng chagum sayong sung'in munje, 1974" [Japanese export of manufacturing plants to North Korea and the controversy over the approval of the use of Export-Import Bank Loans, 1974]. 725.6JA, D-0018 (ROK diplomatic archive).

Iriye, A. "Chinese–Japanese Relations." *China Quarterly* 124, no. 4 (1990): 624–638.

"Japan Lavishes Aid on Pacific Islands." *Associated Press*, May 28, 2006.

"Japanese Prime Minister: The US Will Help in Japan–China Conflict." *Voice of America* [in Chinese], February 26, 2009.

Joint Communiqué of the Government of Japan and the Government of the People's Republic of China, September, 1972. Available at: http://www. mofa.go.jp/region/asia-paci/china/joint72.html.

Jordan, E. C. "The Concept of A Middle Power in International Relations: Distinguishing Between Emerging and Traditional Middle Power." *Politikon: South African Journal of Political Studies* 30, no. 2 (2003): 165–181.

Kang, C. H. *Ethnic Koreans in Japan Victimized by the North Korean Regime's Fraud.* Korean Unification Research Institute of Chosun Ilbo, 2003. Available at: http://www.dailynk.com/english/keys/2003/12/05.php.

Kang, D. "The 100 Years of Kando Convention… 'Returning our Lost Land' is Spreading." *Hankook Ilbo*, September 2, 2009.

"Kang kongsa wa Sunobe asea kukjang kwaui myondamrok" [Memorandum of conversation between Minister at the Embassy in Tokyo Kang Young-kyu and Director of Asian Affairs Bureau Sunobe]. JAW-01025, January 4, 1972. In *Han-Il jongmu ilban* [Korea–Japan political affairs], 722.1JA, C-0051 (ROK diplomatic archive).

Khong, Y. F. "The United States and East Asia: Challenges to the Balance of Power." In *Explaining International Relations*. Edited by N. Woods. Oxford: Oxford University Press, 1996.

Kim, C. "Finding the Baikal Lake, the Symbol of Korean National Origins." *Yŏksa T'amhŏm*, no. 1, supplement to *Wŏlgan Chungang* (2003): 36–46.

"Kim Jong Il, the Tyrant with a Passion for Wine, Women, and the Bomb." *The Independent*, October 21, 2006.

Kim, R. U. T. "Sino–North Korean Relations." *Asian Survey* 8, no. 8 (1968): 708–722.

Kim, T. "China's Ascendancy and the Future of the Korean Peninsula." In *Korea in the New Asia: East Asian Integration and the China Factor*. Edited by F. Nicolas. London: Routledge, 2007.

—. "Gathering Storm or Silver Lining out of the Clouds? The North Korea Nuclear Issue and the Case for Coercive Diplomacy." *Korea Observer* 41, no. 3 (2010): 439–469.

Kim, Y. M. "The Dilemma of North Korea's Japanese Wives." *JPRI Critique*, no. 5 (1997): 10.

"Koizumi's Shrine Visit Criticized." *Xinhua News Agency*, January 2, 2004.

Ku, C. "Uncovering Korea's Past." *Pyongyang Times*, September 22, 2002.

Kurlantzick, J. *Charm Offensive: How China's Soft Power is Transforming the World*. New Haven, CT: Yale University Press, 2007.

Lee, G. "A Theory of Soft Power and Korea's Soft Power Strategy." *Korean Journal of Defense Analysis* 21, no. 2 (2009): 205–218.

Lee, S. H. and J. C. Baek. *Korea–US Relations in Transition: Korea–US Alliance in Retrospect and Prospects for a New Strategic Partnership*. Seongnam: Sejong Institute, 2002.

Leheny, D. "A Narrow Place to Cross Swords: Soft Power and the Politics of Japanese Popular Culture in East Asia." In *Beyond Japan: The Dynamics of East Asian Regionalism*. Edited by P. Katzenstein and T. Shiraishi. Ithaca: Cornell University Press, 2006.

Lind, J. M. "Pacifism or Passing the Buck." *International Security* 29, no. 1 (2004): 92–121.

Lipscy, P. Y. and E. Scheiner. "Japan under the DPJ: The Paradox of Political Change without Policy Change." *Journal of East Asian Studies* 12, no. 3 (2012): 311–322.

Liu, M. "China and the North Korean Crisis: Facing Test and Transition," *Pacific Affairs* 76, no. 3 (2003): 347–373.

Luck, G. and W. Perry. "Testimony at the US Senate." *US Department of State Transcript*, January 15, 1995.

Lynn, H. G. "Vicarious Traumas: Television and Public Opinion in Japan's North Korea Policy." *Pacific Affairs* 79, no. 3 (2006): 483–508.

Mack, A. "North Korea and the Bomb." *Foreign Policy*, no. 83 (1991): 87–104.

Mann, J. *About Face: A History of America's Curious Relationship with China, from Nixon to Clinton*. New York: Vintage Books, 2000.

Manyin, M. E., E. Chanlett-Avery, and H. Marchart. *North Korea: A Chronology of Events, October 2002–December 2004*. CRS Report for Congress, January 24, 2005.

Manyin, M. E. *Japan–North Korea Relations: Selected Issues*. CRS Report for Congress. Washington, DC: Library of Congress, 2003.

Mearsheimer, J. J. "Back to the Future: Instability in Europe after the Cold War." *International Security* 15, no. 1 (1990): 5–56.

—. *The Tragedy of Great Power Politics*. New York: Norton, 2001.

Meyer, A. H. *Assignment: Tokyo*. Indianapolis and New York: Bobbs-Merrill, 1974.

Ministry of Foreign Affairs to President, Abuk 700-11, January 12, 1972. In *Sato Eisaku Ilbon susang Miguk pangmun* [Japanese Prime Minister Sato Eisaku's visit to the United States], January 6/7, 1972, 722.12JA/US, 1971-72, C-0052 (ROK diplomatic archive).

Mochizuki, M. "Terms of Engagement: The US–Japan Alliance and the Rise of China." In *Beyond Bilateralism: US–Japan Relations in the New Asia-Pacific*. Edited by E. Krauss and T. J. Pempel. Stanford: Stanford University Press, 2004.

Morgenthau, H. J. *Politics among Nations: The Struggle for Power and Peace*. New York: Alfred A. Knopf, 1948.

Morris-Suzuki, T. "Lost Memories: Historical Reconciliation and Cross-Border Narratives in Northeast Asia." In *Contested Views of a Common Past: Revisions of History in Contemporary East Asia*. Edited by Steffi Richter. Frankfurt: Campus Verlag, 2008.

Nahm, A. C. *Korea: Traditions and Transformation, A History of the Korean People*. Seoul: Hollym, 1991.

Nanto, D. K. and M. E. Manyin. *China–North Korea Relations*. CRS Report for Congress. Washington, DC: Library of Congress, 2010.

Naotaka, I. *Nichi–Bei kakei to hutatsu no chugoku* [Japan–US Relations and Two Chinas]. Tokyo: Bokutakusha, 1995.

Nikitin, M. B. *North Korea's Nuclear Weapons*. CRS Report for Congress. Washington, DC: Library for Congress, 2009.

Niksch, L. A. *North Korea's Nuclear Weapons Program*. CRS Issue Brief for Congress. Washington, DC: Library for Congress, 2005.

"North Korean Cannibalism Fears Amid Claims Starving People Forced to Desperate Measures." *The Independent*, January 28, 2013.

"N.K Commits 221 Provocations Since 1953." *Korea Herald*, January 5, 2011.

"North Korea Conduct a Second Nuclear Test." *BBC News*, May 25, 2009.

"North Korea Warns against Intercepting 'Satellite' Launch." *CNN*, March 9, 2009.

Nye, J. *Bound to Lead: The Changing Nature of American Power*. New York: Basic Books, 1990.

—. *Soft Power: The Means to Succeed in World Politics*. New York: Public Affairs, 2004.

O'Hanlon, Michael E. "Stopping a North Korean Invasion: Why Defending South Korea Is Easier Than the Pentagon Thinks." *International Security* 22, no. 4 (1998): 153–156.

Oda, S. "The Normalization of Relations between Japan and the Republic of Korea." *American Journal of International Law* 61, no. 1 (1967): 35–56.

Okeshott, M. *Experience and its Modes*. Cambridge: Cambridge University Press, 1933.

Ong, R. "China, US and the North Korean Issue." *Asia Pacific Review* 13, no. 1 (2006): 118–135.

Park, I. "The Northeast Asian International Relations and Korea's National Interest: On the Perspective of the US–China–Japan's Power Balance." *Journal of East Asian Affairs* 4 (2005): 5–32.

Pempel, T. J., ed. *Remapping East Asia: The Construction of a Region*. Ithaca: Cornell University Press, 2005.

Perl, Raphael F. *Drug Trafficking and North Korea: Issues for US Policy*. CRS Report for Congress. Washington, DC: Library of Congress, 2007.

Peterson, V. S. "Shifting Ground: Epistemological and Territorial Remapping in the Context of Globalization." In *Globalization: Theory and Practice*. Edited by E. Kofman and G. Youngs. London: Pinter, 1996.

Petrov, L. A. "Restoring the Glorious Past: North Korean Juche Historiography and Goguryeo." *Review of Korean Studies* 7, no. 3 (2004): 231–252.

"'Pleasure squad' defector sheds light on life of Kim Jong Il." *National*, January 8, 2010.

Pollack, J. D. "The Major Powers and the Two Koreas: An Uneasy Transition." *Korean Journal of Defense Analysis* 21, no. 1 (2009): 1–9.

Prichard, C. L. *Failed Diplomacy: The Tragic Story of How North Korea Got the Bomb*. Washington, DC: The Brookings Institution, 2007.

"Pukgoe ui oechae hyonhwang mit sanghwan kyosop hwaldong" [North Korea's debt and its negotiation activities with regard to repayment]. In *Pukhan ui tae sobang oechae munje, 1976/77* [North Korea's debt to Western countries, 1976/77], 725.6XG, 2007-24 (ROK diplomatic archive).

Putnam, Robert. "Diplomacy and Domestic Politics: The Logic of Two-Level Games." *International Organization* 42, no. 3 (1998): 427–460.

Rozman, G. "Post–Cold War Evolution of Chinese Thinking on Regional Institutions in Northeast Asia." *Journal of Contemporary China* 19, no. 66 (2010): 605–620.

—. "East Asian Regionalism and Sinocentrism." *Japanese Journal of Political Science* 13, no. 1 (2012): 143–153.

Satoshi Amako. *China in Japanese Eyes*. Beijing: Social Sciences Academic Press, 2003.

Schaller, M. "Détente and the Strategic Triangle: Or, 'Drinking Your Mao Tai and Having Your Vodka, Too'." In *Re-examining the Cold War*.

Edited by R. S. Ross and C. Jiang. Massachusetts: Harvard University Press, 1971.

Seiichi, K. "Wielding Soft Power: The Key Stages of Transmission and Reception." In *Soft Power Superpowers*. Edited by Watanabe and McConnell. New York: M. E. Sharpe, 2008.

Simmons, R. R. "China's Cautious Relations with North Korea and Indochina." *Asian Survey* 11, no. 7 (1971): 629–644.

Shim, D. "Hybridity and the Rise of Korean Popular Culture in Asia." *Media Culture and Society* 28, no. 1 (2006): 25–44.

Snyder, G. "Mearsheimer's World—Offensive Realism and the Struggle for Security: A Review Essay." *International Security* 27, no. 1 (2002): 149–173.

Soeya, Y. *Japan's Economic Diplomacy with China, 1945–1978*. Oxford: Clarendon Press, 1998.

Soeya, Yoshihide, David A. Welch, and M. Takokoro, eds. *Japan as a "Normal Country"?: A Nation in Search of its Place in the World*. Toronto: University of Toronto Press, 2011.

Solingen, E. "East Asian Regional Institution: Characteristics, Sources, Distinctiveness." In *Remapping Asia: Competing Patterns of Regional Integration*. Edited by T. J. Pempel. Ithaca: Cornell University Press, 2005.

"South Korea Faces Skeptics at Home Over Evidence Linking North to Torpedo." *Bloomberg*, May 29, 2011.

"South Korean Tourist Shot Dead by North Soldier." *Reuters*, July 11, 2008.

Squassoni, S. *North Korea's Nuclear Weapons: Recent Developments*. CRS Report for Congress. Washington, DC: Library of Congress, 2006.

Steinberg, J. B. Deputy Secretary of State. "Engaging Asia 2009: Strategies for Success." Bureau of the Deputy Secretary, Remarks at the National Bureau of Asian Research Conference, Washington, DC, April 1, 2009. Available at: http://www.state.gov/s/d/2009/121564.htm.

Stephens, P. "A Diplomatic Feint that Looks to Leave Japan in the Cold." *Financial Times*, February 27, 2009.

Tang, S. and X. Cao. "Seeking the Base Point of Mutual Security between China, the United States and Japan." *Strategy and Management* 1 (2002): 99–109.

Tang, S. M. "The Future of Japanese Diplomacy: Challenges and Prospects." *Journal e-Bangi*, 2006.

Takahashi, T. "Japanese Neo–Conservatism: Coping with China and North Korea." *Security Challenges* 6, no. 3 (2010): 21–40.

Taylor, R. "China Arms Spend Prompts South Korea Arms Race Warning." *Reuters*, March 5, 2009.

Telegram from the Ambassador in Tokyo to the Minister of Foreign Affairs, "Kissinger pojwagwan nongil chongnyo" [Completion of National Security Advisor Kissinger's visit to Japan], JAW-08369, August 21, 1972 (ROK diplomatic archive).

Telegram from the Ambassador in Tokyo to the Minister of Foreign Affairs, JAW-01309, January 24, 1972. "Ilbon Il-Cho uhochokjin uiwonyonmaeng taepyodan Pukhan pangmun" [Visit to North Korea by the representatives of the Japan–North Korea Friendship Promotion League], 725.32JA, 1971/72 (ROK diplomatic archive).

Telegram from the Ambassador in Tokyo to the Minister of Foreign Affairs, JAW-02406, February 23, 1972. "Han-Il jongmu ilban" [Korea–Japan Political Affairs], 722.1JA, C-0051 (ROK diplomatic archive).

Telegram from the Ambassador in Tokyo to the Minister of Foreign Affairs, JAW-03297, March 17, 1972. "Han-Il jongmu ilban" [Korea–Japan political affairs], 722.1JA, C-0051 (ROK diplomatic archive).

Telegram from the Ambassador in Tokyo to the Minister of Foreign Affairs, JAW-06068, June 5, 1972. "Ilbon chuyo taepyodan Pukhan pangmun" [Japanese representatives' visit to North Korea], 725.32JA, 1972, D-0012 (ROK diplomatic archive).

Telegram from the Ambassador in Tokyo to the Minister of Foreign Affairs, JAW-09521, September 24, 1973. "Pukhan-Ilbon kwan'gye, 1973" [North Korea–Japan relations, 1973], 725.1JA, D-0014 (ROK diplomatic archive).

Telegram from the Embassy in Tokyo to the State Secretary, February 8,1972. POL 15-1 KOR N (US archive).

"The Cannibals of North Korea." *Washington Post*, February 5, 2013.

"The Commander's Special Pleasure, the 'Pleasure Group'." *Daily North Korea*, September 25, 2005.

Thornton, John L. *China's Peaceful Rise: Speeches of Zheng Bijian 1997–2004*. Washington, DC: Brookings Institution, 2005.

"Treasury Designates Banco Delta Asia as Primary Money Laundering Concern under USA Patriot Act." September 15, 2005. US Department of the Treasury. Available at:
http://www.ustreas.gov/press/releases/js2720.htm.

Trilateral Joint History Editorial Committee. *A History that Opens the Future: The Contemporary and Modern History of Three East Asian Countries*. Seoul: Hankyoreh Sinmunsa, 2005.

US National Intelligence Council. *Global Trends 2025: A Transformed World*. Washington, DC: Government Printing Office, 2008.

"US Congress Likely to Boost Pressure on Japan over Trade, Yasukuni." *Kyoto News International*, November 13, 2006.

"Utsunomiya Ilbon chamindang uiwon Pukhan pangmun, 1974.8.5–15" [LDP Diet member Utsunomiya's visit to North Korea, August 5–15, 1974], 725.32JA, D-0018 (ROK diplomatic archive).

Waltz, K. N. *Theory of International Politics*. New York: Addison Wesley, 1979.

—. "The Origin of War in Neorealist Theory." In *The Origin and Prevention of Major Wars*. Edited by R. I. Rotberg and T. K. Rabb. Cambridge: Cambridge University Press, 1989.

Wang, Y. "China, Economic Regionalism, and East Asian Integration." *Japanese Journal of Political Science* 12, no. 2 (2011): 195–212.

Warwick, J. "On North Korean Freighter, a Hidden Missile Factory." *Washington Post*, August 14, 2003.

—. "North Korea Shops Stealthily for Nuclear Arms Gear." *Washington Post*, August 15, 2003.

Wassterstorm, Jeff N. *Modern History of Three Countries of East Asia*. Beijing: Social Sciences Academic Press, 2005.

Weber, M. "Interpretive Sociology, and the Sense of Historical Science: A Positivistic Conception of Verstehen." *Sociological Quarterly* 18, no. 2 (1977): 165–175.

Wit, J. "Enhancing US Engagement with North Korea." *Washington Quarterly* 30, no. 2 (2007): 53–69.

Wolfers, A. *Discord and Collaboration: Essays on International Politics*. Baltimore: Johns Hopkins Press, 1962.

"Woman to be First South Korean in Space." *New York Times*, March 10, 2008.

Yamaji, H. *Policy Recommendations for Japan: Unification of the Korean Peninsula*. New York: Brookings Institution, 2004.

Yang, Y. *Tong'il chongch'aengnon* [A study on unification policy]. Seoul: Pakyongsa, 1997.

Yasushi, W. and D. L. McConnell, eds. *Soft Power Superpowers: Cultural and National Assets of Japan and the United States*. New York: M. E. Sharpe, 2008.

You, J. "China and North Korea: A Fragile Relationship with Strategic Convenience." *Journal of Contemporary China* 10, no. 28 (2001): 387–398.

Yun, H. S. "Reciprocity and Koizumi Government's North Korea Policy" [in Korean]. *Segye Jiyeok Yongu Nonchong* 25, no. 3 (2007): 191.

Zakaria, F. *The Post-American World.* New York: W.W. Norton and Company, 2008.

Zartman, I. W. *Negotiation and Conflict Management: Essays on Theory and Practice.* London and New York: Routledge, 2008.

Zhang, Y. "Searching the Road to Push East Asian Cooperation Forward." *Foreign Affairs Review* 6 (2008): 7–11.

Zhebin, A. "Some Aspects of Korea's Nuclear Crisis." In *Russia and Korea in the Changing World Order*. Edited by V. Tkachenko. Moscow: Institute of World Economic and International Relations, Russian Academy of Sciences, 2003.

CONTRIBUTORS

Hiroyasu AKUTSU is Senior Fellow in the sixth Research Office at the Research Department, National Institute for Defense Studies (NIDS), Japan. His research focuses on political and military affairs on the Korean Peninsula, security issues in Northeast Asia, and the Japan–US alliance. His selected publications are *The Hegemon's Alliance Security Dilemma: US Accommodation with Japan and the ROK from 1994 to 2004* (ANU, 2006), *Korea–Japan Security Relations: Prescriptive Studies* (co-authored) (Seoul: Oruem Publishing House, 2000) and *US–Korea–Japan Relations: Building Toward a "Virtual Alliance"* (co-authored) (CSIS, 1999). He has also written a number of scholarly articles published in international journals including "The New Shape of Asian Security," *Journal of International Security Affairs* (Spring 2007), and "Tokyo and Taipei Try to Tango," *Far Eastern Economic Review* (January 2007).

DONG Xiangrong is Associate Professor at the Institute of Asia-Pacific Studies, Chinese Academy of Social Sciences. She was also Visiting Scholar at the Arnold A. Saltzman Institute of War and Peace Studies at Columbia University in 2012. She has a special research interest in Korean studies. She has been publishing books and journal articles widely on Korean issues. Recent publications in Chinese include "The Asymmetric Alliance and Anti-Americanism in Korea," *Contemporary Asia-Pacific* (June 2009), *The External Force of Korea's Take-off: The US Impact on Korea's Development in 1945–1965* (Beijing: Social Sciences Academic Press of China, 2005).

JIANG Lifeng is Professor and former Director at the Institute of Japanese Studies, Chinese Academy of Social Sciences. Professor Jiang sits on the China–Japan Joint Committee on History and is widely regarded as China's top specialist on contemporary Japan. His recent publications in Chinese include *Japan: 2005* (co-edited) (Beijing: Shijie Zhishi Chubanshe, 2006), *On Japanese Militarism* (co-edited) (Hebei: Hebei People's Press) and *The Government and Politics in Japan* (co-authored) (Taipei: Yangzhi Chuban, 2002).

Sung-chull KIM is Humanities Korea Professor at the Institute for Peace and Unification Studies (IPUS) at Seoul National University. Before joining the IPUS, he worked at the Korea Institute for National Unification and the Hiroshima Peace Institute. His research specializes on democratization, Korean affairs, and regionalism in Asia. He is the author of *North Korea under Kim Jong Il: From Consolidation to Systemic Dissonance* (Albany: SUNY Press, 2006) and co-editor of *State Violence in East Asia* (with N. Ganesan) (University Press of Kentucky, 2013), *Engagement with North Korea: A Viable Alternative* (with David Kang) (Albany: SUNY Press, 2009), *Regional Cooperation and Its Enemies in Northeast Asia: The Impact of Domestic Forces* (with Edward Friedman) (London: Routledge, 2006). He has also contributed a number of articles to academic journals, including *Systems Research and Behavioral Science*, *Journal of Communist Studies and Transition Politics*, and *Development and Society*.

Geun LEE is Professor of International Relations at the Graduate School of International Studies, and Director of the Institute of International Affairs (IIA), Seoul National University. He was Assistant Professor at the Institute of Foreign Affairs and National Security, Ministry of Foreign Affairs and Trade, Korea in 1997–2000. He is now an advisor to the Ministry of Foreign Affairs and Trade, Working Bee for Strategic Policy Initiative (SPI) for Future Korea–US Alliance, Ministry of Defense, Policy Specialist Committee Member, National Security Council (NSC), Consulting Professor of Government Transition Team (Foreign and Trade Policy) and Advisory Committee Member of the United Nations Association of Korea. He is also the editor of the *Journal of International and Area Studies*, a regular columnist of *Hankuk Ilbo* (Hankuk Daily), and a regular contributor of op-ed articles in *Seoul Ilbo* (Seoul Daily), *Chosun Ilbo* (Chosun Daily), *Joongang Ilbo* (Joongang Daily), *Maeil Economic Daily*, *Korea Herald*, and *Korea Times*. His recent English publications include "Economic Interdependence, Identity Change, and Issue-oriented Balancing in Northeast Asia," in *The Future of US–Korea–Japan Relations*, edited by Tae-hyo Kim and Brad Glosserman (CSIS, 2004), "The Rise of China and Korea's China Policy," in *The Rise of China and a Changing East Asian Order*, edited by Kokubun Ryosei and Wang Jisi (JCIE, 2004), and "Environment Security in East Asia: The Regional Environmental Security Complex Approach," in *Asian Perspective* 26, no. 2 (2002).

Sang-Hyun LEE is a senior research fellow and Director for Security Strategy Studies Program at the Sejong Institute in Korea. He has served as Director-General for Policy Planning, Ministry of Foreign Affairs (MOFA) from May 2011 to April 2013. He received his B.A. and M.A. from Seoul National University and Ph.D. from the Department of Political Science at the University of Illinois at Urbana-Champaign in 1999. He was a research fellow at the Korean Institute for International Studies (1987-88), the Korea Institute for Defense Analysis (1988-90), and policy advisor for Ministry of Foreign Affairs, Ministry of National Unification, and Ministry of National Defense. His main research interests include international politics and security, Korea-U.S. relations, inter-Korean relations, and East Asian security issues. His recent publications include: "South Korea's Foreign Policy Strategy toward Peace and Stability on the Korean Peninsula"(2013), "U.S. Strategy for Contingency Situations on the Korean Peninsula" (2013), "South Korea's Complex Diplomacy for the Network Age" (2012), *New Security Landscape in East Asia* (2011, co-authored, in Korean), *Korea's National Strategy in the Age of Global Transformation* (2011, in Korean), and "South Korea's Nuclear Nonproliferation Policy and Korea-US Nuclear Cooperation" (2010).

Ihn-Hwi PARK is Associate Professor of the Division of International Studies at Ewha Womans University in the Republic of Korea. Professor Park's areas of expertise lie in international security, US foreign policy, and Northeast Asian international relations. He was a Research Professor at the Asiatic Research Center at Korea University (2001/02), and has been a Research Fellow for the Korea–US Exchange Council (2001–04). Since 2011 he has been a member of the Advisory Committee of the Ministry of Foreign Affairs and Trade, and since 2009 a member of the Advisory Committee of the Ministry of Unification. He was a director of the research committee of the Korean Association of International Studies for 2011, and was a director of the editorial committee of the Korean Political Science Association for 2008. Professor Park has edited many books, and most recently published *Korea's National Security in the Age of Globalization: Key Subjects and Significances* in 2010. He has also written many articles on international relations in leading journals, including *Journal of East Asia Affairs*, *Korean Journal of Defense Analysis*, *Korea Political Science Review*, *Korean Journal of International Relations*, and *National Strategy*. Selected publications include "Sino–Japan Strategic Rivalry and the Security of the Korean Peninsula" in the *Korean Journal of Defense Analysis* (in English, 2007), and "Politics of Security and Insecurity on the Korean Peninsula: The Contradictory Combination of the

Korea–US and Inter-Korean Relations" in the *Korean Political Science Review* (in Korean, 2011). He received his PhD from Northwestern University in 1999. Professor Park can be reached at ihpark@ewha.ac.kr.

Leonid PETROV is Research Associate at Australian National University School of International, Political, and Strategic Studies. He taught Korean Studies at the University of Sydney. Dr. Petrov graduated from the Department of Oriental Studies, St Petersburg State University in 1994, where he majored in Korean History and Language. In 1994–1996, he worked as interpreter for the South Korean National Soccer Team and participated in the twenty-sixth Olympic Games in Atlanta. In 1996–2002, Dr. Petrov worked on a doctoral thesis entitled "Socio-economic School and the Formation of North Korean Official Historiography" at the Australian National University (Canberra). Between 2003 and 2005, he conducted post-doctoral research at the Academy of Korean Studies (Seongnam) and taught Korean History at the Intercultural Institute of California (San Francisco) and Keimyung University (Daegu). In 2006/07, he was Chair of Korean Studies at the Institut d'Etudes Politiques de Paris (Sciences Po). Starting from 2007, Dr. Petrov has been involved in a number of projects sponsored by the Australian Research Council: "Historical Conflict and Reconciliation in East Asia" (2007, ANU); "Northeast Asia and the Korean War: Legacies of Hot and Cold Wars in Contemporary Constructions of the Region" (2011, ANU); and "North Korea's Quiet Transformation" (2013, UTS).

Victor E. TEO is Assistant Professor at the Department of Japanese Studies and Modern China Studies Program, the Faculty of Arts at the University of Hong Kong. He is currently Visiting Research Fellow at the Department of Politics and International Relations at the University of Oxford. His research interest is in the International Relations of Asia-Pacific, with particular reference to Sino-Japanese Relations. Victor also convenes the HKU symposium series on Sino–Japanese Relations. Before joining the University of Hong Kong, he was LSE Fellow on the MSc China in Comparative Perspective program at LSE's Department of Anthropology. He has held teaching positions at the War Studies Department of Kings College London, London School of Economics, Chinese University of Hong Kong, City University of Hong Kong, and Hong Kong University of Science and Technology. From 2004 until 2009 he was the editor-in-chief of Studies in Ethnicity and Nationalism published by Wiley-Blackwell. He held the Japan Foundation Fellowship at the University of Kyoto in 2010. Dr. Teo was called to the Bar of

England and Wales in 2004 and received his PhD from the International Relations Department of the London School of Economics in 2007. He is also author and co-editor of three books on Sino–Japanese Relations: *The United States between China and Japan* (with Caroline Rose, 2013), *Southeast Asia between China and Japan* (with Peng-Er Lam, 2012), and *Reconceptualizing the Divide: Identity, Memories, and Nationalism in Sino–Japanese Relations* (with Gerrit Gong, 2010).

Zhiqun ZHU is Professor of Political Science and International Relations and holds the John D. and Catherine T. MacArthur Chair in East Asian Politics at Bucknell University. He received a PhD in political science at the University of South Carolina. In the early 1990s he worked in the information section of the American Consulate General in Shanghai. His research focuses on Chinese politics and foreign policy, and East Asian international relations. Dr. Zhu has published widely on US–Chinese relations. His most recent publications are *The People's Republic of China Today: Internal and External Challenges* (World Scientific Publishing Company, 2010), *China's New Diplomacy* (Ashgate, 2010), *Global Studies: China* (McGraw-Hill/Dushkin, 2009), *Understanding East Asia's Economic Miracles* (Association for Asian Studies, 2007) and *US–China Relations in the 21st Century: Power Transition and Peace* (Routledge, 2006).

Alexander ZHEBIN is Director of the Center for Korean Studies (CKS) at the Institute of Far Eastern Studies (IFES) of the Russian Academy of Sciences in Moscow. He graduated from the Moscow State Institute of International Relations (MGIMO) of the USSR Ministry of Foreign Affairs in 1975. Dr. Zhebin spent twelve years in North Korea as a journalist and a diplomat—as a TASS News Agency correspondent in Pyongyang (1978/79), and as TASS Bureau Chief in Pyongyang (1983–1990). He joined IFES in 1992 and since then has participated in various international seminars on Korean affairs at home and abroad. He received his PhD in political science from the IFES in 1998. During 1993/94 he was a visiting research fellow at the Asiatic Research Center at the Korea University in Seoul, and in 1997 visiting research fellow at the Korea Institute of National Unification (KINU) in Seoul. Between 1998 and 2001 he was First Secretary and Counselor at the Embassy of the Russian Federation in the DPRK. After returning to Moscow he resumed his work at the IFES and has been Director of the Centre of Korean Studies since 2004. His fields of research include political developments in the DPRK, Russia–North Korea relations, and the security situation and nuclear

problem on the Korean Peninsula. Dr. Zhebin has authored three books, many chapters in several collective works, and numerous articles on Korean affairs in academic journals and newspapers at home and abroad. He is author of "Pyongyang, Seoul, then Moscow" (1991, in Korean), "Luster and Misery of the Kim's Empire" (1992, in Japanese) and "The Evolution of the DPRK's Political System under the Impact of Global Changes" (2006, in Russian). His publications in English include "Political History of Soviet–North Korean Nuclear Cooperation," in *The North Korean Nuclear Program: Security, Strategy, and New Perspectives from Russia*, edited by James Clay Moltz and Alexandre Y. Mansourov (New York: Routledge, 2000), "The Bush Doctrine, Russia, and Korea" in *Confronting the Bush Doctrine: Critical Views from the Asia-Pacific*, edited by M. Gurtov and P. Van Ness (London and New York: Routledge Curzon, 2005), "Nuclear Non-Proliferation Challenges on the Korean Peninsula" in *Tuning Priorities in Nuclear Arms Control and Non-Proliferation*, edited by A. Nikitin and M. B. Maerli (Amsterdam, Berlin, Oxford, Tokyo, Washington DC: IOS Press, 2008). Since 1980 he has been a member of the Russian and Moscow Journalist Associations, since 1997 a member of the Association for Korean Studies in Europe (AKSE), since 2003 a member of the Russian Association for Political Science (RAPS), and since 2006 a member of the International Political Science Association (IPSA).